Offering Theory

Offering Theory

Reading in Sociography

John Mowitt

… and offer him there for a burnt offering upon one of the mountains.
(Gen. 22:2)

ANTHEM PRESS

Anthem Press
An imprint of Wimbledon Publishing Company
www.anthempress.com

This edition first published in UK and USA 2022
by ANTHEM PRESS
75–76 Blackfriars Road, London SE1 8HA, UK
or PO Box 9779, London SW19 7ZG, UK
and
244 Madison Ave #116, New York, NY 10016, USA

First published in the UK and USA by Anthem Press in 2020

Copyright © John Mowitt 2022

The author asserts the moral right to be identified as the author of this work.

All rights reserved. Without limiting the rights under copyright reserved above,
no part of this publication may be reproduced, stored or introduced into
a retrieval system, or transmitted, in any form or by any means
(electronic, mechanical, photocopying, recording or otherwise),
without the prior written permission of both the copyright
owner and the above publisher of this book.

British Library Cataloguing-in-Publication Data
A catalogue record for this book is available from the British Library.

Library of Congress Control Number: 2020936151

ISBN-13: 978-1-83998-234-7 (Pbk)
ISBN-10: 1-83998-234-9 (Pbk)

This title is also available as an e-book.

For the recently departed, Jim, Tim and Gary
And for the recently arrived, Sabine Elizabeth

CONTENTS

Acknowledgments ix

The Pretext xi

    Introduction: Theory in Limbo   1
1. Queer Resistance: Foucault and the *Unnamable*   15
2. Stumbling on Analysis: Psychoanalysis and Everyday Life   37
3. Strangers in Analysis: Nationalism and the Talking Cure   59
4. "Jamming"   85
5. WWJD?   103
6. What Said Said   119
7. Apart from Theory   141
8. Conclusion: Theory Is Out There   163

References   173

Index   179

ACKNOWLEDGMENTS

Aware of the countless voices that have pricked my ears, my habit is to be long-winded in acknowledging them. However, "the world" (Brexit, Trump, Hong Kong, Brazil, Venezuela and now COVID-19) has taken my breath away. Not quite speechless, but almost. Thus, beyond Jeffrey Di Leo and Megan Greiving at Anthem, only the bare essentials.

The readings that comprise this text straddle two continents. In 2013 I ended my long affiliation with the University of Minnesota and the department I helped invent, Cultural Studies and Comparative Literature, to join the School of Fine Art, History of Art and Cultural Studies, at the University of Leeds. Colleagues and friends from both institutions deserve my gratitude whether welcomed or not.

At Minnesota I am thinking especially of Cesare Casarino, Vinay Gidwani, Qadri Ismail, Michal Kobialka, Richard Leppert, Tom Pepper, J. B. Shank, Ajay Skaria and Shaden Tageldin as well as Lisa Disch, Andreas Gaillus, Rembert Hüser, Premesh Lalu, Helena Pohlandt-McCormick, Verena Mund, Anaïs Nony, Simona Sawhney, Naomi Scheman and Adam Sitze who, like me, have since moved on.

At Leeds the list is short, but growing. I especially want to acknowledge the provocations of Jason Allen-Paissant, Barbara Engh, Gail Day, Sam Durrant, Eric Prenowitz as well as Adrian Rifkin, Marcel Swiboda (who, among other brilliant things, prepared the index) and Jane Taylor, all of whom have since left.

Since coming to Leeds my more irregular affiliations with the University of Western Cape and with the University of Fort Hare have deepened considerably. Many of the concepts invented in the chapters that follow developed out of these friendships and I want especially to acknowledge the voices of Maurits van Bever Donker, Heidi Grunebaum, Patricia Hayes, Gary Minkley, Ross Truscott and the unfathomably deep talent pool gathered around them.

In this spirit somewhat more formal thanks are owed to the various friends and colleagues who have invited me to address them, their colleagues and students on the matter of Theory: Karyn Ball at the University of Alberta,

Jonathan Bordo and Andrew Wernick at Tent University, Paul Bouissac at the University of Toronto, Griselda Pollock at the University of Leeds, Tilottama Rajan at the University of Western Ontario, Lynn Turner at Goldsmiths, the organizers of "The Humanities Improvised" (notably Premesh Lalu and Jim Chandler) at the Consortium of Humanities Centers and Institutes, seminar leaders (especially Jeffrey Di Leo and Zahi Zalloua) at the American Comparative Literature Association and the organizers at the Cultural Studies Association (notably Patricia Clough and Randy Johnson). Enablers all.

As the bicontinental character of these pieces might suggest, some of them, in various iterations and guises, have appeared in print before. Formal acknowledgment of their sources appears as stipulated by the presses granting permission to recycle. I am professionally grateful to them all: *Canadian Journal of Comparative Literature*, Taylor and Francis and *Symplokē*. More directly though I want to acknowledge and thank Peggy Kamuf for helping me gain access to the Jacques Derrida papers held in Special Collections at the Langson Library at UC-Irvine and for permitting me to cite from the as-yet unpublished seminar, "Language and the Method of Discourse."

But if "essentials" is the watchword of these remarks, two more personal acknowledgments are in order. First and foremost, I want to thank Jeanine, Rosalind and Rachel for their patience and generosity during the interminable gestation of these thoughts. Jeanine Ferguson in particular continues to humble me with her wisdom, her willingness to try out titles, turns of phrase, topics and remain, in spite of it all, in my company. With endless gratitude and affection.

Lastly, I want to thank "mi bibliotecario," Jose Rodriguez Dod, a very early collaborator who, with his wife Eloisa, has routinely welcomed me into his home and its boundless shelves of all those texts you didn't know you needed until you did. A near fatal illness almost broke off our friendship. I am thankful it did not.

THE PRETEXT

This study traces various iterations of the question: when or where is Theory today? Its aim is not to avoid the question, "what *is* Theory?," but to subordinate that question to the prior one. At stake in this subordination is the conviction that the "essential" question, the "what" question, leads too quickly to an archival impasse where movements, debates, national traditions, figures, births, deaths and so on impose an order on Theory that reduces it largely to the intellectual property of publishers and universities. And not just any publishers and universities, but far too typically ones in what have come to be called the North and the West, both designations that Theory now includes within the modes of its own self-doubt. Here, and the problem is a familiar one, Theory immediately undergoes a metamorphosis when confronted with the dilemma of application, whether understood methodologically (*can* Theory x be applied to object y, and to what effect?) or politically (*should* Theory from intellectual heritage x be applied to objects from another?). These are not false problems, it is just that the power of their falsity is too limited to be especially generative. They make the "when or the where" of Theory seem less interesting than they might otherwise be by, in effect, folding a single when and a single where into what Theory is. Or, as is more often heard today, what Theory *was*.

This invocation of the grammatical distinction between the past and the present points to something that will matter in what follows. Hovering, like a "third ear," above or behind the "when or where" of Theory is a proposition about context. More particularly, the question "when is Theory?" reads like a historical question, just as "where is Theory?" reads like a social or cultural question. History, society, culture are all ways to think what context designates in the protocols of critical analysis. That said, at issue here is not a banal "contextualization" of Theory (others have scorched this earth), and this for two reasons. First, what seems worth fussing over in the "when or where" of Theory is something more like its "occasion," "event" or "performance," where what is foregrounded is how what we might provisionally call "theoretical effects" arise, where the enunciation of Theory can be traced in the emergence of its statements or, in the jargon of application, its arguments, those pieces of prose exposition folks trained philosophically are adept at parsing (separating into parts).

Second, at risk in the labor of contextualization is the theoretical presupposition of context itself. To invoke a commonplace, context is typically compared and insistently contrasted with text, but is this really anything more than a gesture of convenience and thus a sign of intellectual impatience? Grasped in its historical materiality, that is, etymologically, "context" derives from Latin where it plainly says: weave (*texere*) with or together (*con*). Here the warp and the woof, the strands woven together and across, cannot be grasped as contrasting with one another in the way that text is now typically contrasted with context. In fact, if one has been paying attention, this weaving is precisely what text came to designate in the mo(ve)ment, now, with some justice, derided, as *post*structuralism. Indeed, it is perhaps only within this derisive posturing that text is insistently deprived of this etymological force, a telling symptom of which is the proposition that texts are simply, strictly or merely linguistic phenomena. Although clearly not his cup of tea, text might also be another word for what Charles Sanders Peirce meant by a "general semiosis," that is, the evolutionary process whereby being "cognizes" itself.

Thus, attention to the "when or where of Theory" must immediately be attention to the event, the occasion of this weaving, both in terms of the moment of its production and also in terms of its moment of reception or the moment of "theorization," that is, when the species of writing and reading meet. Here, one might argue, the distinction between "close" and "distant" reading is especially unhelpful for it allows reading to avoid all of the political complications that arise in approaching a given "when or a where" from a different "when or where" even when this approach is from within a geographically or historically shared "when or where." That said, and there will be more to be said about the logic of devotion, the "friends of the text" have proven to be their own worst enemies. Even scholars and critics who *have* been paying attention note with justifiable exasperation that the weaving one finds in much work inspired by the concept of the text is rather narrow-minded. That is, inclined to follow out only those threads that challenge and therefore satisfy a conception of reading bound by the protocols of a largely disciplinary literacy. As important as this radicalization of reading has been (and this is not in dispute), it has implicitly motivated this radicalization by setting certain threads aside, protecting textual reading from the even more profound radicalization that tracing "weaving with or together" (what Gayatri Spivak once called "textility") might provoke. Thus, at the risk of "unfriending" the friends of the text, the chapters that follow will build toward the invention, perhaps "reinvention," of a concept of context designed to help with this impasse.

How do we read the weave? Not the text in terms of context, nor the context in terms of the text, but the weave.

This concept, that of "sociography," will emerge in the course of a series of readings each seeking to attend to the "when or where" of Theory. Deliberately, these readings will engage rather familiar (and not only within Northern and Western discourses of the university) theoretical figures—Foucault, Kristeva, Derrida, Williams, Said, Lacan, Deleuze and so on—but with the express goal of brushing them against the grain. That is, reading them either in the setting of an occasion—an inaugural lecture, a staged debate/conversation, a graduate seminar—or at the level of enunciation, a form of attentiveness that will facilitate a transition from the musicality of theoretical procedures to musical performance as a site of theoretical articulation. In each case, the task of picking up these particular threads from "here" will prompt refection on Theory as an event, the offering of a reading, and drive the invention of "sociography," that is, the means by which to figure the site of the "when or where" of Theory. Without this those working in the critical humanities and "interpretive" (previously, "qualitative") social science are left to "situate" the objects of their attention against something outside them, a constraining or determining context that responsible, "properly" political scholarship typically speed-reads through the objects of its attention to reach. Again, the snarl of reading has for too long been confused with something like "literacy" and thus needs to be displaced onto the work of weaving with and together, a mode of "handling" that I am proposing to rename Theory. The "sociographic" is designed to facilitate this displacement.

But sociography is also designed to amplify the "or" that conjoins "where" and "when" in the question that animates this project. To amplify here means to sound simultaneously the inclusive and exclusive connotations of the conjunction, the effect of which is to stress that where and when are distinct, but in ways that when juxtaposed make them spatiotemporal renditions of each other. Sociography is pitched so as to encounter this problem, not as a limit but as a provocation. A provocation to what? On the right hand, it is a provocation to consider that humanistic inquiry as such might be committed to problem finding, to stumbling upon when or where Theory could and maybe even should be taking place (a matter taken up at greater length in the introduction that follows). But on the left, the sinister hand, sociography is a provocation to let Theory answer to the demands of those who, to stick with the trope of weaving with or together, work when or where weaving forms part of a world, a planet, in which a theorist is clothed, swaddled, embalmed or enshrouded. Sociography does not, therefore, traffic in either guilt or responsibility. It is not about the professional suicide that even a glimpse at this world or the next might tragically recommend. But nor is it about a practice of responsibility that forgets, in the instant of a ringtone, that response is an insidious ruse. Behind its ocean of zeroes and ones, digitalization makes certain digits count more than others. Some have the wherewithal of responding. It is not an unequivocal virtue.

Very little in what follows is settled. Faithful to its humanistic leanings, this inflammatory device is thrown forward seeking problems, not their solutions. The threads spun out here do not lead out of the labyrinth, they lead in; in where no monster waits to show itself, where no heroes hastily provision a quest the West cannot seem to get enough of.

INTRODUCTION: THEORY IN LIMBO

Surely, now more needs to be said about the "when or where" of *what* precisely. My tedious recourse to capitalization, "Theory," demands it.

As if implicitly demonstrating the principle that the event of decolonization takes place in both the colony and the metropole, the debate over Theory—largely, but not exclusively in the North and the West—has long assumed a necro-political tone. I myself have chimed in. Apart from a certain critique of Mbembe's existential humanism, what seems called for now is less fussing over whether Theory is alive or dead—let's just stipulate that its condition is "chronic"—and more careful consideration of its circumstances. Or, more precisely, how did its condition arise and with what implications for those of us who insist upon handling Theory?

Although Adorno's feelings about Nietzsche are hard to pin down, his approach to *die Liebhaber* in "Bach Defended Against His Devotees" seems obviously to channel the sentiment found in Nietzsche's stinging aphorism (number 298) from the first volume of *Human All Too Human*: "In every party there is someone whose far too credulous expression of the party's principles provokes others to defect" (Nietzsche 2010, 198). Regardless of whether Nietzsche is his source, Adorno's "devotee" is arguably the Doppelgänger of the thinker who knows how to assimilate tradition by "hating it properly." Frankly, I am not especially concerned here to sort the matter of influence. Instead, the point is to situate Theory in the context of a thinking—as my title clearly suggests—about how its offering participates in the logic of devotion challenged by Adorno. More particularly, in a straightforwardly pedagogical mood, my discussion and the readings that follow explore, within the semantic resonances of "offering," how one might work with Theory so as to, as it were, *sacrifice it properly*. Drawing initially on Terry Eagleton and Giorgio Agamben I consider here how Theory is exposed, even risked through its offering, and examine what grasp of Theory emerges from thinking its offering as an act of sacrifice. Theory not as *on* offer, but Theory as offering, or as I will propose, Theory as "giving a reading." How does one handle that? When and where does that handling take place?

Not long ago the medievalist Andrew Cole told us everything we do not need to know about the "birth" of Theory. A more emphatic and thus persuasive account of why Theory ought not be profiled, that is, handled, as having an identity would be hard to imagine. And, so as not to be misunderstood, Cole's text is a *really* good one. However, as with any sort of achievement it exacts a price and here this takes the form of the text's seduction. His text is properly seductive in that it leads one astray—thinking here of Freud's *Verführung*, whether actual or not. More directly, what concerns me in Cole's approach is its devotional tone, a tone that manifests not only in his historicism but in his conviction that Theory is best grasped as exhibiting an identity. So as to cut to the proverbial chase, in order to sacrifice theory properly, it must not be profiled, it must not be given an identity that one can "historicize" or not. This is especially important when thinking about handling theory in the diffuse era of "the peace," that is, in the moment that has survived the Theory Wars, a moment, I will argue, during which Theory obliges us to be thoughtful about when and where we handle it, especially now that Theory has been reduced to a cinder, a glowing coal.

Perhaps then a more direct if less immediate interlocutor here is the late Wolfgang Iser, whose *How to Do Theory*, with its explicitly pedagogical orientation, falls more squarely in the path of these reflections. What Iser and Cole share— and Cole makes only a passing reference to him—is the inclination to treat Theory as a type, a genre of academic discourse. Iser's text is textbook-like in its effort to demonstrate not how various theoretical traditions ought be applied to objects of scholarly attention (although a bit of this occurs), but how theoretical traditions might be taken in their own right as objects of scholarly attention and, decisively, presented in the context of the graduate or undergraduate classroom. The organization of his study says it all: Chapter 2, Phenomenological Theory; Chapter 3, Hermeneutical Theory; Chapter 5, Reception Theory (no surprise) and so on, culminating in a postscript dedicated to "Postcolonial Discourse" (*not* Theory) represented by Edward Said. In his preface Iser somewhat nervously distances himself from his text by stressing its commissioned status and by noting the more or less persistent coaxing of his editor to do this or that. Anyone who has published a book will know that Iser is not making this up. Editors do behave this way. But the issue here is not who *actually* wrote the text, but rather of what is its existence a sign? To respond succinctly: its existence symptomatizes the typecasting, the "profiling" of Theory. As his introductory chapter makes plain: Theory is now (it was written in 1992!) something academic intellectuals can't avoid, so we might as well be clear about how to *do* it. To be frank, I actually think "do" is the most provocative word in Iser's title for the attention it directs to the practice of offering and if I am dissatisfied with his text, and I am, it is because he doesn't do enough with "do," starting with the problem of treating it as a verb that simply precedes a noun. Doing Theory shields Theory from the doing, so as to set Theory off from the work of doing, of offering. Put differently, Iser wants us to understand different types of Theory so as to offer them *competently*, he does not want to offer them *theoretically*, almost certainly a sure path to a low score on RateMyProfessors.com.

If earlier I invoked a certain "necro-political" tone in the debate over Theory it was with an eye toward commenting upon the "marketing history" of what I have called "the peace." Consider then the following "facts," aware that one needs to resist taking the evidentiary force of chronology at face value.

In 1983 the University of Minnesota Press, published Terry Eagleton's *Literary Theory: An Introduction*. A witty, well-informed and unabashedly left-leaning survey of those traditions within critical theory that had transformed the study of literary texts, this book quickly emerged as the best-selling title at the press, surpassing sales of so-called regional books about life in and around Minnesota. Its sales were directly indexed to the book's wide adoption for use in classroom instruction, testifying to the perception among educators that "literary theory" mattered as an offering within the hallowed halls of higher education. Iser's text is obviously modeled on it; indeed its implicit rejoinder is: yes, yes, but how does one *do* it?

In 2003 Eagleton published, now at Basic Books (a trade press), *After Theory*, an equally witty, but far more mean-spirited description of the fate of Theory (no longer simply literary theory) in the early years of the new century. Although not exactly rife with self-loathing, *After Theory* hardened *Literary Theory*'s left leanings, recasting its survey as a form of blood sport in which theoretical propositions about society, culture and the economy that resisted the implicit authority of a certain anti-Soviet orthodoxy were deemed "bloodless," pale shades and thus worthy of the oblivion into which the context of the new century was said to be consigning them. The title thus resonated not only as an anodyne historical descriptor but also as a command to a pack of dogs.

Five years later in 2008, the University of Minnesota Press published what was called the 25th anniversary edition of *Literary Theory: An Introduction* to which Eagleton had added an "Afterword." This last was written more in the spirit of his warm valediction to Jacques Derrida who had passed in October of 2004, a statement pitched almost directly against the sanctimonious obituary for Derrida published by the *New York Times* where it was proclaimed that with Derrida's demise the "theory of everything" was now dead. Without exactly calling off the dogs, Eagleton was here thinking *after* Theory in a less distempered way.

Now, let me quickly correct some false impressions. This is not really about Terry Eagleton. It is not about the press that publishes the academic journal that I edit. It is not even about the first two decades of my professional career. It is about what, in a plainly melodramatic register, we could call the *fate* of Theory, and here not merely literary theory. If one accepts that print capitalism is one of the decisive materializations of Theory, then the dates I have recorded matter in tracing an alternate version of what Said sought to capture in his influential essay, "Traveling Theory," namely, the slackening or attenuation of the perceived urgency of theoretical reflection in both the humanities and the social sciences. Again, in a somewhat awkward rhetorical register, these dates mark the *passing* of Theory as witnessed from the vantage point of a partisan with a trans-Atlantic audience. Although their differences are legion, Eagleton and Iser share the conviction that Theory, unlike many theorists themselves, has a life. It is the type of thing that has a life span, and a finite one at that. Time's up.

We come then to the proverbial heart of the matter. Namely, what should or even can we *do* with the Theory that has passed, whose condition is curiously "chronic"? As my opening paragraphs will have clarified, the strategy of deepening our devotion to this discursive identity is not a viable option. In their most piquant manifestations such strategies manifest as cockfights spurred by the schoolyard idiom of: "is so, is not," or, in Gerald Graff's more sober idiom, "the conflicts." Are those of us who embrace the materialization of Theory that manifests in university curricula, in pedagogical practice, left with no other option than to reanimate and defend a *corpus* whose expiration date has passed? Is the passion of Theory essentially nostalgic? I'll not linger here, but a significant part of what is at issue in what I have called the passing of Theory is precisely the reorganization of the university as a business, begun—if we are to believe James Buchanan's account in *Academia in Anarchy* (Buchanan 1970, *passim*)—during the student movements of the 1960s whose 50th anniversary many around the world began marking in 2018.

To pursue further the matter of how we might carry on within the general project of the critical humanities I will bear down a bit more systematically on the senses of "offering" in my title. As with "passing," "offering" invites distinct but related glosses. In the case of "offering," at least two. Perhaps its more immediate sense arises when we speak, as so many of us do, of "offering" classes or seminars. Here "offering" means presenting or giving, and my title certainly aims to posit the notion that Theory should continue to be available as an area of inquiry in any and every setting that regards itself as a locus of education. At the risk of moving too quickly, I would even go as far as to propose that in the absence of Theory education ceases to be about learning. It becomes about training. And, as an aside, this problem was one among several agitating members of GREPH when they fought to keep philosophy on offer in high school curricula in France during the 1980s.

The less immediate sense of "offering" is surely the sense of it that arises in the biblical formulation of a "burnt offering" where it touches immediately on the matter and practice of sacrifice. Perhaps less immediate still, at least for those unaware that the word "holocaust" derives from the Greek for "completely burned," is the join, the knot within sacrifice between veneration and execration. Indeed, the staggering ambivalence that binds denying and affirming sacrifice is precisely one of those problems that calls insistently for theoretical attention. Thus, with a certain night and foggy vividness, my title is also a call to "sacrifice" Theory, to treat it precisely as a "burnt offering," whence my earlier invocation of Derrida's (and earlier T. E. Hulme's) figure of the cinder. But now what can this mean given that I have also parsed the title to posit the *necessity* of offering Theory as part of what it means today to educate? Am I talking, for instance, about sacrificing the Theory that Theory has passed into, that is, a largely Northern, Western canon of "great ideas," a canon long valued for its role in initiating certain people, largely but by no means exclusively white men (what, e.g., at Duke were once referred to as "Fred's Boys"), into the cult of knowledge? Yes, of course. But one understands vaguely if at all what it might mean to sacrifice Theory properly if we leave it at that. Setting aside the antagonistic theoretical profiles of the four posts—postmodernism, postfeminism, post-Marxism and postcolonialism—the *concept* of Theory that followed in their wake is one whose papers are patently not in order. It is, as Arendt said about the refugee, stateless. In effect, just passing through. Passing through its own peace.[1]

In the book whose argument these remarks introduce, I engage this snarl of issues by thinking about the various tensions between Theory and identity. Two aspects of this tension are foregrounded. On the one hand, when Eagleton in *After Theory* tells us that the context in which Theory mattered is now lost to us, he is effectively giving Theory an identity, even a purpose, and the gist of his analysis is to illustrate that this identity, like the context that determined it, has been lost. Put differently, through the device of the concept of "context" Theory is given an identity, a time and place of belonging, indeed the very identity whose birth Cole has so assiduously reconstructed. If *this* loss can be characterized as a sacrifice, our relation to it is cast as largely devotional if not nostalgic. Through such an analysis we are coaxed to mourn the loss of an identity and to organize the reactive crusade aimed to confront what ineluctably looms up as blasphemy. If we are book publishers we seek out, translate and distribute any shred of paper on which a "theorist" wrote something including a note like "I forgot my umbrella" or, far less trivially, the fragile transcripts of lectures recorded at the College de France. Febrile archiving indeed.

On the other hand, and this point is a difficult one, the tension between Theory and identity also manifests as a *conflict* between Theory and identity, not then the identity of Theory, but the Theory of identity, a Theory that disappears as theorizing, in its prioritization of a practice, the act of identification. Here, Theory is sacrificed to a politics of identity that in its most dangerous forms resuscitates ethnocentrisms of all sorts. The "Nation State Law" mooted in the summer of 2018 by the Israeli Knesset is a handy and glaring example. So, when I *assent* to the proposition that the sacrifice of Theory is part of what must be on offer in a place calling itself a university, this sacrifice of loss, this conflicted pairing of identity and Theory is among the things that must go.[2]

But go how? The takeaway of these introductory remarks can be phrased as a response to this question. Beyond sacrificing the Theory that has passed, how should Theory, in general, be sacrificed properly? Or, rephrased more directly, is there a sense in which Theory sacrifices itself? If so, by what means?

A few more dates. Same cautions as before. In 1995 the first of Giorgio Agamben's multivolume treatment of *homo sacer* appeared. Although much effort of late has been devoted to tracing the shafts of sunlight that separate these studies, they can all be said to explore how political sovereignty founds its constitutive instability on a particular type of political actor, the figure of *homo sacer*. Brazenly collapsing a host of subtleties, I will thus parse Agamben's discussion of sovereignty by foregrounding its provocative juridical character. Following Carl Schmitt, the one who is sovereign, the decider, is the one who is in a position to suspend the law in order to preserve it. In the rhetoric of statecraft this constitutes a declaration of "a state of emergency" where the state, to protect the identity given it by its ruling oligarchy, violates the principles on which it is founded in order to eliminate what the state believes threatens it. In other words, the "one" (the unity of the state) is almost always more than one. Significantly, for Agamben, this structure of standing outside and above the law in order to preserve the essence of its rule is the very same invaginated structure that isolates *homo sacer* as the one whose expulsion from society, from the human community, is precisely what preserves that community as a biopolitical formation. In a different terminological register, this is the scapegoat, and in most contemporary regimes, whether democracies or not, this figure is now (at least since *Covering Islam*) the "terrorist," who, according to Boris Johnson, walks among the people of Britain disguised as mailboxes. Although Agamben has himself offered various iconic incarnations of such a figure, he has consistently placed important stress on the occupants of the extermination camps during World War II, especially the living corpse called "the Muselman," the Muslim. What does this stress clarify?

It clarifies the simple fact that *homo sacer* is not and cannot be a "burnt offering." As Agamben writes: "The protagonist of this book is bare life, that is, the life of homo sacer (sacred man) who *may be killed and yet not sacrificed*"

(Agamben 1998, 8).³ Indeed, the whole point of this inaugural volume is that *homo sacer* is one (or ones) who can be eliminated by the sovereign *without* sacrifice, that is, without producing a significant relation to something, or someone, absolutely other. The sovereign may sacrifice him or herself to the potent instability that sustains it, but *homo sacer* is beyond sacrifice. It is precisely unsacrificable and in this sense "holocaust" may be the wrong word for those consigned to crematoria in the Nazi extermination camps. Those exterminated there may have been "completely burned," but they were not sacrificed. They were purely and simply slaughtered. Hopefully now the reader can sense where I am heading. If, in offering Theory, we sacrifice it, we precisely *do not* treat it as an incarnation, however uncanny, of *homo sacer*. We do not treat it as something we can expel from the sociopolitical order without effect, without losing our constitutive relation to someone, or something, other, even or especially when this otherness might designate the biopolitical plane of immanence on which life itself slips and slides. Although Eagleton, in *After Theory*, has a somewhat different point to make in invoking the "bloodlessness" of Theory (he predictably deplores its apolitical abstraction), the adjective "bloodless" nevertheless invites comparison with Agamben's discussion of *homo sacer*, who as we have seen is a figure whose sacrifice offers nothing *vital* to the gods, a figure whose sacrifice secures no relation to anything or anyone other, in effect, a figure whose sacrifice is not one.⁴

A final date. In 2018, as if anticipating these impatient remarks, Eagleton published a small book with Yale University Press, titled, *Radical Sacrifice*. Given the preceding I can hardly avoid it, but, more to the point, "reading" it (however sparingly) helpfully amplifies the gesture of sacrificing theory properly. In general terms this text continues Eagleton's examination of conscience begun in his first book, *New Left Church*; indeed, it is dedicated to the "Carmelite Sisters of Thicket Priory" and builds steadily to an argument about the deep convergence between radical sacrifice and proletarian revolution. He writes:

> It is axiomatic that men and women must accomplish their emancipation for themselves. It can no more be delegated than the act of dying. The notion of revolution turns on the paradox that what has been reduced by the arrogance of power to a state of inert objectivity is precisely on that account capable of emerging as a new kind of subject. [...] Seen in this light, revolution is a modern version of what the ancient world new as sacrifice. (Eagleton 2018, 180–81)

As the rhetoric of dying, to which Eagleton devotes an entire chapter, and the becoming-subject of the inert object might suggest, radical sacrifice bears an undeclared relation to resurrection or, to reanimate the gothic register of

Capital, galvanization. As a culminating gesture, these formulations clarify where the several preceding discussions of sacrifice were heading. While it is hard not to resonate to Eagleton's utopianism—surely the world can't get much worse—what does not yet hum is his willingness to overlook what is properly different in the various accounts of sacrifice to which he attends. The reader likely will not be surprised to hear that this stands out most conspicuously in his discussion of Agamben. Arising here and there in Eagleton's rambling and allusive exposition (there are pages on which he drops five or six "big names" and he repeatedly solicits an invitation to spend Christmas with the Derridas) when he settles down to "read" Agamben, he concentrates his energies on *Remnants of Auschwitz* where the specter haunting the camps, the Muselman, shuffles out onto the mirror stage. To be truer to convictions I will go on to defend, Eagleton does not actually "read" Agamben. He "comments" on the figure of the Muselman largely to establish its solidarity, perhaps even its kinship, with *homo sacer*, a point on which we agree. What slips away, however, is the difference between the Muselman and the other internees. In effect, if *homo sacer* is the unsacrificable, the one who is simply murdered rather than sacrificed, then the Muselman does indeed qualify as sacred because in an important sense s/he is already dead, s/he contains nothing to offer to anyone or anything. S/he is bloodless. But this ought to complicate rather than confirm the correlations being drawn by Eagleton. This ought to remind us that to sacrifice properly what is offered is not, cannot be drained of value, and while it is true that Eagleton observes this difference in his other commentaries, the drive to funnel all ancient sacrifice toward modern revolution loses nuance worth holding on to.

Agamben himself struggles with this difficult matter, but Eagleton—who, after all, is writing after Theory—cannot be bothered to produce a theoretical encounter between his own aims and those of Agamben. Indeed, although the word "theory" occasionally appears in *Radical Sacrifice*, one has to sift with a prospector's patience for the golden veins that run between this text and *After Theory*. They are there and they manifest in vessels, notably blood vessels, or put less facetiously, they manifest in the rhetoric of sanguinity that calibrates the scales of judgment in much of Eagleton's writing and, as we have seen, nowhere more bluntly than in *After Theory*. Rather than demonstrate this proposition here, I will simply stress that my issue here is not doctrinal. I am not really concerned to establish whether Eagleton gets Agamben "right." Of greater immediate pertinence is clarifying what stands illuminated about sacrificing Theory properly by holding onto the proposition that within the discussion of *homo sacer* sacrifice is at odds with itself, and nowhere more so than in the "zone of irreducible indistinction" (Agamben 1998, 9) wherein the sovereign and scapegoat rub elbows.

So, Theory must be offered and not merely offed. And yes, I am investing Theory with properties that cannot but strike one as exorbitant. With this in mind, consider the well-known formulation that concludes Roland Barthes's "The Death of the Author," a title whose French iteration (deliberately?) echoes Mallory's fifteenth-century text on the death of a sovereign: "We are no longer so willing to be the dupes of such antiphrases, by which a society proudly recriminates in favor of precisely what it discards, ignores, muffles or destroys; we know that to restore writing to its future, we must reverse the myth: the birth of the reader, must be requited by the death of the Author" (Barthes 1986). "Requited" here is a translation for "*doit se payer.*" In an alternative Howard translation it is rendered as "ransomed," but either way the notion of paying for a birth is here connoted in the register of what I have been calling sacrifice, although perhaps more like a pawn than a child. Something offered so as to secure something other. The author (and in the last sentence where the text cites its title, "*Auteur*" is capitalized) must be sacrificed for the reader. It is not therefore, unsacrificable. It is not sacred.

What begins to crown here is not simply the reader but reading, and more specifically, as what arises out of a corpus whose sovereign had been the author. It is not therefore uninteresting that precisely in his function as an educator Barthes, in 1972, addressed a group of lycée teachers on the topic of what he titled, in an oblique evocation of Robbe-Grillet, "For a Theory of Reading." Such talks were designed to bring high school teachers up to speed with developments in the university, and it is therefore proper that Barthes opens by informing them that the traditional and thus familiar pairing of "work and author" has passed. Perhaps more startling, however, is his subsequent declaration that "there has never before been a theory of reading" (Barthes 2015, 157), a counterfactual so glaring—has he actually not read *Reading Capital*, or *Of Grammatology?*—that "reading" directly assumes a provocative idiolectal resonance. Barthes's remarks, brief though they are, quickly then capitalize on this feint by advancing not only a grid of the four levels of reading along with their correlative disciplinary stakeholders but, as if acutely aware of the chiasmus of his title, a Theory of Theory. Theory does not mean, he insists, either "'a philosophical dissertation' or 'abstract system'" (Barthes 2015, 158). Instead, the term designates a "description" that examines problems in their "infinite reach," one "open to criticism," in a word, "responsible." This segues immediately to a bracing attack on interdisciplinarity, confronting his audience with a proper problematic, that is, an echo chamber of questions and answers, in this case those of reading, Theory and discipline.

Of particular pertinence to the task of sacrificing Theory properly is what I have called the chiasmus, that is, the proposition that a Theory of reading is at one and the same time a reading of Theory or, to nudge this toward the motif of offering, that Theory and reading are two words for the "same" gesture. Lest one think that this nudge is utterly without textual warrant, that there is nothing here about sacrifice, about offering, consider not only the context (an address to educators) but even more importantly the following:

> Reading, as we know, is a social object/issue; it is prey to instances of power and morality. [...] For my part, I shall formulate the ethical question in the following way: there are *dead* readings (subject to stereotypes, mental repetitions and sloganizing) and there are *living* readings (producing an inner text, homogeneous with a virtual writing on the part of the reader). Now, this living reading, during which the subject believes what he reads emotionally while also realizing its unreality, is a split (*clivée* thus divided and shared) reading. (Barthes 2015, 160)

Barthes goes on to associate, freely or not, this split with Freud's account of the "splitting (*Spaltung*) of the subject (*le moi*, so the 'self' or 'ego')" and concludes: "'living reading' is a perverse activity and reading is always immoral" (Barthes ibid.).

Written in 1972 this set of formulations about a Theory of reading/a reading of Theory falls directly between *S/Z* (1970) and *The Pleasure of the Text* (1973). It retrieves and complicates the distinction drawn in the former between two types of text, the writable and the readable ("writerly" and "readerly" in the Howard translation), by introducing into the latter a further distinction between the dead and living. Although the touch between the living reading that is homogeneous with a *virtual* writing and what in *S/Z* is designated as the "*scriptible*" is suggestive, I will settle for a more obtuse point. Namely, if reading can be either alive or dead, if it can be perverse, this is because a Theory of reading is obliged to treat it in a way that solicits, that invites, the recognition that we are no longer here talking about literacy, strictly speaking. We are talking about offering, offering as a way to think the practice of separating the living from the dead, of producing the occasion for learning how to "do" Theory by sacrificing it to the reading that Theory becomes.

Several matters follow from this and since they will figure in the "readings" that follow they call for attention. Perhaps the most urgent of these bears on the matter of what it means to treat reading as an offering of Theory that is theoretical. Derrida has, with his usual abandon, aligned reading and mourning (see *The Work of Mourning*), and here Barthes, as if channeling Bataille, aligns it with perversion and ultimately immorality. Whether it is best aligned with one or the other is not as pressing as the following question: What makes such formulations seem exorbitant, or what have we misread in reading in failing to recognize the possibility of such alignments? My response has the advantage of being straightforward: We have failed to recognize what reading does, when and where it brings about what it brings about. Reading theorizes in carrying on, struggling to make sense, within the encounter between the text and a possible world. Put differently, what we offer in sacrificing reading to this encounter is Theory, and yes, at a very basic level I wish to underscore the obvious, namely, that if Theory has mattered for however long it has mattered, it is because it grips and deeply rattles the way reading takes place. In a sense, this is the insight that silently animates any list of the sort adjective ("feminist") or surname (Butlerian) followed by the word "reading." More than a demonstration, this then is a proposal about offering Theory that sacrifices it properly to the readings it propels and the reading it is, the reading by which Theory became what it is. In short, to offer Theory is to offer (its) reading, neither close nor distant, slow nor fast, but reading. Implacably, this pushes us toward what I take to be the opening generated by sacrificing Theory properly, namely, what Barthes sought to delimit, in another context, through the test of commutation, or in my more pedestrian jargon, the when and the where of Theory. When does the reading that theorizes start and stop? Where does this take place?

These evocations of genealogy and geography are, I will propose, helpful ways to think through one of the more generatively enigmatic formulations in Barthes's corpus. It derives from the section named "Interpretation" in *S/Z* and reads (in my translation): "To interpret a text is not to give it a (more or less grounded, more or less free) meaning, but on the contrary to discern of what plural it is made" (Barthes 1974, 5). Immediately dashing the hopes of my students who want to read here license for any interpretation whatever, Barthes pressures the "plural" in ways that matter to the chiasmus of reading and Theory. Specifically, the plural designates a generative potentiality in the gesture of reading that enables theories of the typological sort to emerge. Or, to retrieve a few additional formulations from "For a Theory of Reading":

> What goes on in the total act of reading? Where does reading begin? How far does it extend? Can we assign structure or boundaries to this production? We shall have to draw on many disciplines to answer such questions. Reading is an *overdetermined* phenomenon, involving different levels of description. *Reading is what does not stop.* (Barthes 2015, 158, emphasis in original)

The invocation here of "overdetermination," obviously anticipates the turn to Freud, but also therefore urges us to bring the concept of a "split reading" into urgent proximity with the "plural" of which the text is made, which in turn drives one to consider how the reading that is Theory, its when and its where, is what makes it impossible to know when a reading has begun, while at the "same" time to be convinced that it does not stop.

All such propositions underscore that at some vexed point in the reading/Theory chiasmus the Theory we offer happens when and where we least expect it. While on the one hand this reminds us that pedagogy and improvisation have much in common, it also brings back into range one of the more provocative moments in the meditation on reading that opens *Reading Capital*, a text also called up by Barthes's invocation (unknowing?) of "overdetermination," but not for that reason relevant here. Instead, attention ought to be directed to the footnote in Section 10 of Part One that reads:

> The same applies to the "reading" of those new works of Marxism which, sometimes in surprising forms, contain in them something essential to the future of socialism: what Marxism is producing in the vanguard countries of the "third world" which is struggling for its freedom from the guerillas of Vietnam to Cuba. It is vital that we be able to "read" these works before it is too late. (Althusser and Balibar 1979, 34)

Setting aside the romance of a now jaded "Third Worldism," what insists here is an acknowledgment that the reading that Marxist theory *is* offers itself to "works" that are well off the page. To be sure this resonates with the Althusserian principle of "theoretical practice," but it channels practice more carefully into the gift, the giving, of reading, suggesting perhaps even positing that *what* reading reads is itself reorganized by the reading/Theory chiasmus. To put the matter bluntly, the oft-heard dismissal of Theory as a linguistic phenomenon ekphrastically isolated from things beyond language is at best nonsense and at worst sheer ideology. Whatever can be read can be theorized, and whatever can be theorized *is* read. So, to conclude abruptly, to sacrifice Theory properly, to offer it, is to offer reading. Not reading in the sense of literacy (however crucial it may be), that is, the competence for decoding messages structured by linguistic codes, but reading in the sense of the handling, working in, on and with the split, the plural that makes every text a text. To be continued.

Notes

1 A provocative genealogical angle on the relation between Theory and sacrifice is assiduously traced in Ian Rutherford's study of *Theōria and Theōroi*. The connection between Theory and collective spectating is well established. What Rutherford adds is the connection between spectating and pilgrimage, that is, the practice carried out by Greek city-states, of sending delegations to observe events such as festivals and ceremonies. The delegation, known as *Theōroi*, precisely as a condition of observing, would

typically "offer," as in sacrifice, something to its hosts, securing access and "intelligence." Theory is thus obliged to offer and is conditioned by such offering. Rutherford traces this thinking of Theory to philosophy on the pages of Plato's "Laws." See Rutherford (2013).

2   Interviewed in the spring of 2014 by Clément Petitjean about his then recent book, *The Meaning of Sarkozy*, Alain Badiou takes up the vexed motif of identity in the following way:

> Since commodities are the principal motor of society, each person is called to appear before the market as a subject-consumer. In correlation with this, people fall back on identities, since to be drowned in the abstract world as an individual is a nightmare, wandering without end. So we cling to family, provincial, national, linguistic and religious identities. Identities that are available to us because they refer back to the dawn of time. It is a world opposed to the encounter, a world of defensive retreat. (Badiou 2014, n.p.)

The concluding sentence, in picking up the thread of the encounter, strings these remarks into the preceding conversation with Petitjean, a conversation that concerns itself not simply with Althusser's late concept of the encounter, but with the conflict between philosophy and this particular concept. As Badiou explains, this has to do with the impasse between the logic of necessity (rationalism) and the logic of experience (empiricism) that, for him, defines philosophy. For my part, I am less interested in the concept of the encounter than I am in the provocative relation between philosophy and identity active in Badiou's formulation. In other words, if identity is what the consumer-subject appeals to so as to *avoid* the encounter, and if philosophy avoids thinking this concept, does this mean that philosophy and identity have something in common? Perhaps what they share is what de Man once invoked under the heading, "the resistance to theory?" That is, the reading that, in being resisted by Theory, effects the event of the encounter where Philosophy and identity fear to tread.

3   Jean-Luc Nancy in "The Unsacrificeable" has taken up these matters from a rather different angle, but since he argues strenuously against the relation between sacrifice and what he calls, taking his cue from both Bataille and Heidegger, "an absolute outside," a relation for which I advocate, some comments are called for. Nancy is concerned here with the violently ecstatic character of this relation and its destructive sublation of the spiritualization of sacrifice (see Nietzsche's aphorism number 55 in *Beyond Good and Evil*). I take the point, but much hangs on what is meant by "absolute" in Nancy's formulation. For my part, if one recognizes in it Foucault's concept of "break," that is, the radical historicity (the point at which history is no longer history) of the Kantian "noumena," then the onto-theological disaster feared by Nancy and fended off by the principle of the "unsacrificable" loses much of its horror. Not its gravity, but its horror. To sacrifice Theory properly is to offer it to the possibility of onto-epistemic transgression. The political history of "absolutism" should reassure us in the regard.

4   Although perhaps overstated, what is clear about *After Theory* is that it is deeply invested in what Agamben calls the "politicization of death." This does not first and foremost concern the politics of killing (who, e.g., authorized and executed the murder and quartering of Jamal Khashoggi), but rather the sovereign power over the zone of indistinction wherein life and death brush insistently up against one another. From such a perspective one reads Eagleton's persistent rhetorical appeals to death and

blood (the basic binary is "bloodless," bad; "full blooded," good) with pricked ears. Even correcting for a certain Lawrencian identification, Eagleton is plainly involved in struggling over the matter of the political meaning of death, proposing both implicitly and explicitly that the bloodless blood of Theory (his figure is that of the "bloodstained coin" (Eagleton 2003, 161)) will be on the hands of those who, in denying the blunt facticity of the body, abandon any means by which to protect themselves from a death unchecked by moral condemnation. Theory will aneurysmalize itself. Like the fundamentalist martyr, the postmodern theorist is, apparently, always already hurling toward the instant but empty paradise of self-immolation. There are moments, alas, when Eagleton appears to want a piece of this action. One might then propose that Theory—perhaps uniquely in its postmodern incarnation—assumes the status of "bare life" in Eagleton's analysis. Precisely to the extent that it has become bloodless, or is otherwise already dead ("cold-blooded" in Eagleton's parlance), it cannot be sacrificed. It cannot be sacrificed because it has nothing to give, it has nothing of value to secure its status as a totem. Even if we interpret Eagleton's argument to say that Theory must be sacrificed to or for politics, what seems clear is that in aspiring to an articulation of sovereign power, that is, the authority to exempt from life that which menaces it, he founds his politics on the very zone of indistinction that distinctly complicates the difference between Theory and politics. Indulge me as I then uncharitably suggest that this dilemma appears to suit Eagleton to, as we say, a T, the very letter whose introduction converts morality into mortality, the very letter *tau* that in the Semitic alphabets marked the brand, indeed brand x, that rendered an animal, for example *taurus*, one's property. T, it so happens, also sounds out the name with which Eagleton signs *After Theory*, "TE" (Eagleton 2003, 227).

Chapter 1

QUEER RESISTANCE: FOUCAULT AND THE *UNNAMABLE*

A crucial aspect of the thinking of context bears on the when–where–who of that which is to be contextualized. As I have suggested, the "who" of this series, as the index and avatar of identity, has come illegitimately to operate as a metonymy for the whole. It has done so at the expense of Theory, or so I contend. To develop this argument one might pose a rather direct "methodological" question, namely, *where* is it that Theory takes place, or, *when* does it happen? While this might appear to submit to a preemptive gesture of contextualization, consider that the bizarreness of the question, particularly as it avoids the standard attributive maneuver—who wrote it?—indicates that there is more here than meets the ear. Matters become even more challenging when we consider that Theory's uncanny status as the "chronic" implies that wherever and whenever it takes place, it isn't quite. Instead, however, of sitting stunned before this aporia, let me propose that it is precisely under such circumstances that the attractions of reading assert themselves. This never-quite-happening or always-having-happened quality of Theory calls out for attention. Not an interpretation. Not a production of the sense of Theory's situation, its identity under these circumstances, but a *reading* of the potential ensnarled in the chronic condition of Theory. As this clearly implies, reading is more than literacy, or if it is literacy, then literacy is more than the exercise of a narrowly defined linguistic competence. Put differently, and to use an expression whose evocativeness we have grown deaf to, what must reading be if one can "read a or the situation"? Is it a "decoding" as Stuart Hall once famously argued? If so, what is the code of the situation, or the encounter, that is deployed in the act of decoding? To be clear, the drift of such questions derives not from the now compulsory impatience with "language" that one hears everywhere and every time we speak of affect, body, technology, objects, matter and so on, but with the distinctive pressure put on the work of reading Theory when its character *as* reading is taken seriously.

To draw this out, even in some sense to parade it, I turn to the work of Michel Foucault, not the now canonical statements about madness, reason, the clinic, things, discipline, knowledge, power, sexuality and so on, not even the lectures in which these statements were vulcanized and whose insistent contemporary circulation testifies to our refusal, as with Elvis, to live without him. No, I want to read the event of his inaugural lecture at the Collège de France in 1971, the talk titled, "The Order of Discourse." I want us to ponder in what way we can read Theory as occurring within, while also generating, the dispersed contexts of this event. As the title of this chapter makes clear, "queerness" and Theory will rub each other here and perhaps even in the right way.[1]

What's in an acronym or, as some prefer, initialism? As I write we have just marked the 50th-year commemoration of the so-called Stonewall Riots, that is, the uprising that developed in response to vice squad raids that took place at and around the Stonewall Inn in New York City during June of 1969. I trust then I will be forgiven for having the acronym LGBTQ in mind. Initially, the acronym took form as both a protest against inaccurate labeling and the assertion of a certain coalitional consciousness. It included only three letters: LGB. Over the course of the ensuing decades it became alphabetically enhanced assuming its current form, and the matter is in dispute, in the late 1990s. A politics of coalition among communities has gradually given way to a metaphysics of intersectionality, with each letter a "proxy" (Gayatri Spivak might insist) for an identity, so, Lesbian, Gay, Bisexual and Trans-gendered (as opposed to cis-gendered). The odd letter out is Q. It is the one letter that has consistently denoted two separate things: a community (Queers) and a practice (questioning). At the very least, Q is a proxy for a split identity, and this is part of what makes "queer" into a concept whose power is far from exhausted even if it is stopping more frequently at march oases.

The title of the path-breaking volume, *Queering the Pitch*, is an expedient way to elaborate the point I am concerned to make here, which is embedded, as it were, in the titular pun (Brett, Wood and Thomas, 1994). Queering a pitch invites immediate comparison with the musical practice of "bending a note," in effect, with the means by which a "blue" or slurred note is produced. Queering thus becomes a technique, a practice that makes a virtue of tonal intemperance. By the same token, queering *the* pitch (especially in a musicological context where the study of pitch-class sets has set the standard for a certain type of disciplinary knowledge) means altering, or problematizing, the very concept of pitch. Here, "queering" becomes the articulation of an alternative paradigm for reading and therefore constituting pitch.

It is this second connotation that I am interested in evoking through my chapter title, and it is this aspect of queer theory that, one might argue, has prompted the critical scrutiny it has sustained. Queer resistance is not exclusively or even primarily about the resistance carried out by subjects willing, under still unbearable circumstances, to bear the designation "queer." It is not resisting queers. As the very structure of paronomasia would suggest, queer resistance resituates the queer subject within the articulation of an alternative paradigm of resistance. In other words, queers may well become where their resistance was (to misquote Freud). However, to avoid falling prey to the embarrassment of a circular argument (if queers do not precede queer resistance, then in what sense is *their* resistance queer), it is crucial that one delineate what is distinctive about the resistant practices that secure or enable queer identities. Historically, one might argue that this lesson was most emphatically relearned when it became possible for men to be feminists. Feminist resistance, in spite of the tenacious link between "females" and feminism (a link with an identitarian strategic value within the broadly professional sector), does not, in fact, presuppose a specific engendered identity as its agent. Moreover, the gains of feminism have often been embodied in alternative paradigms, for example, in the pedagogical field, where the otherwise attenuated paronomasiac aspect of "feminist resistance" clearly reasserts itself.

This said, it remains to specify what constitutes the distinctive tactical profile of queer resistance. It is what I will call inauthenticity. If queer theory has come to serve as the odd beacon of so many nomadic strains of poststructural, postmodern and even postcolonial analyses, it is because it has distilled the precipitate of the inauthentic from the politics of representation. In Adorno's polemical assessment, authenticity, at least in its rigorously phenomenological sense (a sense, I would argue, which props up even the most quotidian of its recent applications, say, in debates about the difference between digital and analogue sound signals), rests on a misrecognized fusion of language and being (Adorno 1973, *passim*). By contrast, partisans of the inauthentic (and here I too am rehabilitating an epithet) insist upon the ontologically consequential antagonism between language and being, where identities become the unstable effect of the discourses that break up and socialize being. As the "feminist" scholar Judith Butler might say, performance precedes both existence and essence, where the point is not, as some have charged, to translate everything into language. Instead, the stress on the performative was designed to radicalize the philosophy of praxis by delimiting a problem (namely, if we are always already making sense and the world, then we ourselves are this interminable labor) whose subtleties require that it be explored outside the field dominated by the neat opposition between being and language. In Nick de Villiers's provocative study of "opacity," this point is given a formulation in which we recognize that the matter concerns not merely performance but the opaque performance of a Warhol or a certain "masked philosopher."

Under the broad heading of the politics of representation, as is well known, literature and literary theory came to have a cortical status. The socio-genesis of this phenomenon is not what requires immediate attention especially since it has been discussed innumerable times before. Instead, what I want to draw attention to is the way inauthenticity and, what Nietzsche might call, the transvaluation of all literary values figure within the same genealogical constellation. Let us just say, for the sake of provocation, that literature was decisive here because of the way its study prompted many to rethink the relation between language and being, especially once language had been reconceptualized within the purview of structural linguistics where literature was stripped of its elevated status. Foucault, who along with Deleuze and Klossowski participated centrally in the Nietzsche revival of the 1960s, was among the first (one would, as Badiou might insist, also have to include Lacan here) to begin subjecting this relation to sustained historical and philosophical scrutiny. Though initially, at least in *The Order of Things*, this took the form of an archaeological, that is, spatiotemporalized, reconstruction of the "being of language," after 1970 these archaeological preoccupations gave way to a radicalized concept of discourse and the distinctly genealogical hybrid of power/knowledge. What deserves special emphasis here is the fact that though literature (roughly, the Eurocentric tradition of letters that extended from the picaresque to the "new novel," with special emphasis on the masculinist pantheon of Sade, Hölderlin, Artaud, Bataille and Roussel) played a decisive role in Foucault's early analyses, it becomes all but entirely absent in the later work where, through the treatment of disciplinary power and the apparatus of sexuality, he lays out the theoretical principles that really underpin the concept of inauthenticity as it figures in the debates in and around queer theory.[2]

This overstates the case to some degree (there is, after all, a brilliant microgenealogy of crime fiction in Part One of *Discipline and Punish*), but it enables me to pinpoint the problem whose exploration will help us come to terms with what is at stake in the concept of queer resistance. Though *Discipline and Punish* and the first volume of *The History of Sexuality* (in English, *The Will to Know*) are separated only by a year, one cannot help but be struck by Foucault's extravagant insistence upon the possibility of resistance in the second book. This was prompted by the fact that the concept of power mapped out in *Discipline and Punish* seemed to have thrown the baby of resistance out with the bathwater of truth. If revolt, which grounded itself in truth, justice and the rational law of history, could not reliably be separated from the field of power/knowledge in which it made sense, then perhaps it was groundless or, worse, nonexistent. As Foucault himself once provocatively put it, "is it useless to revolt?" To counter the obviously unacceptable political implications of this, he moved quickly to reinstate the possibility of resistance, an activity with which he was well acquainted in a variety of practical contexts. Unfortunately, this was not enough. For, to reinstate the possibility of resistance is not yet to establish either its necessity or its efficacy, and Foucault's critics, particularly those within the legions of scholars influenced, directly or indirectly, by Jürgen Habermas, have not hesitated to point this out.

My point in redirecting our attention to Foucault's inaugural lecture—the "performance" or event I will read here—is as follows. Countless commentators have read the lecture as the hinge between the archaeological and the genealogical Foucault, between the Foucault of epistemes and the Foucault of power. Implicitly, this gives the lecture the status of a site of "emergence" for the notion of power that allegedly disallows or ineptly preserves the concept of resistance. I do not dispute that the lecture marks a significant event in the intellectual trajectory of Foucault's career, but I see this in terms of the way he encounters and initiates an alternative paradigm of resistance; an alternative he later assumed, wrongly, could be taken for granted in the book on the prison and which, therefore, required specification in the book on sexuality. Crucial to the articulation of this alternative paradigm is the discourse of literary modernism, and the work of Samuel Beckett in particular. Indeed, if I stress the crucial character of this evocation of Beckett it is because I believe it can be shown that it is through the strategic, and institutionally specific, deployment of *The Unnamable* that Foucault carries over his engagement with literature into his elaboration of the terms of what I am calling inauthentic, and therefore queer, resistance.

A word about the madness of method. I was not present when Foucault delivered his inaugural lecture on the evening of December 2, 1970. I would have liked to have been, but I was not. According to an archivist at Les Fonds Michel Foucault, no recording survives. Nevertheless, I would prefer not to express my regret as an implicit apology for the inauthenticity, and therefore defiantly compromised character, of my analysis. Instead, what seems called for is a reading of the text of the lecture, a reading that unfolds in a "sociographic" echo chamber where architectural space in winter, speaking and listening bodies, furniture, media of various sort (including paper and words written on it), even smoke, drift in and out of contact with each other. This requires that one then read such a text as though it were, in the evocative words of Barthes—later Foucault's colleague at the Collège de France—"cruising" us, sizing us up, down and around. As those familiar with Barthes's *The Pleasure of the Text* know, cruising (a term, *drager*, with wide resonance in the gay subculture of Paris and elsewhere) designates a reading of a "writable" text; that is, a text in which the scriptor's body figures as a phantasy for the reader who is called upon to invest in the collaborative labor of making the text produce sense (Barthes 1975, 4). In addition to interrupting the "readable" obsession with what the author means (either consciously or unconsciously), this approach queerly "sexualizes" the experience of this interruption. I say "queerly" because Barthes is openly corroding the authentic link between sexed bodies and sexuality, replacing it with a concept of sexual practice that bleeds into a field of activities that would appear, at first glance, to have little or nothing to do with sex. And while some have criticized this as the quintessential expression of Barthes's troubling, even closeted, asceticism, I think his effort to specify the practical, ordinary field of what Foucault calls the "apparatus" (*dispositif*, so, the nonpositive or negative) of sexuality is crucial intellectual and political work. Barthes, after all, was not advocating reading instead of having sex. Read *Incidents*. Nor, for that matter, was he advocating reading (a book) while having sex, although the "thinking of another" underscored in *A Lover's Discourse* might in a pinch be construed in such terms. Instead, he was inviting those of us who "enjoy" the roughness of reading to see it as a way to proliferate the angles that might be explored for the production of carnal knowledge.

Thus, my reading of the inaugural lecture approaches it as though Foucault were "cruising" me, that is, reading him as though he were inviting me to participate in his desire to speak without knowing either where or who I am. As we shall see, this slippery drama of the voice, one's encounter with it, is an absolutely crucial aspect of the inaugural lecture. Indeed, it is here in this when and where of the lecture that Theory happens; not precisely its queer theory, but a queerness that resonates, that sounds within the Theory we misname by calling it "Foucauldian."

Anyone who has read the inaugural lecture carefully has probably been struck by the peculiar self-reflexivity of its opening.

> I wish I could have slipped surreptitiously into this discourse which I must present today, and into the ones I shall have to give here, perhaps for many years to come. I should have preferred to be enveloped by speech [...]. I should have preferred to become aware that a nameless voice was already speaking long before me, so that I should only have needed to join in, to continue the sentence it (*lui*) had started and lodge myself [...], in its interstices [...]. I should have liked there to be a voice behind me which had begun to speak a very long time before, doubling in advance everything I was going to say, a voice which would say, "You must go on, I can't go on, you must go on, I'll go on, you must say words, as long as there are any, until they find me, strange pain, strange sin, you must go on, perhaps its done already, perhaps they have said me already, perhaps they have carried me to the threshold of my story, before the door that opens on my story, that would surprise me, if it opened." (Foucault 1981, 51)

Jean Lacouture, who covered the lecture for *Le Monde*, was clearly struck by this opening gambit in which he heard the faint sound of a repudiation of May '68 through Foucault's refusal to execute a bold *prise de parole* (a "taking" of the floor) (Lacouture 1970, n.p.). And, Lacouture was not alone. When interviewed in the mid-1980s by Foucault's later biographer, Didier Eribon, another member of Foucault's audience, Claude Lévi-Strauss—when asked about his opinion of Foucault's work—said this about the lecture:

> His work touches me because of its stylistic qualities—I recall his inaugural lecture at the Collège de France. It was very beautiful in a literary way, tinged with feeling. On the other hand, I have reservations about an attitude that seems to repeat at every turn, Watch out, things are not as you believe, it is the other way around. In a word, an attitude that says black is white and white is black. This enlightens me concerning the author's opinions, but tells me nothing else: a photographic negative and positive both contain the same amount of information. (Lévi-Strauss 1991, 72)

A faint refusal tinged with feeling ("strange pain, strange sin") manages to attract the attention of both journalism and anthropology. However, what makes Foucault's delineation of the enunciation of the lecture especially interesting is not chiefly the sentiment of humility or anxiety that it gives expression to (both are perfectly comprehensible given the occasion) but the details of the desire that it enunciates. Why this fascination with slipping into someone else's discourse, or being addressed from behind by a voice without a name—a fascination given concrete expression through Foucault's extended citation of Samuel Beckett's *The Unnamable*? To answer these questions, as well as those raised at the outset, our reading has to trace this intertextual ping through the page, through the lecture hall, through the bilingual border between French and English.

The citation from Beckett comes from the tail end of *The Unnamable*. It is where Beckett's text coils back on itself, devouring everything that has preceded that moment as the "prehistory" of a story readers assume they have, in fact, just read. The tortured temporality of this characteristically "modernist" moment is duly reflected in the voicing of the passage where the narrator shifts back and forth between the position of subject and object, the speaker and the spoken. In this respect, one might argue that the allusion to Beckett is motivated by the symmetry between his staging of the instability of the narrator and Foucault's problematization of the moment of enunciation; his own acting of lecturing and thereby entering the order of discourse. This line of argumentation is encouraged when, later in Foucault's lecture, he takes up the problematic status of the author. Aside from the fact that Foucault's discussion of the author stresses its function in the immanent channeling of discourse—the very theme of his own opening remarks—this development prompts us (as if whispered to) to return to Foucault's nearly contemporaneous essay "What Is an Author?" where one of the only two other sustained published allusions to Beckett's work is to be found.

This essay, written in 1969 and revised during the early 1970s, opens and closes with a citation from the opening of Beckett's third text in his collection, *Texts for Nothing*. It reads, "Leave. I was going to leave all that. What matter who's speaking, someone said what matters who's speaking" (Beckett 1967, 85). As many will know, Foucault exploits the citation to question the traditional importance assigned by literary criticism to the author as the presumed guarantor of a text's meaning. His point is not to dismiss the author as a sociohistorical being, but to challenge the way this being is abstracted and made to function as an interpretive device. Now, even at this rudimentary level of analysis it is not hard to hear how this line of inquiry converges with the one inaugurating the inaugural lecture. In both cases, the boundaries, the lips of discourse—particularly as these might be conceived in relation to the agency of its enunciation—are not only raised as issues, but they are figured into the contours of Foucault's texts (the *beginning* of the lecture and the *end* of the essay) at their own boundaries, as if to execute formally, almost anatomically, the interplay of voices wished for in the inaugural lecture. Once we sense this, it becomes difficult to treat these references to Beckett as mere citations or allusions. They are reaching for more. In addition, if we continue to treat these references as though they were motivated by nothing more than Foucault's perception of a certain analogy or symmetry between his immediate situation as an inductee at the Collège de France, and Beckett's quintessentially modernist experience of writing, then I think we risk missing something decisive about the gestures being carried out by—not simply in, but by—the inaugural lecture. We miss our encounter with Theory in its reading.

Let us then return to the lecture and detail its rhythm more carefully. It is divided into eight segments (parts of which were suppressed, on the evening of its delivery, for reasons of time), the last of these reiterating and giving concrete expression to the theme of locating or losing one's voice in the voice of another. Thus, the suspension opened in the first segment is provided with closure in the eighth. Aside from the fact that the final segment testifies to Foucault's ability to master the rigors of organic form, it is striking because this segment takes the lecture in the most traditional of directions, as if the space of the occasion were writing itself into the lecture. In effect, it converts it into an homage. Specifically, Foucault discusses his debt (and the economic vocabulary is not coincidental) to three men: George Dumézil, a comparative historian of religion (later credited by Foucault with solving the riddle of Socrates' debt to Asclepius), George Canquilhem, a historian of science and persistent benefactor, and, most importantly, Jean Hyppolite, then probably the most significant French interpreter of Hegel after Alexandre Kojève. In fact, it is precisely the impact of Hyppolite's reading of Hegel that Foucault cites as the motivation for his homage, though one ought not forget that it was Hyppolite's death that created an opening for Foucault in the Collège, thus rendering the homage simultaneously an epitaph. To those unfamiliar with the philosophical issues at stake here this may seem peculiar, but Stanley Aronowitz, among others, has argued that Foucault's restless repudiation of the dialectical tradition embodied in the work of Hegel is what gave his own philosophical project its specificity (Aronowitz 1981, 306). Obviously, and Foucault says as much, Hyppolite is worthy of homage because his reading provided Foucault with a model for recognizing "what is still Hegelian in that which allows us to think against Hegel" (Foucault 1981, 74). Before we tease out how such a formulation resonates with the slippery drama of the voice staged at the opening of the lecture, let us make some effort to read the rich complexity of Foucault's relation to Hyppolite.

The book that launched Foucault's career, *The History of Madness*, was also one of the two "theses" that permitted Foucault to receive his *doctorat d' état* in philosophy. Though we might be inclined to think that this is the very least one ought to be given for writing such a book, the fact that it read like a history of institutional practices nevertheless made its strictly philosophical credentials suspect. The man who Foucault first contacted to shepherd this text through the French academic bureaucracy was his old teacher, Jean Hyppolite. Though Hyppolite felt unqualified to present the main thesis (*Madness*), his *piston* helped Foucault secure the crucial support of Georges Canguilhem. To this extent, Hyppolite did not only provide Foucault with the intellectual means *to think* the specificity of his own philosophical project, he quite literally facilitated Foucault's *access*—both pedagogic and professional—to the discourse of philosophy. Shortly after Foucault was given his first chair as the director of the philosophy department at the University of Paris at Vincennes, Hyppolite died.

In the wake of Hyppolite's death two official "homages" appeared. Foucault was involved in both of them. The first of these, the special issue of the French philosophic journal *Revue de métaphysique et de morale*, contains a remarkable tribute to Hyppolite by Foucault. The second homage appeared in book form as *Hommage à Jean Hyppolite*, where Foucault published "Nietzsche, Genealogy, History"—the paper that grew out of the courses offered at Vincennes. What makes the journal essay so evocative is the insistent attention Foucault devotes to Hyppolites's *voice*. Consider the opening paragraph of the essay:

> Those who took the preparatory courses for entry into the Ecole Normale Supérior after the war remember the course offered by M. Hyppolite on *The Phenomenology of Mind*: in that voice which never ceased taking stock of itself as if it were meditating on its own movement, we not only perceived the voice of a professor; we heard something of the voice of Hegel, and perhaps as well the voice of philosophy itself. (Foucault 1969, 76)

The focus here reminds one immediately of the inaugural moves of the inaugural lecture. In fact, the resemblance is so strong one is tempted to read the entire lecture as little more than a disguised homage that seeks to deflect attention to this by locating the homage proper in the explicit and plainly generic language of the final segment. To justify such a temptation one's reading must follow out the voice's relation to homage.

Homage, as a literary gesture, is a ritualistic vestige of feudalism. In the feudal context, at least within Europe, homage (from Medieval Latin, *hominaticum*) designated the ceremony through which vassals publicly recognized and affirmed their responsibility to the Lord. Interestingly, this recognition was a two-way street: the vassal agreed to serve as the Lord's delegate and tenant, and the Lord assumed responsibility for the vassal's protection.[3] With the slow dispersion of feudalism this ritualized ceremony spread beyond the religioeconomic sphere into the cultural sphere, where, despite this displacement the distinctive Hegelian logic of recognition remained intact. Accompanying this logic was the entire rhetoric of debt, but as homage became increasingly important to the reproduction of intellectual kin(g)ship systems, this irreducibly economic rhetoric had to alter in order to map itself onto the peculiar commodity of the voice. The reciprocity of homage was thus reconstituted as a dialogic exchange where "the subject's entry into language" was restaged as an economic and ultimately political relation. This aspect of homage is intensified when, as is often the case today, the fecundity of the voice being celebrated has been silenced by death. Under these circumstances, the voice of homage draws attention to its derivation from a voice whose authority derives solely from the homage's own projective power. Literary homage is thus almost always a form of self-enlargement, a swelling up.

Perhaps more importantly though, homage is also a site for the cultural construction of masculinity. As the term implies, homage is all about ritualizing the recognition of a man, not simply as the subject of a particular ceremony, but as a particular entity within the social division of gender—*ecce homo*.[4] Although feminist scholars have urged us to be deeply suspicious of rituals wherein the feigned reproductive power of men is being affirmed, it is important not to confuse affirmation with the sort of deliberate complication introduced within the ritual of homage by Foucault. Specifically, by focusing on the interplay of voices Foucault presents masculinity not merely as an effect of speech, or discourse more generally, but as a construct that, while remaining indissociable from the field of sexuality, nevertheless provokes us to encounter and thus question the limits of this field. In Foucault's hands, homage becomes a site where declaring oneself to be another's "man" is presented less as an occasion for fantasizing one's birth than as an occasion wherein one man discovers his own manhood in the mouth of another man. To this extent, Foucault backs away from the model of reproductive heterosexuality latent within traditional accounts of literary kinship. I am thinking here of the preemptive drama of the epigone, where the follower or adherent is explicitly modeled on the child (the *gonos*). What he retains is the figure of promiscuous interpenetration, but by attaching this to the problem of negotiating influence at the level of reading he revises the "sexual," even "erotic," sense of this gesture altogether. What we have then is a critique that is doubled over. That is, at the very moment that homage is homosexualized, sexuality is extended beyond the domain of corporeal intercourse.

But we have gotten ahead of ourselves. Surely there must be more evidence for such a reading of the lecture than the slim rhetorical details gathered so far. Indeed there is. To elaborate this evidence it is necessary to return to the citation of Beckett that led us to anticipate the interplay of voices in Foucault's homage to Hyppolite and the other men. I have already emphasized the way this intertextual gesture enables the split opening of Foucault's lecture to engorge the tail end of Beckett's "novel," but at this point we ought to ask ourselves, why *The Unnamable*?

I would like to propose that it is precisely because Beckett's novel prefigures the chain of associations I have been exploring in the lecture that it comes to serve as the focus of Foucault's interests. Since such a proposition contradicts the obvious, namely, that as the quintessentially repressed, homosexual desire is ideally figured as "the unnamable," we must return to the novel in order to justify it. Consider the following passage:

> One might as well speak and be done with it. What liberty! I strained my ear towards what must have been my voice still, so weak, so far, that it was like the sea, a far calm sea dying—no, none of that, no beach, no shore, the sea is enough. I've had enough of shingle, enough of sand, enough of earth, enough of sea too. Decidedly Basil is becoming important. I'll call him Mahood instead, I prefer that, I'm queer. It was he that told me stories about me, lived in my stead, issued forth from me, came back to me, entered back into me, heaped stories upon my head. I don't

know how it was done. I always like not knowing, but Mahood said it wasn't right. He didn't know either, but it worried him. It is his voice which has often, always, mingled with mine, and sometimes drowned it completely. Until he left me for good, or refused to leave me any more, I don't know. (Beckett 1958, 309)

This is one of innumerable passages in the novel where it reflects upon the activity of its own production. Here we witness the birth of Mahood from Basil, a birth that—through the device of a certain pronominal ambiguity—shuffles the positions of author, narrator, character and reader. Of course, particularly suggestive about this passage is the explicit association made within it between the interpenetration of voices and the "narratorial" declaration, "I'm queer," followed by various evocations of positions whose "sexual" character would be hard to deny. Although the French version of the tale obscures the homosexual allusion (*Je suis bizarre*), it is important that in his translation Beckett allows what in British (or Irish) slang is more than an innocuous allusion circulate. Moreover, the couple Basil/Mahood is quite suggestive in its own right. In particular, the name "Mahood," with its intense orthographic evocation of "ma(n)hood," invites one to read the displacement of Basil (potentially a Wilde allusion) as an event rather than like an homage, that is, a moment where one's manhood is, if not publicly declared, then certainly withdrawn from another man. Perhaps this is why the issue of whether one is at liberty to speak figures so prominently in this textual episode.

Of course, Foucault is likely to have read Beckett in French. Significantly though, in the one other extended treatment of Beckett, Foucault's response to questions put to him by Jean Domenach of *Esprit*, he explicitly links the peculiarities of his own identity with the themes activated in the passage from *The Unnamable*. Just two years before the inaugural lecture Foucault writes:

I must admit that you have characterized with extreme accuracy what I have undertaken to do, and that you have at the same time identified the point of inevitable discord: "to introduce discontinuity and the constraints of system into the history of the mind." Yes, I accept this diagnosis almost entirely. Yes, I recognize that this is scarcely a justifiable move. With diabolical pertinence you have succeeded in giving a definition of my work to which I cannot avoid subscribing, but for which no one would reasonably wish to assume responsibility. I suddenly sense how bizarre my position is, how strange, how illegitimate. (*Soudain, je sens toute ma bizarrerie, mon étrangeté si peu légitime*). And I now perceive how far this work, […] has deviated from the best established norms, how jarring it was bound to seem. (Burchell et al. 1991, 53)

As we have now been led to expect, Beckett enters this text at its tail end. In fact, the very last sentence of Foucault's response is the same cited phrase that concludes "What is an Author?": "What matter who is speaking; someone has said, what matter who is speaking." Again, Beckett's language is invoked as Foucault's voice trails off, as if to enact formally the slipping into the other's voice that inaugurates the homage of the inaugural lecture. What is more, in the passage cited above, especially in the original French, the difference between Foucault and his intellectual position (advocating the introduction of discontinuity in the history of the mind) is blurred to the precise degree that the exclusionary rhetoric of clinical discourse is invoked to describe both. Specifically, Foucault characterizes Domenach's analysis as a "diagnosis" that illuminates not only his bizarreness but also the illegitimate and deviant character of, as we say, what he is doing. Here is an elegantly forceful articulation of Foucault's wry awareness of the link between his experience of homosexuality and his work; both significantly deviant, even as Huffer would say, erratically deviant. Introducing discontinuity into the life of the mind is thus made tantamount to a refusal of reproductive heterosexuality, where the libidinal economy of the continuity of generations is made explicit. Moreover, and this is the concern that motivated my turn to the response to *Esprit* in the first place, Foucault uses virtually the same word that Beckett translates as "queer" to name the position Domenach's "diabolical" (the irony would not be lost on the editor of a Catholic monthly) questioning exposed. Is it not also suggestive that Foucault's French biographer, Didier Eribon, found it necessary to invoke the term "bizarre" when describing the way Foucault was perceived by his colleagues at Clermont-Ferrand where, in the period immediately preceding the texts we are examining here, he created quite the stir by giving his lover, Daniel Defert, a post in the philosophy department (Eribon 1991, 141)?

Of course, the passage from *The Unnamable* is also inscribed with the oblique thematics of an homage (the extraction of Mahood from Basil). But, even if Foucault were to have overlooked this, it is hard to deny that there is a strong affiliation between what is staged in the opening of the inaugural lecture and Beckett's novelistic inscription of the sexuality of speaking. Yet what does this really tell us about the tactical register of Foucault's presentation? I do not think that we should conclude that what I have constructed here are the surreptitious means by which Foucault "came out" to his audience at the Collège de France. This gesture would have been unnecessary since many of those in attendance were aware of Foucault's status as a *gai* scientist. Moreover, "coming out" would have been of paramount importance primarily to a gay man who would regard failing to do so on such an occasion as an act of personal "dishonesty." As we have seen, Foucault is not committed to the notion of authenticity that grounds this sort of conclusion. Nevertheless, Foucault *does* make a point of characterizing the fate of his desire throughout the lecture. My sense is that there is thus a broader political issue inflecting Foucault's self-presentation, one that addresses precisely the problems of power and the discursive articulation of queer resistance. Queer (/) questioning.

In emphasizing this I do not mean to imply that the question of homosexuality is either subordinated to or displaced by a more general political problematic. In fact, what is intriguing about the lecture is the way Foucault plays out the relation between power "in general" and homosexual politics. To explore this, however briefly, consider the following remarks on power from the first volume of Foucault's *History of Sexuality*—a study announced in the lecture.

> Where there is power, there is resistance, and yet, or rather consequently, this resistance is never in a position of exteriority in relation to power. [The existence of power relationships] depends on a multiplicity of points of resistance: these play the role of adversary, target, support or handle[.] These points of resistance are present everywhere in the power network. [...] Resistances do not derive from a few heterogeneous principles; but neither are they a lure or a promise that is of necessity betrayed. They are the odd term (*l' autre terme*) in relations of power; they are inscribed in the latter as an irreducible opposite (*l' irreductible vis à vis*). Hence they too are distributed in irregular fashion: the points, knots or focuses of resistance are spread over time and space at varying densities, at times mobilizing groups or individuals in a definitive way, inflaming certain parts of the body, certain moments in life, certain types of behavior. (Foucault 1980, 95–96)

These remarks appear in the section of Foucault's text devoted to methodology. As such, they formulate the conviction that if one treats power as a mode of productivity (rather than prohibition, as exemplified in the concept of the law), then resistance to power must be understood to arise from within the general field of power relations. As suggested earlier, this formulation seeks to make explicit what Foucault believed he could take for granted, namely, the irreducibility of resistance as a methodological category. Although Foucault addresses the problem of resistance, both theoretically and practically, in the remaining volumes of *The History of Sexuality*, I want to explore it in relation to the context created here by my reading of the "sociographic" echo chamber of the lecture.

Is there not a rather suggestive symmetry between the self-reflexive opening of the lecture—an opening which, as we have seen, immediately swallows the tail end of Beckett's tale—and the intercourse between power and resistance as it is mapped out in *The History of Sexuality*? All that has really dropped out in the six years separating the two texts is the subjunctive mood wherein a wish to slip surreptitiously into the voice of authority has given way to an implicit affirmation of the mouth as a bizarrely inflamed point of resistance *within* the spiral of power, here figured as a face-to-face (vis-à-vis) encounter. What this observation implies, of course, is that the lecture is being presented to us as a sample of institutional resistance. However, the lecture assumes this status not merely because it formulates a political theory of discourse but because it *performs* resistance even before its Theory has been written (assuming, for the moment, that this was done in earnest during the mid-1970s). Perhaps this belatedness of Theory is only the most subtle inscription of Foucault's Hegelianism?

Significantly, this performance takes the form of what deserves to be considered a queer and to that extent "homosexualized" rendition of the ritual of homage. Seen in this light, Foucault's manipulation of the honorific formula, "Since I owe so much to him [Hyppolite], I can well see that in choosing to invite me to teach here, you are in large part paying homage to him[,]" (Foucault 1981, p. 76) becomes most provocative. In effect, by drawing his auditors into the sexuality of his own articulation of the homage, and then fusing their respect with his desire, Foucault manages to pervert (literally, to turn it back around) the entire ceremony from within. He was not so much "coming out" as, so to speak, "coming in." Of course, the question arises as to whether any of his auditors sensed what was taking place. I would suggest that the following remarks of the intrepid Jean Lacouture indicate that at the very least he did.

> Hesiod or not, a good talk is incomplete without praise. M. Michel Foucault had chosen not to open in a traditional way, but to enclose his opening in an homage to three of his masters: Dumézil, Canguilhem and Jean Hyppolite, his predecessor and the chief voter in these places. One could not have accomplished this task with greater warmth, and by the way, there was something even a little diabolical that burned in his flickering (*scintillant*) discourse which appeared to found itself on a fugitive harmony. (Lacouture 1970, n.p.)

Even if Lacouture was unaware of the public exchange between Domenach and Foucault, where the diabolical character of the former's "diagnosis" of Foucault's deviance figured prominently, it is clear that in teasing out the details of Foucault's "warmth" he is doing more than perfunctorily noting its irony. In fact, as my earlier evocation of Lacouture's report implies, he was quite struck (mentioning it twice) by the maneuvering that opened the lecture, a maneuvering that was deeply and diversely structured by "*l 'inommable*" (not only the unnameable but also the undeniable, the un-no-able). What is politically important here is not whether the auditors truly recognized that they were being positioned as *gai* scientists, but rather that by participating in the oral drama staged in the lecture, Foucault's audience could no longer recognize where, in their immediate experience, "homosexuality" started and stopped. This is precisely the effect sought after by queer theory where—in the piety of questioning—no one is either as straight or as gay as s/he thinks. Obviously, if one begins by grounding homosexual being in the notion of authenticity then the importance I am attaching to Foucault's tactical decision is greatly diminished, if not negated altogether. But what exactly would have been gained from confronting an audience with a pose whose political effects might well have been exhausted in the shock of scandal or neutralized in the complacency of tolerance? It seems to me that the political question raised here can only be resolved by appealing to an analytical framework wherein the general principles to be tested at the practical level are elaborated in some detail. I will address this impossible task by briefly delineating how Foucault's theoretical convictions surface within the tactical gestures of the inaugural lecture.

Though much of what I have argued so far might lead one to expect that the convictions animating Foucault's "micro-physics of power" flow directly out of his being gay, seeking to delineate these principles in such a context would lead off in precisely the wrong direction. Instead, I want to underscore how the interpenetration of resistance and power—a structural relation Foucault treats as a methodological principle—organizes the tactics of the lecture. As we have seen, the lecture responds to an institutional solicitation by activating a perfectly traditional ritual—the homage. At this rather generic level, Foucault permits power to dictate the form of his statement. But, by dragging this form into contact with the modernist literary problematic of authorial voice, an exchange is effected wherein the lecture/homage, as a rite of passage, is mixed up with a writing practice that, by virtue of its articulate reticence, evokes another problematic passage: does Beckett belong within the field of *belles lettres* or not, and more importantly, if he does belong, to which national field does he belong—English/Irish or French?[5] This exchange transforms or certainly rattles both the ritual and literary modernism. The ritual, as a rite of *passage*, cannot avoid the issue of the contact between what is proper to an institution and what is not, or at least *not yet*, while literary modernism—often defined in terms of the anti-institutional and therefore redemptive power of the difficulties encountered by readers in penetrating its linguistic insularity—is forced to confront the socio-institutional conditions of its effects. When this relation, or exchange, is enveloped by the "homosexualized" drama of the voice, it is doubled. I have already indicated how homosexual desire (Hocquenghem's formulation) and speaking in, or through, another are *both* altered when brought into thematic proximity (speech is embodied or sexualized, sex is disembodied or signified), but when we superimpose this alteration on the exchange between the lecture/homage and literary modernism it becomes possible to detect a significant cluster of resistance within this tactical configuration. Thus, supplementing the alteration of sex and speaking is an alteration of canon formation and intellectual genealogy, where "belonging" is sexualized to the precise degree that sexuality is again conceptualized as a setup, an apparatus. Taken in isolation these alterations mean little, but brought into configuration they trace the incoherence and irrationality of the social field which otherwise appears to order the instances (sex, speech, homage, etc.) defining it. This cluster of resistance arises within power, but precisely at those points where the historically sedimented heterogeneity of the social field obliges power to enter into conflict with itself. Rather than further elaborate the conditions of this resistance, I will flesh out the fate of "homosexuality" as it fans out here and draw on this to delineate what I take to be its specifically queer character.

Put succinctly, "homosexuality" is here definitively detached from the notion of authenticity, that is, the idea that one's sexual identity comes *before* the conditions of its articulation, its performance (in Butler's terms). What is more, the political struggle for the freedom of sexual orientation is connected, within the lecture, to the task of forming hegemonic practices—practices that resist power from within power by establishing relays among different sites of contestation that are no longer protected from one another by the notion of authenticity. Within the lecture, Foucault involves his auditors in his erection of relays between those sites where practices of contestation are defined by struggles over institutional boundaries, namely, the troubled canonization of a radically bilingual modernist, the paradoxical acquisition of "one's *own* voice" and the uneven social reproduction of sexual norms. In each case, the bearer of authenticity—tradition, voice, nature—is displaced by the arrangement (or setup) in which conflicted and contending bearers of authenticity are made to occupy the same structural position. In fact, as I interpret the lecture and thus labor to put words in the mouth of this dead author, the context of my own activities is drawn into this "sociographic" echo chamber. Accordingly, the objectivity that would otherwise authenticate my reading is itself displaced. While it is certainly true that this ensemble is neither exhaustive nor universal, it is irreducibly and decisively unstable. What is more, literary discourse, as embodied in the work of Beckett, comprises an indispensable component of this ensemble, an ensemble that exemplifies the very possibility of resistance in Foucault's late conceptualization of power. While it is true that such a reading does not, in itself, rescue queer theory from either its detractors or its devotees, it does nevertheless clarify that the burning question for all parties is actually about the link, at once theoretical and practical, between resistance and revolt.

When Foucault invites us to read the orally complicated homage as a site of gay struggle, he is not merely sexualizing public speaking, he is remapping "homosexuality." The point is not to trivialize the latter, to make speaking equivalent to the struggle to survive homophobia, but to proliferate the contexts wherein interventions designed to contest and upset compulsory heterosexuality might take place. Obviously, this is not simply a matter of terrain, it is more fundamentally a matter of constituencies—in fact, precisely those constituencies mobilized by the relays delineated above. If one attempts to either restrict or order the proliferation of constituencies by invoking authenticity as a theoretical principle, then one risks either conflating the political with the immediately personal or sacrificing one's political aims to the restricted aspirations of social tolerance and assimilation. Against this we have the sort of convictions articulated by Foucault—principles that the lecture can be read to show need not be interpreted as sacrificing resistance to power. Clearly, I am urging that the sample of resistance offered to us in the inaugural lecture is one we ought to taste. If I designate this resistance as queer, it is because it does not proceed from a "coming to consciousness" that then seeks out the appropriate vehicles and organizations for the articulation of its interests and/ or desires. What is queer about Foucault's resistance, as others have noted, is that it situates the contestation of sexuality within a field of antagonized and conflicted constituencies that is abounding with inauthenticity. In other words, precisely because no one can be what s/he wants to be, can the different fights be made part of a hegemonic struggle? This possibility is not latent within the wills or the desires of the agents, it is something that must be fabricated in the conditions of the agents' agency. Foucault's account of power only shows that there is no inherently resistant quality that conditions the struggle of agents. I really see no point, in the present historical conjuncture, of pretending we know exactly who our friends are when it may very well turn out that our desires converge in many ways with those with whom we have no desire to sleep. If, on the other hand, politics do indeed make strange bedfellows, then perhaps it is time for these strange bedfellows to make equally strange politics.

Really? In and as the lecture on the evening of the 2nd of December 1970? A theory of queer (/) questioning? Why not? Consider this friendly, if intricate, echo.

> I suppose the main way I coped with it at the time was to see the history of philosophy as a sort of buggery (*une sorte d' enculage*) or (it comes to the same thing) immaculate conception. I saw myself as taking an author

from behind and giving him a child that would be his own offspring, yet monstrous. It was really important for it to be his own child, because the author had to actually say all I had him saying. But the child was bound to be monstrous too, because it resulted from all sorts of shifting, slipping dislocations, and hidden emissions (*émissions secretes*) that I really enjoyed. (Deleuze 1995, 6)

As part of the *Negotiations* collection, these remarks were written by Deleuze in response to "a harsh critic" (*un critique sévère*) now widely acknowledged to be Michel Cressole, a gay activist and journalist who studied with Deleuze, but who turned against him when Deleuze politely refused to help with a book Cressole was attempting to write about him (it appeared in 1973). Cressole died in 1995 from HIV/AIDS.

The "it" that Deleuze is addressing here is Cressole's charge that Deleuze is trapped, unable to think outside the philosophical training that undeniably informs his early studies of Hume, Kant and Nietzsche. Although the terminology is not introduced, Deleuze responds by producing an "image of thought" in which philosophy is at once as the male lover and as the Virgin Mary who is slipped into and filled with emissions (the French *secretes* amplifies the sense of secretions). The result is a birth, a child/monster who, in actually saying *everything* that the author says, is also thus a reading, a reading that produces within philosophy the crack that empties into a potential departure from it. As Deleuze clarifies: his book on Bergson whose afterword, "The Return to Bergson," describes this monster in more traditional detail. Whether in explicit evocation of the inaugural lecture or not, Deleuze is also here responding to Cressole's provocation by speaking his own fantasy of working "on" Deleuze, being stuck in philosophy. This gesture echoes Foucault's embrace of homage (Cressole had drawn attention to their mutual admiration) and in *that* sense brings the letter and the lecture into an alignment that queers/questions resistance, in the letter phrased emphatically as the fraught intensity of pedagogy. Here then again, the when and the where of Theory.

Notes

1 Parts of this chapter were written and initially published in 1996 at which point the question of whether Foucault's concept of power from the mid-1970s made room for the possibility of resistance mattered in general, but also in particular to an emergent queer theory in which Foucault came to play a certain evangelical or Pauline role. As some readers will know, this is also well before Lynne Huffer's *Mad for Foucault* where, largely through a tenacious and principled reading of *The History of Madness*, she argues precisely this point. Since in her chapter on Diderot's "Rameau's Nephew," she too tracks the effects of queering through formulations like "metaphorical ass kissing,"

I know that I would have benefited from the existence of her work. The point is not about precedence. It is all about the proposition regarding Foucault's foundational relation to queer theory about which we agree. She, of course, may not agree entirely since Huffer touches down on the queerness of "erratic deviance," while I entertain the possibility that queer and resistance may define a "bizarrely" pleonastic structure. Recent attention to the inaugural lecture has also drawn attention to the differences between its published version on which both English translations are based and the version circulated by the Collège titled, "Leçon inaugurale faite le Mecredi 2 decembre, 1970." Stuart Elden at Progressive Geographies has usefully isolated all the differences, however slight. Consulting them, one discovers that they do not challenge the reading offered here.

2   Serendipitously, the University of Minnesota has recently brought out a sumptuous volume of Foucault's early writings on literature. See *Language, Madness and Desire: On Literature* (Foucault 2015). This follows by a couple of years the earlier publication of *Speech Begins after Death* (Foucault 2016) an interview with Claude Bonnefoy on language, speech and death that resonates distinctly with themes in his writings on Roussel et al., but "focalized" through his own approach to writing. Both of these, however differently, can be read as confirmations of the point I am making.

3   Significantly, the reciprocity of the power relation at the heart of the homage ceremony is indirectly underscored by Foucault in an interview with the Parisian Lacanians entitled, "Confessions of the Flesh," from 1977 (Gordon 1980, 201). In his remarks Foucault directly anticipates the connection I later make between his model of productive power and the queer character of his homage.

4   Because this proposition may strike one as "far-fetched," it is perhaps worth quoting from Marc Bloch's description of the homage ritual at some length.

> Imagine two men face to face; one wishing to serve, the other willing or anxious to be served. The former puts his hands together and places them, thus joined, between the hands of the other man–a plain symbol of submission, the significance of which was sometimes further emphasized by a kneeling posture. At the same time, the person proffering his hands utters a few words–a very short declaration–by which he acknowledges himself to be the "man" of the person facing him. Then chief and subordinate kiss each other on the mouth, symbolizing accord and friendship. (Bloch 1961, 145–46)

The difference between being *a* man and being *one's* man is not sufficient, to my mind, to warrant a dismissal of the proposition that homage bears on the social construction of masculinity. But in addition, what Bloch's description makes clear—and this regardless of whether one has read Foucault on male friendship—is that this particular ritual construction of masculinity is laced with what the contemporary reader would regard as homoerotic themes. My point here is not to contradict the scholarship that has rightly problematized the transferability of categories such as "homosexuality." Instead, I want merely to stress that Foucault's performance takes place in a world where he can rely on a recognition that may or may not have been available to the members of what Bloch terms "feudal society."

5   In *Beckett and Babel*, Brian Fitch has made a compelling case for the uniquely bilingual character of Beckett's modernism. In particular, he notes not merely the complexity of Beckett's texts (nearly all of which exist in two distinct versions—French and

English—versions that only in rare cases can be characterized as "translations") but also the resulting complexity of the national character of his texts. Predictably, French scholars making a case for Beckett's relation to modernism in France tend only to read the French texts, and vice versa for English or American scholars. These problems are duly reflected in the then definitive French bibliography of Beckett's work that appeared in 1972 (see J. J. Bryer et al. *Samuel Beckett 1 (2) Calepins de Bibliographie 2*, Paris: Lettres Modernes, 1972), indicating that Beckett's status in France was undergoing revision during the very period when Foucault was actively invoking him as, if not a borderline case, then certainly as, a case wherein the problem of the border figured prominently. Would it be going too far to emphasize that this border was explicitly articulated as a relation between tongues?

Chapter 2

STUMBLING ON ANALYSIS: PSYCHOANALYSIS AND EVERYDAY LIFE

In stressing the issue of the when and where of Theory, consideration of the site—at once, socioeconomic, institutional and disciplinary—of reading, the reading that Theory is, becomes unavoidable. Not necessary; just unavoidable. Thus, in this chapter this inevitability will be staged in relation to a meditation on the discipline of cultural studies—the field in and on which I work— that seeks to examine both how the concept of everyday life (*Alltagsleben* in the German, *la vie quotidian* in the French) has steadily emerged to ground its enabling concept of "culture" (think here of Raymond Williams's title, "Culture Is Ordinary") and also how the concept of everyday life both inscribes itself within the theoretical legacy of psychoanalysis and assumes, takes on, from that inscription certain properties not typically foregrounded in the aims of cultural studies. To invoke it again, in the gesture of adumbrating, everyday life can be read as the point at which both cultural studies and psychoanalysis broach the matter of their "sociographic" inscription. If, as my reading will establish, "parapraxis" (*Fehlleistung* in the German) is the decisive manifestation of the "everyday," then the "stumbling," the mis-stepping of my chapter title is to be read as part of the manifestation of the "sociographic," especially as it registers in Freud's thinking about the when and the where of his science.

The argument in this chapter will be staged in two parts. In the first, the conceptual and institutional difficulties currently besetting cultural studies (the Birmingham Centre for Contemporary Cultural Studies was closed in 2002) are characterized in relation to what I deem to be a vulnerability in the concept of culture when construed as the object of cultural studies. Because my immediate interest lies in motivating a reflection upon the concept of everyday life, I settle in this part for proposing that what troubles the concept of culture as a disciplinary object is its restless relation to the concept of socioeconomic determination. Indeed, at issue again is the problem of context in general, not as the opposite of text but as a weaving together in which the specific effect of one strand upon any other is not well rendered through the concept of determination.

In a second movement, Freud's *The Psychopathology of Everyday Life* (1901) will be read (about which more in a moment) so as to glean not only what it has to teach one about the concept of everyday life but also, and of equal importance, what the key concept of parapraxis discloses about the relation between Theory (if not psychoanalysis itself) and society. While the dream, in all its ontological rigor, may indeed constitute the "royal road" to the unconscious, what, I will ask, stands illuminated about everyday life if parapraxis turns out to be the "footpath" (perhaps even *der Holzweg*) leading specifically to or through it? En route further attention will be paid to what I am calling sociography, that is, a problematic within which the very perplexities long associated with the relation between history and historiography can be posed vis-à-vis society. Again, everyday life figures centrally here because—at least in some construals—it has emerged as the means by which to conceptualize the unsettled and ill-defined space where writing and life, Theory and society, persistently rub. If, as Freud implies, everyday life is where accidents can and will happen, and if parapraxis, in leading us to the very logic of everyday life, writes the theory of psychoanalysis into modern Western society, then how might we gauge the significance of the necessary contingency that thus appears to belong to the very genealogy of psychoanalysis? Does it bear on psychoanalysis alone, or does this insight, in shedding light on the reciprocating—and therefore contingent—determinations of life and consciousness, prompt us to consider that psychoanalysis may actually harbor a provocative account of the material relation between Theory and society?

By determination I do not mean, as an existentialist might, the opposite of freedom. Instead, by determination I mean the principle, variously defended by various Marxisms, that the superstructure is caused by the base, that, to put it another way, culture—in both form and content—is decisively and inevitably shaped by the economic institutions and relations that underlie it. My path to it will be circuitous, starting with further thoughts on the practice of reading and then turning to determination proper.

In some of its incarnations cultural studies appears to be stunned by what Paul de Man once called, "the resistance to theory." Not only has the field often defined itself as the disciplinary materialization of the end to which pragmatism, the new historicism and now the new materialisms put Theory, but, and this is the blinding insight behind de Man's formulation, cultural studies has put an end to reading. Although much separates what de Man thought could be read, and what "textuality" rendered legible, it is plain that cultural studies resists the interminable labor of theorizing the enabling conditions of its own reading effects. Such preoccupations are, its partisans often claim, *just*

Theory. Cultural studies, by contrast, is about identities, resistance, hegemony, in short, Theory that is just. Either way, Theory chronically persists, but typically obscured behind the ambivalence besetting its detractors and its devotees alike. Yes, this means that cultural studies has "been there, done that" with regard to a certain genre of so-called secondary texts, but also—and this is the more difficult problem—that the field has generated something like an interdisciplinary object blinded to the theoretical convictions that sustain the disagreements about it. Believing that this state of affairs is far from necessary, this chapter will consider what might actually be gained for cultural studies from a "reading" of the concept of everyday life.

There is much to ponder in the superimposition of Theory and reading in de Man's account of resistance, and yet no amount of pondering will turn up much in the way of an elaboration of the extracurricular conditions of any reader's readings. Better here is Raymond Williams even if, at the end of the day, he too resists reading. It is not, contrary to what one might think, Williams's stature in cultural studies that makes him important here. Instead, what makes reference to his work vital is that in it, he struggles repeatedly with the question of how the conditions of reading and its effects engage the problem of determination. First in "Base and Superstructure in Marxist Cultural Theory" from 1973, then in *Keywords* (1976) and later in *Marxism and Literature* (1977) he airs and re-airs the basic issues, establishing both their importance to Marxism and also Marxism's misrecognition of their importance. Although tempted by a formulation later used by Terry Eagleton, to wit, Marxists worthy of the name accept that, when all is said and done, the base determines the superstructure, Williams presses on in these essays to link the long history of Marxism with various permutations on the theme of determination. Particularly in "Base and Superstructure," where his preference for practices over objects could not be plainer, it is clear that he wants to resist a tendency now common in cultural studies, a tendency we might designate, shadowing a different de Man, as the becoming-symbolic of allegory. Though a thorough airing of the complexities embedded here would take us far afield, suffice it to say that when de Man used temporality to separate symbol and allegory he was placing a restless concept of time at the heart of literary expression and insisting that the full and stable referentiality of the symbol was deeply challenged by allegory. When cultural studies scholars read a novel as a national allegory, the alterity of allegory, the *allos* at its etymological heart is largely factored out. Reading concludes when what Williams calls "components" (Williams 2001, 175) can be shown to "stand for" a national event or faction. This "standing for," beyond mere representation, is the mark of determination in an allegory that has become fully symbolic. Clearly, as the all too familiar example indicates, disputes center on whether the nation can or even ought to be a determining instance. In many respects the *différend* (as in the late Lyotard) that pits Marxism against cultural studies orbits around this precise matter.

As *Marxism and Literature* unfolds Williams draws on the theme of determination and his own effort to nudge it away from vulgar economism to underwrite some of the key formulations of cultural materialism, for example, "structure of feeling" (actually first teased out in *Preface to Film*), the "dominant, residual and emergent" and so on. As important as this work is, it is also unfinished. Specifically, Williams never here crystallizes his philologically driven retheorization of determination as a setting of limits into a new concept. Nor does he bring his reflections to bear on the task of elaborating a disciplinary object for cultural studies, one that would comprehend the place of Theory/reading in such an endeavor. In his late essay, "The Future of Cultural Studies," determination appears only in the plural (Williams 1996, 160) and never factors into his deft probing of the "subject" of cultural studies. In effect, reading is left as a practice among practices pressured or limited by the social intentions active within it. How reading produces the intentions mediating between projects and formations is not taken up. Even Stuart Hall, who in extending the critique of determination to the point where Marxism hits, as it were, the post (as in post-Marxism), has not revisited the unfinished business of articulating an object for cultural studies. This, perhaps, is where the concept of everyday life, especially as it might be brought into relation with the Freudian notion of overdetermination, a concept elaborated by Althusser and discussed by Williams, assumes its contemporary importance for cultural studies.

I turn then to the bungled action figure who is Freud. More specifically, I am interested in Freud as the "founder of a discursivity" (Foucault 1998, 217) as Michel Foucault once provocatively described him, and of the role of *The Psychopathology of Everyday Life* in that founding event. This means, in certain respects, that I am pursuing the line of inquiry opened by Jacques-Alain Miller when, in his contribution to the conference marking Foucault's passing, he called for "an archaeology of psychoanalysis" (Armstrong 1992, 59). No doubt, Miller's intervention was spurred by the direction taken in Michel Henry's *The Genealogy of Psychoanalysis* (1985), where archaeology's shady twin, genealogy, was bent to the task of situating Freud's breakthrough within a yet more resourceful phenomenological account of consciousness. As tenacious as the French encounter with phenomenology has proved to be, it has not always sharpened the wits of its partisans, and while I am sympathetic with the way Miller complicates Foucault's dispute with psychoanalysis, important problems lie buried in his preference for the archaeological metaphor.

Everyday life, for instance. Or, put less flippantly, what the call for an archaeology of psychoanalysis fails to discern is the necessity of clarifying all that it proposes to address. To avoid repeating this mistake let me say plainly that here I am hoping to address and thus account for two things. First, for something like the *Entstehung* or emergence (as Foucault translates Nietzsche) of psychoanalysis, thinking specifically of Freud's "workstation," his routines both professional and familial, and not, as others have emphasized, the transformation of clinical medicine, the development of the cinema, the consolidation and intensification of anti-Semitism, the crisis of hermeneutics and other such broadly institutional phenomena. And second, I hope to account for the registration or inscription of this emergence in the text of *The Psychopathology*, specifically in its animating concept of *Fehlleistung* or, as it is rendered in "English," parapraxis. In a concession to tradition I will maintain the Strachey translation, though in German both *Fehl* and *Leistung* carry an extraordinary range of importantly ordinary connotations. Taken together these two aims suggest that in some yet to be determined sense I regard psychoanalysis itself *as* a parapraxis, but for that very reason it is important to stress that everyday life cannot be treated as the background out of which emerged the concept of parapraxis. Rather, everyday life emerges in Freud's text as a way to designate the very event of sociogenesis whether that of psychoanalysis or any other theorized consciousness. As should be plain from the proceeding remarks about the failed success of cultural studies—particularly as these converge in the problem of its disciplinary object—it is this theoretical function, this work, done by the concept of everyday life that ought to be made to matter more to cultural studies. The reading that follows will turn the text to this end.

In foregrounding the concept of emergence, *Entstehung*, as opposed, for example, to that of "origin," one is nevertheless obliged to come to terms with the Freud/Fliess correspondence. After all, doesn't received opinion tell us that psychoanalysis arose in the interval between the *Project for a Scientific Psychology* (1895) and the *Interpretation of Dreams* (1900), an interval in large part defined by the Freud/Fliess correspondence? Indeed it does. However, instead of tracing through this epistolary exchange something like the birth of an idea, why not treat it as part of an overdetermined conjuncture whose significance may not best be captured in the sieve of intellectual history. What happens if, for example, while reading the correspondence we track Freud's depression, a depression that shines brightest in the dark sentence from letter 133 when he writes, "Otherwise, Vienna is Vienna, that is to say extremely revolting" (Freud 1977, 317). What makes Vienna be Vienna? Or, for that matter, what makes this fact—the fact of Vienna being Vienna—extremely revolting?

Pieces of a possible reply to such questions are much in evidence in the correspondence. Of particular interest are the various places where Freud, though convinced that the secret of dreams had been revealed to him, expresses persistent anxiety about the fate of psychoanalysis. For example, in letter 135 Freud complains bitterly of the pressure being put upon him by his publisher who is complaining about the slow sales of *Interpretation*. Let us recall that in its original press run, 600 copies of *The Interpretation of Dreams* had been printed and that it took the better part of 8 years to sell them. This coupled with the "trickle" of patients—in the course of the 13-year correspondence with Fliess we hear of no more than a handful—and the anti-Semitically motivated irregularity of his academic lecturing doubtless brought home to Freud the fact that his "mental child," as Ernest Jones referred to psychoanalysis, was far from *simply* mental. However, what interests me here is not so much the depression (about which more later), but the way its etiology sheds light on the link between psychoanalysis and *The Psychopathology*.

To discern what stands illuminated in this light one needs to read carefully the preface to the first edition of *The Interpretation*. After confronting those committed to the insights of "neuro-pathology" with the paradigmatic and ultimately theoretical significance of the dream, Freud goes on to draw attention to the "deficiencies" of his text. The first of these bears on the vexing substance of the correspondence with Fliess, namely, the mind/body problem. The second, which Freud introduces under the heading of "difficulties of presentation," bears more thorough consideration. The rhetorical trajectory of this discussion is itself of interest.

In a gesture designed to underscore the "break" constituting the Freudian breakthrough, Freud notes that his text could not make use of dreams reported and analyzed in preexisting literatures. Obviously, this left him with a simple alternative. Either he could use the dreams of his own few patients or he could use his own dreams. In conceding that the "neurotic" character of the former would taint them in the public's eyes (here he anticipates the oft-heard repudiation of psychoanalysis, that it only ever theorizes the normal through the abnormal, or humanity through members of the Viennese bourgeoisie), he turns to his own dreams and writes:

> But if I was to report my own dreams, it inevitably followed that I should have to reveal to the public gaze more of the intimacies of my mental life than I liked or than is normally necessary for any writer who is a man of science and not a poet. Such was the painful but unavoidable necessity; and I have submitted to it rather than totally abandon the possibility of giving the evidence for my psychological findings. Naturally, however, I have been unable to resist the temptation of taking the edge off some of my indiscretions by omissions and substitutions. But whenever this has happened, the value of my instances has been very definitely diminished. I can only express a hope that readers of the book will put themselves in my difficult situation and treat me with indulgence; and

further, that anyone who finds any sort of reference to himself in my dreams may be willing to grant me the right of freedom of thought—in my dream-life, if nowhere else. (Freud 2001: 4, xxiii)

If I have indulged myself with this lengthy citation it is because many remarkable things happen within it. In the passage one finds both the claim to separate psychoanalysis from literature (here "the poet") and something like an advertisement for the confession contained in the much combed dream of Irma's injection, that is, the confession of Freud's anxiety about (among other things) his professional competence. In addition, the passage—which begins apologetically and ends on a note quavering between defiance and exasperation—acknowledges that the evidence upon which psychoanalysis rests suffers from constraints or limits that require the supplement of identification. In other words, the very sort of details that might convince the public that psychoanalysis is indeed an understanding of dreams that is at once scientific and new are precisely those that would expose Freud as either a neurotic, like the very patients whose testimony his prefatory remarks have impugned, or a quack. Hardly a medical man. To compensate for their withdrawal Freud first teases the reader with the notion that this withholding of details is precisely why his text falls short of full persuasiveness (at once predicting and outmaneuvering the reader's incredulity), and then, as further compensation, he solicits their identification, explicitly asking the readers to "put themselves in my difficult situation." In this deft maneuver Freud hails what Michel de Certeau called "the ordinary person" that all theories, including psychoanalysis, erect themselves upon (de Certeau 1984, n. p.). Not only does Freud here become "normal" like everyone else, but everyone else becomes neurotic like Freud, that is, the subject whose dreams contain the perverse logic of everyone's dreams.

The declaration of independence—in my dream-life if nowhere else—with which the passage concludes underscores the important way in which the entire discussion places psychoanalysis on the contested border between scientific thought and what Jürgen Habermas would call the public sphere, here, *das Publikum*. Normally, a man of science would have to expose only so much of himself to the public in order to gain from it the credibility that might nurture the birth of a new science. Freud, in anticipation of a rather cool reception, enters the public sphere by conceding that psychoanalysis is precisely that which has no place there. This is not, however, Freud's problem. Or, if it is Freud's problem, it is so only to the extent that it is everyone's problem. It is a perfectly ordinary problem, indeed it is both an everyday problem and, as we shall see, part of the problem of the everyday.

The preface to the second edition, written ten years later, makes it clear that though psychoanalysis remains controversial, when not simply ignored, the new science has nevertheless arrived. At the end of its first paragraph, the new preface flags the existence of a small group of "gallant supporters," practicing psychoanalysis under Freud's supervision, a group whose very existence is invoked as having necessitated the publication of a second edition of the text. It is in this decade of latent gestation where *The Psychopathology* belongs both temporally and structurally. If I link it intimately to the emergence of psychoanalysis this is not only because of the anecdote related in Jones's biography where we learn that Freud himself became convinced of the survival of his "mental child" when, cruising across the Atlantic to deliver the Clark lectures, he caught sight of his cabin steward reading it. Rather, *The Psychopathology* figures decisively here because of the way it puts psychoanalysis in play in the place where everyday ordinary people live. In effect, *The Psychopathology* restructures the logic of identification that produced the "ordinary person" of the first preface, by extending this logic into the lives of individuals who, by sharing with Freud the entire field of bungled actions and mis-steps, thereby acquire everyday, or perfectly ordinary lives. Thus, a science whose significance might otherwise have been recognized only by those willing and able to seek its curative powers slips into the everyday experiences of everyone, that is, a collective formation subsequently comprised of individuals, none of whom are who they thought they were any longer. Under such circumstances even those who insist that psychoanalysis has no relevance to them live their lives in a way haunted by the presence of a science offering to make sense of precisely what slips through and by those lives. In effect, resistance to it becomes futile, not because the truth of psychoanalysis is powered by denial and repudiation but because its explanatory potential saturates the very field renamed through the concept of parapraxis, that is, the field of everyday life. The question is, of course, what precisely constitutes this field, and how is it theorized in *The Psychopathology*?

One of the most remarkable things about this book—even if I have not yet convinced you of its genealogical significance—is that, despite the fact that everyday life is everywhere at stake within it, Freud never so much as defines it, much less theorizes it. Apparently, like Vienna itself, everyday life is, well, everyday life. In its very thereness, everyday life is thought to slip below the threshold of theorization. Or does it? If one pauses to note that *Fehlleistung*, parapraxis, is theorized at considerable length and that parapraxis is regarded as only taking place within the field of everyday life—indeed, parapraxis appears to constitute the very psychopathological texture of something properly called everyday life—then perhaps everyday life and parapraxis are two names for the same thing. Moreover, if this is so, then everyday life is indeed theorized in *The Psychopathology*, but—and this becomes crucial—in a way that inflects it with the very obliqueness, the misdirection (calling something, in this case, everyday life, by its other name, parapraxis) of its theorization. Or put differently, everyday life may precisely be that which compels a rather particular strategy of theorization, one that relies fundamentally upon the faulty function of parapraxis. Which tells us what? It tells us that everyday life is not only where accidents can happen, it is precisely that which consistently fails to take place *every* day. Earlier I evoked this state of affairs by appealing to the concept of overdetermination. I will try to say why.

In letter 143 of the correspondence with Fliess, Freud writes of his "tremendous dislike" for *The Psychopathology*. The context makes it clear that this affect is linked to the tedious process of correcting the page proofs for the book, a book that perhaps predictably—given its thematization of slips of all kinds—contained, in its first printing, more errors than any of Freud's other texts (although fewer than 2,467, the number that famously "popped into" Freud's head when complaining to Fliess about correcting the proofs of *The Interpretation*). Such mis-calculations notwithstanding one might nevertheless say that while *The Interpretation* was continually revised, *The Psychopathology* was continually corrected. It was nothing but errata (or, as Adorno quipped, "exaggerations"). In spite of Freud's misgivings—whatever their motivation—they did not prevent him from using his discovery of parapraxis for the purpose of introducing ordinary people to psychoanalysis. Indeed, the first four lectures of the *Introductory Lectures on Psychoanalysis* (1917) are devoted to parapraxis. In the course of the second lecture, indeed in its opening paragraphs, Freud provides us with a classificatory schema of parapraxis that sheds considerable light on the concept. It reiterates remarks that appear at the beginning of the last chapter of *The Psychopathology*, thus acquiring a certain, albeit belated, promotional quality. He lists six kinds of "faulty functioning": *Versprechen* (slips of the tongue), *Verlesen* (misreadings), *Verhören* (mishearings), *Vergessen* (forgetting), *Verlegen* (mislayings or misplacings) and *Verlieren* (the losing of things). Freud himself draws attention to the important fact that what links these various kinds of parapraxis is the German prefix *ver-* although he seems content to underscore the mnemonic utility of this fact, rather than elaborate the more theoretically important insight into the way language—here through the device of the prefixial "mis"—traces a certain potential for screwups, a certain necessary contingency, into the ordinary everyday acts of speaking, reading, listening, remembering and doing. Jacques Lacan in "Function and Field of Speech and Language in Psychoanalysis" addressed himself to this missed opportunity, but without recognizing how profoundly parapraxis (whose prefix, by the way, is the etymological source of the German *ver-*) might condition his insight that the unconscious is, as he liked to say, "outside." Be that as it may—and I have no wish to evaluate Lacan's turning back to Freud here—what Freud's accent on the *ver-* invites us to ponder is something like the morphology of everyday life. By which I mean that just as the prefixial "mis-" haunts language with its own faulty functioning it attaches itself to, and thereby assembles, a diverse array of practices all of which belong together by divvying up this faulty functioning. The point here is not that language mediates experience, or that all action is structured like a language. But rather, that everyday life comprehends the entire field of functions susceptible to prefixial attachments of the mis- variety, attachments that mark these functions as contingencies, that is, necessary accidents. Things happen not because they are determined, but because everything that takes place could have failed to take place, but somehow did not.

Of course, this applies to psychoanalysis itself, and it can hardly be insignificant that in 1917, while delivering *The Introductory Lectures*, *Vergreifen* or "bungled actions" is omitted from Freud's classificatory list of the types of parapraxis. To appreciate why it is appropriate to bring the problem of overdetermination to bear more directly on the matter of *The Psychopathology*'s role in the founding of the discursivity we call psychoanalysis. Much of the foregoing has implied that *The Psychopathology* is crucial in founding psychoanalysis because it made the latter matter to a public otherwise ignorant of its existence or openly resistant to its conclusions. While I understand the attraction of seeing Freud's "mental child" as rather more Athenian, I think this does a profound disservice to the rigor of psychoanalysis, while at the same time needlessly exposing it to the charge of idealism. To counteract this, one needs to read Freud's footnote (fn. 15 in chapter 12) in which he insists upon the "popular" character of *The Psychopathology* as a negation. True, there is no extended presentation of the concept of the unconscious, but this matters only to those already familiar with it and thus expecting it. Rather, *The Psychopathology* should be read as a truly "trivial" (in the strict etymological sense) or even pedestrian text that situates the founding of psychoanalysis in a Vienna that is, alas, Vienna. That is, in a world of mis-steps.

Such a reading obviously cannot avoid grappling with the discussion of determinism that dominates the final chapter of *The Psychopathology*. I say this not only for the reason that determinism bears obviously on the questions of contingency and founding, but because the discussion of determinism is framed in terms of an encounter between psychoanalysis and superstition. In other words, there is a crucial strategic issue to be recognized here, namely, that in order to found his science Freud proceeds by acknowledging a public and widespread belief in superstition—it is not for nothing that the epigraph of *The Psychopathology* is in German (unlike *The Interpretation* where the epigraph is in Latin) and derives from the scene in *Faust II* where Faust says: "Now the sky is so full of spooks, that no one can escape"—and then proceeds to substitute the unconscious for either "pure" accident or fate. It is clear though that what Freud sees as his opening, his way in, is the widespread indeed popular belief in unknown forces, a belief that might serve as the nest in which he can lay the "cuckoo eggs" of psychoanalysis. Although the general problem raised here about the genealogy of science in the nineteenth century is fast becoming an urgent one, in this context it is a distraction. I turn instead to the observation that Freud's critique of superstition predicts his entire engagement with religious discourse, an engagement premised upon the wager that if he can explain such things as "oceanic feelings" and so on in ways that have no recourse to the "irrational" premises of faith, then psychoanalysis ought to be allowed to, as it were, dislodge religion. Foucault is thus perhaps only the most recent in a long line of those who have sought to, as it were, turn the strategic tables on Freud locating psychoanalysis within the practices of faith. While doing so does indeed contribute to an elaboration of the genealogy of psychoanalysis, it neither illuminates Foucault's often disavowed debt to Freud nor does it help us capture the texture of superstition as it appears in chapter 12 of *The Psychopathology*. This appears most clearly in the examples. They are numbered.

The chapter opens with a discussion of the Dora case, a discussion that while purportedly illuminating the parapraxis at work in the genesis of her pseudonym nevertheless tugs on the thread that ties this chapter to the first preface of *The Interpretation*. It is not for nothing, one supposes, that when listing fantasy titles for this book in a letter to Fliess (#111) Freud actually started with "The Psychopathology of Daily Life." In any case, Freud follows the discussion of Dora by turning to the Fliess correspondence itself where he reveals the unconscious functioning at work within the number 2,467 to which reference has already been made. Several other examples are adduced (eight in all) and then Freud addresses the theme of superstition head-on. He begins by acknowledging the important question of motivation. What, he asks, motivates faulty functioning or, as he stresses here, symptomatic actions? Then, in a surprising, or better, symptomatic move he introduces the theme of paranoia, a term which, lest it passes unremarked, shares a prefix with parapraxis and therefore *ver-*. It is as if he needs to account first for the very interest, perhaps itself pathological, in small details such as slips of the tongue. Essentially, what the paranoid allows him to do is to set up superstition. In other words, just as the paranoid projects his/her own fantasies onto others, thereby attributing to them his/her own mis-recognized agency, so too does superstition attribute motivation to events or forces that in fact belong to the superstitious person. To make the point stick, Freud introduces a final telling example. He reports that once, shortly after returning from a holiday in the immediate environs of the city, he was summoned to the bedside of one of his patients. He runs to the cab stand outside 19 *Berggasse*, gives the carriage driver the address who then, in spite of the fact that he has delivered Freud to this very address numerous times, takes him to the right house number on the wrong street. Because his patient dies within a year of this episode, Freud proposes that the superstitious person might well see in the cab driver's mistake an omen, perhaps even the workings of fate. Freud, on the other hand, represents himself as recognizing this for what it is, namely, a simple mistake, a "pure" accident. He then turns back to the discussion of paranoia in order to establish precisely where psychoanalysis touches both it and superstition without becoming either. Key here is that both indulge in endopsychic projection (and at this point Freud unhesitatingly fuses superstition and religious faith), while psychoanalysis seeks the causes of such projections not in things—whether rational or irrational—but in thoughts. With this Freud can then place the motivation for parapraxis squarely in the domain of the psychical, suggesting that all mis-hearings, mis-placings, mis-readings and so on result from the disturbance of one thought by another. Disturbance is more than confusion, it is the effect of another mental functioning. Thus, we have taken the back entrance into the unconscious, where, as it turns out, superstition had been squatting all along.

This is all well and good, but we cannot help but ask why *this* example, and does it actually clarify things as neatly as it appears to? In other words, are we dealing here with a so-called pure accident or not? The first thing that strikes the reader of *The Psychopathology* in this regard is that Freud has, as it were, circled back to this patient over and over. Indeed, she (it turns out) appears twice in the earlier chapter devoted to "bungled action" and traces both the zenith and nadir of Freud's professional self-image. In her second appearance, this woman—whom Freud visits twice a day to administer eye drops and a morphine injection—comes to represent his quackery, for it turns out that due to a *Vergreif*, Freud reverses the drugs, putting morphine in her eyes and catching himself just before putting collyrium in her arm. Again, and surely this qualifies as a symptomatic reiteration, parapraxis marks the spot where psychoanalysis seeks to advance itself as a new science. In the first appearance of this patient, she represents Freud's triumph, that is, his steady climb ever upward. However, the particular bungled action involved is one in which Freud—who has been to her home dozens of time—walks past her door and continues on up her staircase to the next floor and the door immediately above his patient's flat. While it is easy to see why Freud interprets the parapraxis as he does, one cannot help but notice that this episode bears a strictly uncanny resemblance to the episode of the cab driver. Indeed, since the story of Freud's futile efforts to leave an Italian red light district—he returns repeatedly to the same street regardless of which compass point he follows—figures centrally in the essay on the uncanny, the uncanny is, like Goethe's *Spuk*, very much in the air here. Thus, even if we were to concede Freud's claim that the cab driver could not be subject to Freud's parapraxis, not only would we have to admit the possibility of the cab driver's own parapraxis (Freud tells us that the cab driver had often taken Freud to this woman's house and would, presumably, be in a position to share Freud's anxious concern about her), but we would have to think carefully about whether recourse to the cab driver's story is not itself a "symptomatic action" on Freud's part. Is it a "pure accident" that as Freud elaborates his interpretation of the mis-injection (and here one cannot forget Irma), he identifies as the thought disturbing his ministrations one involving the Oedipal scenario, a scenario whose importance for psychoanalysis cannot be overestimated, and which Freud describes in this text as something he was "*on the way* to grasping"? The fact that in the midst of all this looms the legitimacy, the viability, of psychoanalysis—can it actually help people, is it really different from paranoia (we know that Freud was to come to have his doubts about this), does it know where it is heading?—is, to my mind, decisive, for it suggests that psychoanalysis arises when and where its founder repeats a faulty functioning, a bungled action. It comes to be where it fails, among things, to heal, to separate itself from superstition, to, as is said, arrive.

A final point then about superstition and psychoanalysis. We know that Freud's relation with Fliess was to break off a year after the publication of *The Psychopathology*, and this despite the fact that many of its parapractical examples are drawn from their correspondence. I would certainly not be the first person to point out that this "moment of conclusion" brought to an end the transferential relation that supported Freud's self-analysis. However, what has not yet been given sufficient attention is the way magic, and specifically "thought-reading," figured in the breakup. When, in letter 143, Fliess's reaction to *The Psychopathology* comes up, Freud invokes a distinction between magic and "thought-reading," rebuking Fliess for characterizing psychoanalysis as parading as magic. As Steven Marcus has pointed out, this correspondence resembles a phone conversation in which one hears only half of what is said. It is therefore difficult to know precisely what Freud is resisting. Nevertheless, the resemblance between magic and superstition is one that invites us to recognize psychoanalysis in "thought-reading." Indeed, Freud lays claim to the latter while casting aside magic. Moreover, when Freud actually addresses the breaking off of their relation "thought-reading" figures prominently. The following is from letter 145:

> There is no concealing the fact that we have drawn somewhat apart from each other. By this and that I can see how much.... In this you come to your limit of penetration, you take sides against me and tell me that "the thought-reader merely reads his own thoughts into other people", which

deprives my work of all its value. If I am such a one, throw my Everyday Life unread into the wastepaper basket. (Freud 1977, 334)

Poubellication indeed. Because the phrase, "the thought-reader merely reads his own thoughts into other people," is in quotes, it would appear to represent at least a portion of that half of the conversation previously missing. Obviously, Fliess treats psychoanalysis as a variant of mind-reading, a charge that stings Freud both because it confronts him with the risk of his strategy of rethinking superstition from within and because it exposes the contradictory logic of the everyday, ordinary person. To wit, if anyone can be asked to put him/herself in "my" position, then this is because I am always already in his/hers. What then of Freud's declaration of independence? In Freud's final letter to Fliess, the one that concludes with the line, "cordial greetings from the culminating point of the journey" (Freud 1977, 45), no mention is made of thought-reading, but, in its place, is Freud's acknowledgment that as a result of their estrangement, he has "lost his only remaining audience," an observation that condenses in one phrase the entire fate of psychoanalysis as a science vying for public legitimacy and, truth be told, a client base. Freud goes on to convey his decision to accept a state-sponsored professorship in Vienna, a decision that turns out to have been a decisive step for both men, indeed for psychoanalysis. Perhaps not surprisingly, as Freud's letter concludes, the theme of steps and mis-steps resounds, and the resignation with which Freud communicates his decision to take "appropriate steps" is recast in closing as recrimination when he tells Fliess that these were steps he *should* have taken three years earlier. Presumably, Fliess is here cast as the cab driver, the one whose actions help bungle the arrival of psychoanalysis.

Jacques Derrida, as some readers will know, was the first to choreograph the fancy footwork of psychoanalysis (see *The Post-Card*), but in seeking to void the beyond of the pleasure principle he stumbled past everyday life. And while his recognition of the fate of psychoanalysis in the rhetoric of mis-stepping is invaluable, important resources remain untapped, especially as regards what I have called the object of cultural studies, if the parapractical character of everyday life is left unspoken. To proceed a return is in order. Specifically, let's come back to Freud's depression and ask ourselves, is Vienna after all Vienna? And if it is, by virtue of what determination?

Regardless of how it may seem, this is not yet another way to speculate on Freud's state of mind. It is, however, a way—perhaps even an irresponsible way—to speculate on the state *in* Freud's mind. Carl Schorske has already drawn attention to the fact that Freud's Virgilian epigraph to *The Interpretation* is one he may well have found on the title page of Ferdinand Lasalle's pamphlet, *The Italian War and the Task of Prussia* (1859) where "the depths," as one would expect from a nineteenth-century socialist, referred to the masses antagonized by Hapsburg conservatism. However, if one begins by recognizing in Vienna the capital of the Austrian state, other more immanent ways to discern the profile of urban space in psychoanalysis become accessible. I am thinking, for example, of the use Rome is put to in the opening chapter of *Civilization and Its Discontents* (1930). There, the eternal city is invoked as a way to flesh out Freud's rethinking of the "oceanic feeling" thought to motivate and sustain religious faith by Romain Rolland. I have already drawn attention to the strategic stakes here, stakes which, in conjunction with the constant thematization of Rome in the Freud/Fliess correspondence (indeed Freud refers, in letter 74, to a visit from Emmanuel Lowy, his source for the archaeological prints referred to *Civilization*), make this discussion matter to a moment thirty years earlier without thereby presupposing the concept of afterwardsness. To "materialize" his suggestion that experiences unavailable to consciousness persist in the mind, Freud, after summarizing the early history of Rome, presents us with the following analogy:

> Now, let us, by a flight of imagination, suppose that Rome is not a human habitation but a psychical entity with a similarly long and copious past—an entity, that is to say, in which nothing that has once come into existence will have passed away and that all the earlier phases of development continue to exist along side the latest one. (Freud 2001, 21, 70)

Freud then goes on to sketch a map of trans-historical Rome, teasing us with something like a hologram in which every building, monument and ruin becomes visible with only the slightest adjustments of perspective. Sensing that Rolland is not likely to be content with an analogy Freud draws this flight of imagination to a close by taking up the question of the difference between a city and the psyche, conceding that loss afflicts each of the two cases quite differently. For the psyche, loss is always due either to illness or to wounding, whereas for the city, loss, which may indeed result from catastrophe, more typically occurs as a result of "development." He refers explicitly to the "demolition" and "replacement" of buildings. The normal/healthy, abnormal/violent binary at work here might ring more true if it were not being deployed by the founder of the discursivity known as psychoanalysis. This coupled with Freud's earlier caveat, to the effect that the inadequacies of his analogy—specifically the paradox of a space containing two contents that results from spatializing historical time—stem from our inability to picture the psyche, makes his concessions to Rolland's suspicions feel hollow. Indeed, if Freud's topography of the psyche rests upon anything, it rests upon the possibility, nay the necessity of two contents struggling to occupy the same space. This logic, applying as it does to the very structure of analogy, renders every analogy *more* than simply an analogy. But it also, mutatis mutandis, makes Vienna more than Vienna.

My point here is manifestly not to suggest that there was no basis for Freud's depression because, at day's end, Vienna is not Vienna, but rather to suggest that Freud's formulation, in its pleonastic irony, traces a mis-step that marks where Vienna, as the urban site of his daily life, is inscribed in the psychoanalytical theory of the psychical apparatus. In other words, Freud mis-reads the site of *The Psychopathology*, but in doing so in a text devoted to prefixial missing provides us with a theory of everyday life that can be made to matter, perhaps even urgently, today. Let me unpack this by stating the obvious, namely, that perhaps due to the illustrative character of *The Psychopathology*, most of the text is given over to reports about the comings and goings of the city of Vienna. We hear about Freud's vacations, his consultations, his cab rides, his card games, his sundry interactions with family, friends and colleagues. We hear as well about his entering and exiting buildings, his encounters with people on the street, the rearranging of his desk and office space so brilliantly traced by Diana Fluss. Indeed, we hear about similar goings-on of his correspondents and colleagues. In other words, the reading that is *The Psychopathology* constitutes a writing, what I have earlier called a sociography, of everyday life in Vienna. De Certeau who, three-quarters of a century later, came to appreciate the narrative character of walking would thus appear to be, literally, following in the footsteps of *The Psychopathology*. My point here is not simply to underscore the routinized character of Freud's Viennese existence, although it is overlooked far too often, even by those eager to emphasize the importance of his subsequent exile to London where he made his one and only English-language film. Instead, I want to stress that it is precisely within the snarl of these routines, these *dérives*, that Freud recognized the faulty functioning binding him to his fellow citizens, a recognition that cleared the ground for the royal road he had contracted his science to pave. Even the concept of *Bahnung* or path-breaking which was to figure so prominently in *The Project*, by participating in the associative paradigm of circulation, would also thus appear to derive, at least in part, from Freud's effort to think the psyche and city in one space.

There is, however, much more to tell about the urban space of Vienna, and it bears on the matter of displacement, that is, the volatility that arises as two contents encounter one another in the same space. We know that during his correspondence with Fliess, Freud and his family moved from *Marie Theresienstrasse* to the *Berggasse*. Not long after the move Freud also rented the ground floor flat, essentially taking over the entire space at number 19. I'll not repeat here all the wonderful work that has been done on Freud's "scene of writing." Instead, I will focus attention on the process of "bourgeoisification" that was reorganizing the topography of Vienna during the later part of the nineteenth century. Beginning in 1857, that is, the year following Freud's birth, Emperor Franz Josef began an architectural and urban process that might be construed as effecting the transition from feudalism to capitalism. Specifically, he instructed engineers to demolish the fortifications that had long encircled the thus named *Innere Stadt* of Vienna (where stand Saint Stephens and the Imperial Palace), replacing them with a series of streets that came to form the *Ringstrassen* that can now be traversed by tram from Augarten bridge in the Northeast to Aspern bridge in the Southeast. On the outside edge of the Ring, in effect, outside the walls, appeared virtually all of the institutional structures that, since Habermas's study, we have come to associate with the bourgeois "public sphere," notably the Austrian parliament building, but also a variety of encyclopedic museums. To be sure, the bourgeois public sphere did not come into existence with these developments. Nor do they simply represent its institutionalization. Instead, precisely to the extent that they herald and mark the displacement of a center, in this case the *Innere Stadt* the development of these institutional structures represent the inscription of something like public opinion in urban space. If I stress this, and express it this way, it is because I want to refer back from this vantage point to the preface of *The Interpretation* where Freud worried openly about his position vis-à-vis the public, developing the logic of the "ordinary person" in order to negotiate this anxious frontier. True, the anxiety there was very much about his reception by ordinary and scientific publics, but let us not forget that the university is also on the outer edge of the Ring and that anxiety is precisely for Freud an affective state whose cause—its link to sexual repression notwithstanding—is difficult to localize. And, if we remember that the move to 19 *Bergasse* is essentially a move from the inside to outside the Ring, a strictly reiterative move designed to give the family more room, but also to give Freud's consulting room a different kind of visibility, then perhaps we can recognize the activity of a certain spatial politics in the "state of Freud's mind," a mind, let us not forget, that will come to model the psyche on holograms of ghostly, and for that reason, eternal cities. The Ring, which facilitates a certain traffic flow from the urban core outward, replaces the fortification that inhibited it. Yet, for Freud, the apparition of the wall, of the feudal fortifications, is still there. His circulation is thus both enabled and blocked. Vienna, in this sense, is a trip.

Perhaps this helps us approach a question posed earlier from a different direction, namely, why is the story of the mistaken cab driver so crucial to the demonstration that psychoanalysis is not superstition? Specifically, why given the associative richness of the anecdote, does it seem decisive or otherwise appealing to Freud? The preceding discussion of the urban history of Vienna suggests two answers: first, that in a city undergoing a decisive reorganization of the spatial distribution of the classes an acute and pervasive form of disorientation obtains. As in Freud's account of his visit to the female patient where he walks up past her door to "greater heights," much of the Viennese bourgeoisie and urban working class find themselves in new traffic patterns of mobility. Phantasy, whether daydreaming or simply hope, is rampant and Freud is aware that everybody, especially ordinary people, is/are getting lost, going too far or not far enough, everyday. Second, precisely to the extent that Vienna is a trip, that is, a place where mis-steps are necessary, an anecdote centered on how one can, *precisely* when circulation is urgent, end up in the wrong place confronts the reader with a richly theorized encounter with the everyday that never whispers its name. In other words, the anecdote of the cab driver appeals because of the compact way it brings together utility (as a common example, it is a useful one) and rigor, that is, the specific way it effects the theorization of everyday life by writing it into Freud's missed encounter with it. In a word, the anecdote is exemplary. Perhaps, but of what? Of the fact that Vienna both is and is not Vienna.

To conclude, a provisional sketch—however incomplete—of how such a reading/Theory of everyday life might supplement cultural studies would not be out of place. Having earlier stressed that I am concerned with the "object" of cultural studies (what do its partisans work on, with, through) let me now add that I want especially to think about two things: (a) overdetermination as a way to designate how various moments or instances of the social (including here the work of intellectuals and other professionals in handling its theorization) cohere as a conjuncture and (b) the distinctive role Theory plays in the construction of such an interdisciplinary object. In faulting cultural studies partisans for their disavowal of both Theory and reading, I did not mean to deny that the Theory is capable of internal diversification and proliferation. On the contrary. However, I do want to resist the idea, much ballyhooed by the more anti-intellectual partisans of cultural studies, that anything like everyday life can be approached without it. Not because—as the cliché has it—everything is theoretical, but because—as my reading of Freud has attempted to establish—everyday life may be, if not a construction of analysis, then certainly a mis-construction of analysis. In other words, it is not a given. Indeed, everyday life teeters on paradox in that precisely what constitutes its routine (the banalities that, by definition, recur *every* day), render all days indistinguishable, thereby erasing the very ground of the diurnal. Theorization must intervene, not from nowhere, but from elsewhere within an uneven configuration it may, in principle, always mis-name. Thus, everyday life might be construed to provide cultural studies not with a substitute field of material objects (although it does that too) but with a way to think its encounter with what it claims to know as part of a more general overdetermination.

What is at stake in invoking Althusser's well-known essay here is best clarified by citing it. The moment of "Contradiction and Overdetermination" (1962) that interests me is where Althusser is drawing the theoretical consequences of his discussion, arguing that a Marxist account of contradiction has to deprive the economic dialectic of its teleological and ultimately Hegelian ambitions. He writes:

> This overdetermination is inevitable and thinkable as soon as the real existence of the forms of the superstructure and the national and international conjuncture has been recognized—an existence largely specific and autonomous, and therefore irreducible to a pure *phenomenon*. We must carry this through to its conclusion and say that this overdetermination does not just refer to apparently unique and aberrant historical situations [...] but is *universal*; the economic dialectic is never active *in the pure state*; in History, these instances, these superstructures, etc.—are never seen to step respectfully aside when their work is done or, when the Time comes, as his pure phenomena, to scatter before His Majesty the Economy as he strides along the royal road of the Dialectic. From the first moment to the last, the lonely hour of the "last instance" never comes. (Althusser 1970, 113)

True to the very logic of afterwardsness, the Freud evoked everywhere in this passage was only named as such a year later in "On the Materialist Dialectic." However, even there, overdetermination was understood as belonging to the dream-work, and this despite the fact that, as the lonely hour of the last instance recedes with the horizon, and with the problem of structural determination hanging in the balance, Althusser goes out of his way to stage an urban encounter of the very sort we have witnessed repeatedly in *The Psychopathology*. Picture the scene. Along the royal road of the dialectic, stroll the economy and the superstructures in opposite directions. Will they step aside as did Jakob Freud, when the young Freud first witnessed the spatial politics of anti-Semitism, or will they collide? Will the economy yield, recognizing that like Zeno's arrow it will forever come without arriving? Will it mis-step? Will there be a bungle in the asphalt jungle? All reasonable questions—however rhetorical—all in some sense underscoring the stubborn way in which Althusser's theorization of overdetermination feels *entirely* underwritten by the concerns and conceits of *The Psychopathology*. Thus, my first point is that the very obliqueness of this underwriting is its confirmation. Clearly, although the word passes unspoken, overdetermination belongs to the Freudian problematization of determination that transpires in chapter 12 of *The Psychopathology* both thematically and strategically. By strategic here what is meant is that Althusser, like Freud, routes his theorization of overdetermination through a reference whose very obliqueness registers its parapractical character. It just so happens (by accident?) that this rerouting involves Freud. My second point, then, is the obvious one, namely that Freud's equally oblique reference for the everyday is not simply parapraxis, but, if not Althusser (and how could it be?), then the emergence within Marxism, as Williams has shown, of the notion of overdetermined contradictions as the motor of historical development. Although a proper airing of all the issues involved would require yet another detour, few key points must be made. First, that although Althusser zeroes in on the overdetermined interface between the national and the international, it is clear that the concept is meant to comprehend spatiotemporal dispersions *in general*. In other words, just as we need to think about how the economic and the cultural interact both nationally and internationally, we need to think about the interplay of what Williams called the emergent, residual and dominant in both the national and the international. In challenging the centrality of class antagonisms within a given society, cultural studies partisans have acted as though class can therefore be written out of the analytical equation (if not central, then irrelevant), effectively proceeding as though social mediations of the economic (of which class is one) do not participate in what is otherwise deemed a space of differentiation. In the long run, this promotes the dubious notion that the only constraints informing thought and action are those to be chalked up to the whiles of self-deception, where the exorbitant radicality of critique is itself the index of liberation. As I see it, the challenge is to develop a critique capable of addressing the overdetermined elements and forces that comprise the detail of the society to be overcome. Cultural studies is not there yet, but nor, for that matter, is psychoanalysis.

Second, and one wonders whether it bears repeating, if determination can come at the end, that is, in the lonely hour of the last instance, it is because thought echoes within the social process. In other words, not only is Theory woven into cultural critique, but it is also subject to the work of overdetermination. As a result, theoretical practice must be exercised with a certain touch to avoid losing touch with what binds it to, and separates it from, the society to be overcome. Reading, if run through both de Man and de Certeau, and distinguished from both the mechanics of literacy and the project of hermeneutics, is not an altogether bad way to gloss touch, to handle, differently. Bringing, as this would, reading back into touch with the task of engaging its enabling conditions makes Theory not simply relevant to but part of the construction of disciplinary objects. Since Freud's example has already broached the matter, we have only to draw the obvious conclusion, namely, that everyday life may well constitute the active, but occluded, disciplinary object that cultural studies is otherwise busy resisting. In effect, overdetermined contradictions constitute, in the register of political analysis, the contingent necessities we have located in our lived encounter with everyday life. In this sense, everyday life (as both concept and event) is the poorly bounded and volatile space that emerges along the overdetermined interface between, to use Althusser's categories, economic, social and cultural constraints and the practices (both national and international) that articulate them. This is where cultural studies wants-to-be.

To avoid a simple misunderstanding, I am not urging that cultural studies subordinate itself to a Freudian or even psychoanalytical paradigm. That would simply disguise the problem in its reiteration. I am, however, insisting that when Freud wrote in his late *Autobiographical Study* (1935): "I do not believe even now that I forced the seduction-fantasy on my patients, that I 'suggested' them. I had in fact, *stumbled for the first time* upon the Oedipus complex [...]" (Freud 2001, 20, 34) he was telling us something we remain poised to mis-read.[1]

Note

1 In German the sentences from which this passage is cited read: "Ich glaube auch heute nicht, daß ich meinen Patienten jene Verführungsphantasein aufgedrängt, 'suggeriert' habe. Ich was da zum erstenmal mit dem Odipus-Komplex *zusammengetroffen*, der späterhin eine so überragende Bedeutung gewinnen sollte, den ich aber in solch phanttastischer Verkleidung noch nicht erkannte." There is much to comment on here beginning with the presence in "seduction" (*Verführung*) of the mark of parapraxis, that is, the prefixial missing that I have been tracking throughout my essay. This then, in light of the founding importance attached by many to Freud's abandonment of the "seduction theory," places a "mis-lead," a leading astray, at the origins of psychoanalysis. However, more important is the term Strachey (Freud's translator) renders as "stumbled upon," that is, *zusammengetroffen*. While one might rightly insist that this is not about stumbling, it is not for that reason unrelated to my point. Even if we translate it somewhat more literally as "ran" or better "bumped into," the bungled pedestrian maneuver persists. The accident of discovery feels less conceptual, but no less overdetermined.

Chapter 3

STRANGERS IN ANALYSIS: NATIONALISM AND THE TALKING CURE

Must we mean what we play? Those familiar with Stanley Cavell's path to philosophy—he trained initially as a pianist—will hear in this rephrasing the matter around which the following reading of Julia Kristeva's meditation on nationalism, *Strangers to Ourselves*, will elliptically orbit. In Cavell's text, actually titled *Must We Mean What We Say?*, he elaborates a rejoinder to the tradition of logical positivism that, among other things, probes the role of intention in language use so as to pry apart saying and meaning, allowing for a robust form of ambiguity in human linguistic communication. Meaning does not exclusively adhere to sayings that are either true or false. Meaning can arise in ambiguity. Indeed, most ordinary language use is meaningful in precisely this way.

But is there something like ordinary piano playing (and it is worth noting that Cavell has written powerfully about improvisation)? To approach such a question it helps to phrase it under one's breath while reading Adorno's fragment, "Music and Language." Written in 1956 after he had resumed his teaching responsibilities at the University of Frankfurt, this piece, despite its terse density, explores provocatively what Adorno insistently, even anaphorically, calls the "resemblance" between music and language. It is clear that *die Sprache* in question is one we speak and write. Ordinary. Significantly, Adorno explores this resemblance (he also invokes the concepts of "analogy" and "similarity") by contrasting musical expression and the language of intentionality, a contrast that does not deny intentionality to music, but that orients it beyond the event of communication. As Adorno says: "Every musical phenomenon points to something beyond itself [...]" (Adorno 1994, 6). In a sense, music always says more than it means, but in this very excess it resembles language most closely. In the Livingston translation the point crystallizes in the concluding sentence: "It is by distancing itself from language that its [music's] resemblance to language finds its fulfillment" (Adorno 1992, 6). In this distance lies the intention that Adorno seeks to attribute to ordinary language, suggesting, I will argue, that while one must mean what one plays, that meaning is perhaps even more ambiguous, more infectious, than the meaning Cavell contrasts to statements that purport to be either true or false.

Several if not consequences then possibilities follow. In attempting to handle this ambiguity one might sense within it Cage's probing of the border between sound and music. In other words, the ambiguous intentions active within musical expression might also manifest in bafflement, shared by performer and audience alike, over whether "musical" expression is taking place at all. Or, if it is, where and how is it taking place? To put the matter *ex negativo*, when one listens to Elizabeth Fraser (of Cocteau Twins renown) sing, it is pretty clear that music is taking place, but is language? By the same token, the question of how one tracks the "curse of ambiguity" (Adorno op. cit.) especially as it manifests in modes of expression that, while linguistic, are musically oriented presses with equal urgency. Here, certain methodological precisions seem warranted. Without committing to a thorough elaboration of the doctrine, a few observations about Louis Hjelmslev's reading of Saussure are relevant. Concerned that Saussure had compromised too early with the linguistic concept of the phoneme, Hjelmslev pressed on to elaborate the glosseme, the deep structural building block, the dark matter, of all language. This required that adjustments be made, most significantly at the level of the sign. Four new concepts come into play: expression and content, form and substance. The details are less interesting than the concept of expression (what Saussure had understood by the signifier) as inflected by the form/substance distinction. What this helps us concentrate on is how the substance of expression takes form, and it is this that I want to think about in relation to the question of tracking how musical expression might take form in nonmusical expression. More particularly, how can we read a text, in this case Kristeva's *Strangers*, attentive to how its theoretical context is, as it were, predicted (said in advance) by its form of expression. The point is not about theoretical form but about where enunciation figures in the reading that is Theory.

In 2016 a bit more than a third of the British electorate voted, via the instrument of a national referendum, to "leave" the European Union. Although the margin of victory was slim, it was decisive. It is now routinely invoked in the subsequent debate about how precisely to do this as the unambiguous expression of the will of the British people, and this despite the torturous math involved in such an assertion: a third of the electorate constitutes little more than a quarter of the population of Britain, reminding us that "the people" is as always a rhetorical assertion. As one might then expect "sovereignty" has trumped solvency (the health of UK finance and capital) as the means by which to designate what is to be secured, even enhanced by leaving the

EU. All efforts to clarify that within the regime of global capital "sovereignty" (whether national or not) is at best a misnomer, go nowhere. Thus, within the current impasse (I write prior to Halloween 2019) anxiety about borders, and the free flow of labor, reveals itself to be prejudice in search of an alibi. As in Trump's "America," the border is just another way to pronounce "foreigners" (all, effectively, "illegal" in democracies grounded in fraternal bonds). It is in relation to the pressing "problem" of the foreigner and the nation-state that I want to read Kristeva's text, a text written at an earlier moment in the monotonous global emergence of xenophobic nationalism. Moreover, because her intervention cuts across debates that have galvanized the encounter between postcolonial and cultural studies, this also deserves attention, both because it registers important sociographic detail and also because it raises the stakes on a reading of Kristeva that seeks to attend to her enunciative gestures. What is she playing at? Does it, can it make any relevant difference?

Those who have been following the postcolonial debate, joined now for some 40 years (Said's *Orientalism* appeared in 1978), know that the very concept of the "postcolonial" is disputed. Predictably, this dispute and the ambivalence it gives voice to concentrate itself in the prefix "post," and though the literature articulating this ambivalence is vast and growing (what does "post" mean, is de- or anti- more accurate and so on), I will not attempt to summarize its intricate rigor here. Suffice it to say that if there is something that, in spite of this ambivalence, seems to warrant the persistent invocation of the postcolonial, it would appear to be the various national projects that either spurred or, in some sense, resulted from the struggle *with and against* colonialism. Since already in 1955 Aimé Césaire had designated the nation a quintessentially European and ultimately bourgeois concept, it has been important—particularly in postcolonial scholarship—to associate the temporal break signaled by the prefix "post" with articulations, at once local and specific, of distinctively non-Western national projects. Thus, perhaps the distinctive achievement of Benedict Anderson's *Imagined Communities* is that, through its appeal to the dynamics of creolization, it was able to locate the concept of the nation outside Europe, in fact, in the very struggle against it. In such a context nationalism emerged as a progressive political strategy, as pertinent to the Palestinians as to the Basque separatists in Southern Spain.

Of course, latent within Césaire's repudiation of the nation is the tradition of Left internationalism, a tradition deeply attentive to the political risk of building socialism in one country, but also to the world system through and by which capitalism antagonizes its gravediggers. From within this tradition nationalism is seen as a reactive, anticosmopolitan traditionalism that, in the final analysis, matters only as an initial site of struggle but whose walls must ultimately give way to the manifest battering rams of international capital.

In recent years, Left internationalism has been at pains to differentiate itself from the current ideology of globalization with which it shares a certain impatience with nationalism, but especially with those nationalisms most politically vulnerable to being named as such, chief among them being the United States. It just can't seem to stop becoming great again and again. In the precincts of postcolonial studies this difficult state of affairs has prompted Gayatri Spivak, among others, to at once sharpen and displace the attack on nationalism, insisting—as she has—that transnational capital flows have produced the need for quite different ways for thinking the locus of Left politics, a locus she gingerly designates as the "planetary," with an eye toward the cultural mediations in dispute around the concept of "world" literature.

Thus, put bluntly, the issue is to what extent should the organized Left—however defined—defend the politics of nationalism and, if so, on what terms? Frankly speaking, it is indeed the matter of "terms" that most concerns me, for if I find Kristeva's writings on the nation pertinent here and now it is not only because of the considerable theoretical rigor they deploy in approaching these issues. It is also because of the idiosyncratic, and ultimately instructive, way that psychoanalysis sets both the "terms" and the "technique" of her analysis. Since here I will be especially concerned to draw out the political implications of the strategic link between psychoanalysis and the nation, I hope I may be indulged for placing Kristeva's discussion in dialogue with the work of Jürgen Habermas and, to a lesser degree, Slavoj Žižek, both of whom have—from rather different points of departure—been pursuing like matters for some time.

Though she has been criticized for a variety of sins, I don't think anyone has yet complained that Julia Kristeva's work is "unprovocative." The reason for this is certainly underscored in *Strangers to Ourselves*. In this text Kristeva composes an analytical framework within which it becomes possible to claim that less separates, say, a Bulgarian student in France from a Mexican migrant laborer in Texas, than one might immediately think. Ultimately, both are foreigners. More importantly though, both are foreigners *in the same way*, that is, they are both strangers to themselves. What accentuates the provocation of this argument is the fact that Kristeva intends her text as an intervention within then contemporary political debates in France concerning the political status of foreigners. In fact, much of her appeal within *Strangers* to the "inner cosmopolitanism" of Montesquieu and Freud was soon repeated in her extended exchange with the spokesperson of *SOS Racisme*, Harlem Désir, that coincided with the French publication of *Strangers* and that is available in English as *Nations without Nationalism*. Nevertheless, Kristeva's arguments, while tempered by this immediate sociohistorical context, are meant to bear on any and all contemporary situations in which "foreigners" have become political forces and/or targets, situations such as those evoked earlier in my allusion to Brexit. This itself is sufficient reason to consider carefully both the argument and the "technique" of Kristeva's text, for the matters she raises continue to press. And, if I insist here on the importance of technique this is because it plays a decisive role in *Strangers*, while also prompting us to reflect carefully upon the analytical significance of the medium of her interaction with M. Désir, that is, the "open letter."

Those familiar with Kristeva's career, or—for that matter—her novel *The Samurai* from 1992, know that my earlier evocation of the "Bulgarian student in France" was not fortuitous. If I begin my reading of *Strangers* here it is because of the special kinship between the text's general preoccupations and the personal history of the woman who wrote it. Many readers have remarked upon the insistently "autobiographical" character of Kristeva's work (beginning, perhaps, with "Stabat Mater" in 1977), but this tendency reaches its apogee here in a rather intricate way. While I too welcome the modulation of voice that attends this development, I prefer to situate the issue in terms of the vexed theoretical problem of the antagonistic relation between the personal and the political, or, if you prefer, between Freud and Marx.

Kristeva has routinely articulated this relation in a distinctive manner. So much so, in fact, that when *Semeiotikē* was reviewed by her mentor, Roland Barthes, he was moved to emphasize the specifically "*foreign* mark" (Barthes 1986, 171) left on French debate by her work, work which insisted upon an approach to literary production that comprehended the unsettled historicity of the speaking subject. Initially, the turn to Freud was marked by her prior training as a linguist and her lived relation to the ideology of historical and dialectical materialism in the former East bloc. But unlike many who, in the wake of the political defeats of the 1960s, simply sought refuge in "the personal," Kristeva moved to extend her problematization of subjectivity by deepening her dialogue with psychoanalysis, leading during the 1980s to her entering into analytic training. In what might qualify as an exemplary "irony of history" her becoming, what in an earlier period was called an "alienist," developed out of, and might appear to resolve, her status as an alien, a foreigner. This is perhaps why psychoanalysis plays such a pivotal role in *Strangers*; pivotal not only because her analysis hangs upon it, but because it embodies the practice wherein Kristeva herself has labored to rearticulate—if not reconceptualize—the personal and the political.[1]

The argument of *Strangers* proceeds along two lines: one historical, the other theoretical. Needless to say, the two lines depend on one another, and though I will not have the opportunity to trace their interaction in satisfying detail, suffice it to say that what I have called her "technique" derives from the compositional logic the interaction of these lines embody. The historical line seeks to clarify how "foreigners" (*étrangers*) were differently constructed during the course of Western history beginning with the Greeks, and culminating with Freud. While in many respects this is the most satisfying and sustained historical research Kristeva has conducted to date (we learn, e.g., about the relationship between pilgrimage and passports, the early link between women and foreigners, the origins of the notion of barbarism and the symptomatically "foreign" character of travel literature), it resonates dissonantly with the theoretical line. I would argue that this is due to the fact that Kristeva's theoretical material includes a meditation on the problem of the foreigner's entry into the writing process, a problem she evokes quietly in the trope of the journey, if not, in fact, the journal. Coupled with the culminating historical role of psychoanalysis (Freud, in ways that rhyme with Said's reading of *Moses and Monotheism*, is both powerfully and provocatively situated within the general framework of the West's encounter with foreigners), this meditation makes the reflexivity of Kristeva's text strain under a significant burden.

The theme of the foreigner's entry into the writing process is where the line of theoretical reflection in Kristeva's text picks up the problem of reflexivity. Thus, we have the problem of a text, written by an erstwhile foreigner, addressing itself to foreigners, about foreigners and seeking to do so in a "foreign" manner (a problem both intensified and acknowledged by the otherwise dexterous English translation). In the virtuosic opening chapter, "Toccata and Fugue for the Foreigner," these issues are addressed directly. Specifically, Kristeva rehearses the theoretical issues that caution against either rushing ahead to speak breathlessly on behalf of (and therefore, as the proxy for) others or demurring to the point of complicity with their oppressive silencing. In approaching the foreigner Kristeva argues that one ought to "merely touch it, brush by it, without giving it a permanent structure" (Kristeva 1991, 3), thus avoiding the twin disasters of demurral or preemption.[2] Those familiar with the musical notion of the toccata will recognize that Kristeva is here both justifying what I have called her "technique" as well as her chapter title. A toccata is a musical piece written (more often than not for keyboard) to be played with a characteristically rapid and light *touch*. Clearly, her aim is to present the way she has selected and organized the subsequent historical materials as warranted by the theoretical convictions animating her approach itself. Those who might otherwise condemn her for her "selectivity" and lack of "detail" are thus implicitly challenged to elaborate and defend their own theoretical convictions about the relation between analytical discourse and politics. Reflexivity is thus made here to at once involve, and implicate, the reader. We read about our reading.

The second musical term evoked in Kristeva's chapter title is that of the fugue. It is vital here because it serves as the figural matrix out of which she forges the link between her technique and the two lines that define her argument: the historical and the theoretical. Pivotal to this link is the reflexive trope of "the journey," evoked earlier.

What such a figure has to do with the fugue can be clarified if we begin by recalling that a fugue is structured musically like a chase (hence the term, from Latin, *fuga*). Typically, what constitutes the dynamics of the chase is the interaction between two distinct melodic lines: one typically identified as the Subject and the other as the Answer. Since the fugue is partially defined by its allegiance to the logic of tonality, the melodic material introduced initially in the Tonic key undergoes a development that drives it away from, and then back to, its point of departure. In this sense the chase between the Subject and the Answer is formally organized like a circuitous journey, or perhaps more to the point, a homecoming where harmonic resolution provides the aesthetic gratification we in the West are inclined to confuse with ontological well-being or comfort in general.

Plainly, this complements Kristeva's notion of the toccata in significant ways. It allows her to incorporate the twisted, Freudian topography of the speaking subject into the register of technique so that her writing *about* the foreigner is already an engagement *with* the foreigner. Moreover, the foreigner thus engaged is at once the answer, the interlocutor and the disquieting plurality that courses through Kristeva's own discourse, a coursing that touches without grabbing the reader. In fact, it is here, as a quintessentially technical effect, that the Freudian uncanny, the stranger within, first lodges itself in the argument of *Strangers*. We are not therefore surprised when in Chapter 8, at the culmination of the historical presentation, Kristeva characterizes psychoanalysis itself as "a journey into the strangeness of the other and oneself" (Kristeva 1991, 182). In effect, the journey the reader has taken from sixth-century Athens to nineteenth-century Vienna, from the encounter with the Danaïdes to the return of the repressed, is here being resolved in accordance with the logic of the fugal form itself. We have, thereby, rejoined the subject of the journey as a trope for the unfolding of her analysis, from the vantage point of the answer, that is, the journey seen as the theoretical warrant for that very unfolding. *Strangers* is thus "on" its own plane of expression.

What complicates and perhaps even compromises this technical achievement is the fact that it occurs in the thematic context of the uncanny; the home that is strangely un-homey, familiarly unfamiliar. Thus, to continue the musical analysis, resolution does indeed take place within the Tonic (the "home" key), but in the theoretical register of her meditation the Tonic has been relieved of its function.

As I have indicated, the Freudian breakthrough is situated at the end of the historical "long march" of the foreigner. What was glimpsed in Rabelais, namely, the presence of the exotic outside within the neurotic inside, is given deliberate theoretical elaboration by Freud. In this sense psychoanalysis, which inherits the Enlightenment contradiction between the rights of Man and the rights of citizens—a contradiction which discloses the irreducibly constructed character of the foreigner (someone who *is* a "man," but not a citizen)—reframes this contradiction by locating the differences of family and nation (sites of "belonging") within the structure of what makes us human. Each one of us, as speaking beings, is structured by a differentiating dynamic that at once bonds us to, and separates us from, others *and* ourselves. From Kristeva's point of view Freud's achievement was to recognize that the West's investment in its "others" sprang directly from its repressed relation to an "otherness" that structured its relation to itself, a point she has been making in various ways since her studies on abjection and the ultimate alien—ET.

Through a terse and audacious reading of Freud's "The 'Uncanny,'" Kristeva shows how Freud's discovery of the antithetical meanings of the term *unheimlich* leads him to anticipate the insights of *Civilization and Its Discontents*, namely, that the production of Oedipal guilt leaves us forever uneasy in our cultural homeland. Though she does not walk us through the psychoanalytic model in detail, Kristeva makes it clear that the unfamiliar or strange is strangely familiar because, as speaking beings, we are constitutionally marked by the repressed familial origins that buckle us to the maternal/feminine body, the drives and death. In other words, what haunts the house of our identity is the personal history of its construction, a history that our independent—and therefore unstable—identities require that we commemorate, that is, bury and revere. Though Habermas would be loathe to admit it, Kristeva's analysis actually resonates deeply with aspects of his formulations concerning the ethicopolitical status of communicative behavior, in that her reading of "The 'Uncanny'" is designed to secure a transcendental foothold for the cosmopolitanism of Montesquieu, that is, the perspective which linked, as a matter of principle, universal homelessness with a commitment to humanity as such. Instead of locating this homelessness in the geopolitical world where "the homeless" hustle homeowners, renters and passersby alike, or, for that matter, in Lukács's post-epical novel, Kristeva draws on Freud to locate it within the very structure of the speaking being. Thus, her political stance implies that only by recognizing the extent to which we are all estranged from ourselves, that is, foreigners, can we begin to resist the balmy nationalism that, like the Lacanian ego, provokes us to locate the foreign outside or around us, a provocation which, under present social conditions, manifests itself as virulent xenophobia and racism. Here psychoanalysis is deployed, if not to institute then certainly to disclose the commonality of transnational self-alienation.

This, of course, is the theoretical perspective that would permit Kristeva to compare herself with a migrant laborer.[3] It is not that the two are identical since neither has a secure identity, but that at the most fundamental level she and the laborer are *alike* in lacking such an identity and are therefore capable of reciprocal recognition and compassion, in effect, she and the laborer are capable of affirming national identifications without appealing to nationalism. However, this bold and innovative attempt to identify a nonessentialist basis for what is called "identity politics" threatens to buckle under the strain of its own technical execution.

This becomes most apparent in relation to the obviously personal theme of France, the place where Kristeva first lived her own national construction as a foreigner. When France enters the thematic register of the text, Kristeva, in a troubled ironic voice, moves discreetly to objectify—and therefore legitimate— her own case by arguing that since France nationalism still confuses itself with civilization as such, no one is *ever more* a foreigner than in France. In other words, her experience reaches below the merely accidental (and therefore didactically compromised) to the necessary. While she is clearly critical of French national identity, when she later reprises this theme in Chapter 7, her critique is decidedly softened. Here, she challenges the equation between France and culture by problematizing it in precisely the manner she later affirms in her subsequent discussion of Freud. In fact, in her savaging of the ideological function of the French national media she argues that in France, "[t]he romantic or terroristic seriousness of strangeness in itself becomes dissolved in this glittering of polymorphic culture that returns everyone to his or her otherness or foreign status" (Kristeva 1991, 147) a rebuke that resonates more than dissonantly with the positive assertion in Chapter 8 that "[b]y recognizing *our* uncanny strangeness we shall neither suffer from it nor enjoy it from the outside. The foreigner is within me, hence we are all foreigners. If I am a foreigner, there are no foreigners" (ibid., 192). The difference between being returned to one's otherness and recognizing one's uncanny strangeness—an experience also, as we have seen, structured by a return—is exceedingly difficult to discern. In fact, one might well argue that these two propositions collapse into one another, and with them a considerable portion of the critical force of *Strangers*. For, if it is true that the French national public sphere, dominated as it is by the centralized mass media, condemns *every* attempt to pose the radicality of strangeness in itself (whatever *that* is) to spectacular irrelevance, then Kristeva's intellectual intervention—her "authenticity" as an immigrant notwithstanding—is likewise compromised. Instead of brushing past the foreigner, Kristeva seems condemned to brush him/her off, in the guise, perhaps, of self-effacement.

What goes awry here is that Kristeva's otherwise ingenious integration of technique and argument turns against her. Her return to the Tonic ought to be uncanny, but is not. In order for the homecoming required by the logic of tonality to work, the musical material unfolded during the journey must sustain the differences that give it contrapuntal power. What happens in Kristeva's performance is that due to the collapse noted above—a collapse which could be uncharitably reformulated as a mere superimposition of the political and the personal—she exhausts the harmonic resources of her material, and instead of there being a sustained tension between the Subject and the Answer that might allow for an uncanny repetition of the Tonic, all her "voices" are singing in unison. In other words, the technical force of her compositional form ends up exerting itself in a way that pressures her argument to build the very house it will return to, a place which her argument has otherwise moved to dislodge.[4]

In an effort to implicate myself in the strategy of my own reading, let us then turn back to the beginning and revisit the question of Left internationalism. As framed earlier, this question would oblige us to conclude that, in her embrace of an uncanny cosmopolitanism, Kristeva is prepared to side with an internationalist repudiation of national ambitions, a position which places her in the surprising—and no doubt unwelcomed—company of Ted Turner (a Centrist at best), who not long ago boasted in an interview with David Frost, "I was an internationalist before anyone else was." This reappropriation of one of the cherished values of both Marxism and modernism by the multinational, corporate Right must give pause even to those intellectuals who—like Kristeva—have distanced themselves from the Communist Left, and this despite the fact that her excoriation of the "myth of national origins" in "What of Tomorrow's Nation?" is compelling indeed. Quite apart from the conundrum glimpsed here however, it seems pertinent to consider—albeit perfunctorily—the possibility that Kristeva's repudiation of nationalism aligns her with neither Lenin nor Turner, and, further, that her nonaligned status is premised upon a perspective on psychoanalytic politics she herself has yet fully to disclose, a perspective that—I will propose—derives from psychoanalysis' persistent reflection upon the problem of technique.

It is useful to recall at this juncture that the book that followed *Strangers* was titled, *Nations without Nationalism*, where a clear distinction is drawn between something like a geopolitical phenomenon and an ideology, a place and an idea. True, Kristeva herself never titled the essays collected here in this manner (it appeared in French as *Lettre ouvert à Harlem Désir*)—though I find it hard to believe that M. Roudiez did not confer with her about the English title—this is a distinction that is indeed theorized in the book's contents. If I emphasize this, it is because here one can see that Kristeva is prepared to retain, at least provisionally, the concept of the nation—and in this sense distance herself from a certain internationalism—while letting nationalism, internationalism's terrible twin, go. While this invites us to recognize that her perspective is more nuanced than it might otherwise appear, precisely what it enables us to think—about either nationalism or internationalism—cannot be clarified without coming to terms with the status of the nation within the theory of psychoanalysis.

I confess that my interest here lies less in the articulation of a thorough genealogy of psychoanalysis than in a truncated symptomatic reading of the appeal to the concept of nation within psychoanalysis. Though it would be tempting to regard Ernst Renan's observation that "[…] the essence of a nation is that all individuals have many things in common, and that they have also forgotten many things" (Bhabha 1990, 11) as the origin of the encounter evoked above, clearly Freud is, as always, the innovator. In "Thoughts for the Times on War and Death" from 1915 he writes:

> Within each of these nations ["the great world-dominating nations of the white race"!] high norms of moral conduct were laid down for the individual, to which his manner of life was bound to conform if he desired to take part in a civilized community. These ordinances, often too stringent, demanded a great deal of him, much self-restraint, much renunciation of instinctual satisfaction. (Freud 2001, 14, 276)

It is striking, of course, that the nation—though mentioned in an introductory section (and adumbrated at the close of "On Narcissism")—does not otherwise figure in the discussion of Le Bon's *The Crowd* that opens, "Group Psychology and the Analysis of the Ego," and this despite Le Bon's (a police psychologist) belligerent ethnocentrism which the preceding citation might lead one to believe represented the source of Freud's interest in *The Crowd*. Instead, "Group Psychology" concentrates on what Freud calls "artificial groups," as if the nation is to be kept apart from such things as the army or the church. This is noteworthy, I believe, because it prompts us to search for a motivation for Freud's interest in the nation other than that of his desire to confirm the hermeneutic power and pertinence of psychoanalysis. In other words, unlike the army or the church—forms of collective identification that the psychoanalytic hermeneutic is deemed uniquely capable of illuminating—the nation assumes the properly meta-psychological burden of bridging the distance between the individual and the collective. The point is not simply that the nation-state achieves super-egoic status—perversely stockpiling and enjoying the *jouissance* it denies the subject—but that it provides psychoanalysis with a veritable base camp on the climb from phylogeny to ontogeny. As we have seen, this "form" of argument is manifest in Kristeva's discussion in *Strangers*, where the dynamic of the uncanny subtends both individual and specifically national identifications. It invites us to consider then that what is redeemable in the nation—as opposed to nationalism—is precisely this function, that is, the meta-psychological establishment of a Moebian node where the theory of psychoanalysis addresses itself to the subject and the nation at one and the same time. Is the nation the only such concept? No. But as is clear from Freud's cagey invocation of Left internationalism in "Why War" from 1932, the nation is the one clearly politicized instance of such a function.

But what then of nationalism? Consulting the essays and letters gathered in *Nations*, one is prompted to see that, in spite of its various national inflections, nationalism operates as a "myth of origins." By this she does not mean that nationalism represents a simple investment in territorial derivation (*jus solis*, in the discourse of nationality). Nationalism is, instead, the logic that links such an investment to its opposite, that is, the repudiation (Renan might even say, forgetting) of territorial derivation, a repudiation which, more often than not, returns as the repressed or—as Mathieu Kassovitz might say—*la haine*. It is significant that in thus characterizing nationalism, Kristeva slips psychoanalysis into the discussion as a way to, as she says, "transcend" the myth of origin, a formulation that sounds untempered coming from the mouth of someone long affiliated with *la pensée '68*. However, transcendence is deployed here to designate the possibility of working through an impasse once it is clear that all sides, and all techniques of analysis, are equally compromised. Thus, the signal virtue of psychoanalysis is that it presupposes this compromise and seeks to give it methodological proportions, in other words, it is the very emptiness of the origin that fills it with psychoanalytical meaning.

Recognizing this clearly complicates what I have otherwise characterized as Kristeva's repudiation of nationalism. In other words, if psychoanalysis differs from nationalism primarily in the *way* it shares the latter's relation to the "myth of origins," then psychoanalysis can no more repudiate nationalism than it can repudiate itself. Which is, I suppose, the point: psychoanalysis can and must repudiate itself, while nationalism remains trapped in an angry and ultimately mythic binary. Obviously, this places a special premium on the way, or as I prefer, the technique, psychoanalysis deploys in negotiating its unique compromise with the myth of origins. In particular, Kristeva's perspective prompts us to consider carefully how a recognition of psychoanalysis' investment in a myth of origins—an investment which links a clinical practice and scientific institution to a broad-based ideological formation—articulates itself in a meta-psychological protocol that, as it were, makes a difference. That is, that prevents psychoanalysis from simply collapsing into a nationalism. Though such concerns might urge that we preoccupy ourselves with the politics involved in the emergence of "national traditions" within psychoanalysis (most famously Hungarian and now French and Argentinian), or even with the distinctly international dynamics of the emergence of psychoanalysis—two themes elaborated with provocative rigor by Elisabeth Roudinesco in her useful history of psychoanalysis in France—instead, I want to linger on the issue of technique and replay Kristeva's analysis of the foreigner.

Strange though it may seem, I want to effect this return by invoking the theme of touch. Let us therefore call up the parallel between Kristeva's unabashedly psychoanalytical approach to the foreigner and the relation between psychoanalysis and nationalism, the myth of origins. In the former—as exemplified in her musical allusion to the toccata—touch enters as a way to reflect upon the delicacy of speaking to and for others. Lightness sets the tone. As concerns the relation between psychoanalysis and the myth of origins, though touch does not enter the conversation, technique does, at least insofar as technique designates the locus of what differentiates psychoanalysis' mythic compromise from that of nationalism. Thus, one might say that psychoanalysis—precisely to the extent that it transcends nationalism—does so by touching the myth of origins differently, perhaps, in fact, by doing so in the reflexive domain of technique rather than in the domain of *doxa*. However, a further consequence of this particular line of development is that the collapse traced in *Strangers* between the fugal subjects, that is, between being returned to one's own strangeness by the mass media and discovering the stranger one is, repeats itself in the *pas de deux* of psychoanalysis and nationalism. As such an outcome manifestly bodes ill for the maintenance of a distinction between nationalism and the nation—a distinction that, to my mind, is crucial to Kristeva's hesitation regarding both Lenin and Turner—it requires further consideration.

Before, however, turning away from the theme of technique and its avatar, touch, let us secure what is to be gained from stating the obvious. I am thinking here of essentially two things: first, as Kristeva reflects upon her approach to foreigners or nationalism, she is involving psychoanalysis in self-reflection, that is, she is obliging it to touch (upon) itself as she draws upon it to consider how one might touch others; and second, she—in associating self-reflection and technique—is reminding us that psychoanalytical technique is, at least optimally, curative. That is, the capacity for self-reflection and the capacity for healing are indissociably linked. Thus, insofar as her investment in the nation is destined to participate in the healing that will allow nations to transcend nationalism, she is implicitly conceptualizing psychoanalysis as a mode of what Foucault once called "pastoral power." How, under circumstances such as these, are we to conceptualize not simply the role but the resources of technique? This, ultimately, is the question my reading seeks to pose.

To sharpen the terms of my response I turn at this juncture to the work of Habermas who has thought carefully about two things that matter in the present context, namely, psychoanalysis and the public sphere. If one consults the analysis of psychoanalysis that transpires on the pages of *Knowledge and Human Interests* (1968) s/he discovers that it is subsumed under a sustained preoccupation with "self-reflection." On the one hand, psychoanalysis is characterized as mired in self-misunderstanding with regard to its theoretical comprehension of the relation between its knowledge and the social interests that condition its production. In this, Habermas is reiterating the Frankfurt School's fidelity to Lukács. On the other hand, and here he is sublating Adorno and Benjamin's more patient engagement with Freud, Habermas sees psychoanalysis as committed to a form of radical self-reflection—a form that countenanced the necessity of, as Ricoeur might have said, self-suspicion. In fact, in the chapter devoted to "Psychoanalysis and Social Theory," Habermas argues that it is precisely this quality of psychoanalysis that recommends it as a model for turning knowledge back on itself in an effort to comprehend its own capacity for self-delusion, for not knowing what it does, but doing it. While it is clear that in displacing desire with interests Habermas largely avoids the epistemological consequences of the unconscious, this should not obscure the fact that he does indeed recognize psychoanalysis' decisive role in the domain of ideology, an insight now consummately embodied in the work of Žižek and the Slovenian School.

Though Habermas himself does not establish the link between this early account of psychoanalysis and his earlier discussion of the public sphere, it is a link that is there for the making. In *The Structural Transformation of the Public Sphere* (1962) Habermas finesses the problem of the public sphere's virtuality, that is, the fact that strictly speaking it never existed, by insisting upon its role during the bourgeois period in instantiating what he regards as its principles: accessibility, tolerance, consensus. To the extent that this sphere served to articulate the emergent interests of the bourgeoisie, and did so in conformity with its principles, would it not then follow that psychoanalysis—as the definitive guard against self-delusion in the domain of interests—is theorized as bearing political responsibility for monitoring the observance, by participants, of the principles of the public sphere? In effect, psychoanalysis is conceived as the means by which the public sphere labors to overcome its own virtuality. Perhaps because Freud's discovery arose in the context of the public sphere's disintegration—a matter I have treated elsewhere (Mowitt 1989, 274–84)—Habermas avoids taking up the technical question of *how* psychoanalytical knowledge is to enter the public sphere. One can only assume that, when push came to shove, he would appeal either to the notion of public intellectuals—presumably themselves products of analysis—or to citizens *already* capable of sufficient self-reflection that they would recognize the indispensable role of psychoanalysis in protecting the principles organizing their collective interaction. In sum, Habermas is long on principle, short on technique.

As I believe is well known, the problems of difference and privilege are what Habermas has been chastised for overlooking in his articulation of the principles of publicness (one thinks immediately here of Nancy Fraser's work), and while Kristeva does not appeal directly to his notion of the public sphere, her focus on foreigners within the national context raises these problems directly. Even in his more recent efforts to find ways to protect *Gastarbeiten* and former East Germans within a constitutional framework, Habermas emphasizes the importance of downplaying differences and, perhaps most tellingly, has altogether abandoned any substantive reference to psychoanalysis. Clearly, his devotion to the liberal democratic project of legitimating democracy by grounding it within rationalism has itself passed through desire to principle. If, however, we pressure Kristeva's discussion with the concept of the public sphere—whether virtual or not—then we will be in a position to assess what indeed is at stake in her emphasis on technique in the domain of critical self-reflection.

Since I have already drawn attention to Kristeva's orthodox commitment to the curative aims of psychoanalytic technique, it is no doubt necessary here to at least acknowledge an ancillary matter that I can no more resolve than avoid. I am thinking of what in the French context goes by the name of "ethnopsychoanalysis," a perspective associated with the analyst George Devereux. What is at issue here can be efficiently called up by recalling that when Albert Memmi reviewed Geismar's and Caute's books on Fanon in 1971, he attacked "the voice of the African revolution," as an analyst who could not speak a word of Arabic: "[N]either in Algeria nor in Tunisia did he understand the language, so he like other foreign doctors, had to hold consultations with his patients through an interpreter" (Memmi 1971, 5). Memmi's point was that, in spite of Fanon's impressive credentials as a critic of colonialism, his own analytical practice was nevertheless implicated in the former because the "talking cure" perforce had to transpire in the colonial tongue. The less charitable of Fanon's critics have even suggested that this is why his therapeutic innovations, such as they were, took the form of forming football squads among the residents at Blida-Joinville. Of course, Kristeva encounters this problem on a rather different terrain. Foreigners, and let us assume that those among the postcolonial middle and upper classes number among her clients, *expect* to be addressed in French, because they are in Paris. But, precisely because she is attentive to the profound link between psychoanalysis and strangers, one can only imagine that Fanon's dilemma haunts her own practice as well: can one, just to construct an example from the analysand's perspective, freely associate with an unveiled infidel who cannot understand your maternal tongue? While it is certainly true that psychoanalysis has consistently struggled with the problem of so-called foreign languages—one thinks here of the Wolf Man or, for that matter, Louis Wolfson—it is only since the mid-twentieth century that this struggle has been openly waged upon the ethnically and nationalistically charged terrain of the postcolonial condition. However, as important as these matters are I'll not pursue them further here.

To my mind the more urgent question bears on the relation between the discursive practice of psychoanalysis and the public sphere. If I stress here the issue of technique it is precisely because I want to avoid the pitfalls of Habermas's approach to this question where, as I have indicated, he seeks to delimit principles that, presumably in accordance with the Hegelian logic of "the concept," simply establish themselves in the deep structure of dialogic practices. To the extent that these principles might be brought to bear on the critique of nationalism, they would appear to do so only as a component of rational self-reflection in which the antagonism between nationalism and "the ideal speech situation" would *already* have to be established. What I find especially provocative about Kristeva's touch, despite the difficulties noted earlier (to which I will journey back), is that precisely in her formal attentiveness to the technique of analysis she obliges us to consider the *means* by which a psychoanalytic critique of nationalism might enter something like a public sphere. In other words, when she writes of "brushing by the foreigner," she is not merely characterizing how psychoanalysis might think the foreign, but—precisely to the extent that she remains committed to the curative force of psychoanalysis—she is offering up a technique for approaching the foreigner as a position, or ensemble of positions, *within* the public sphere (what Sara Ahmed might call the "other other"), perhaps even a public sphere convulsed by debates over the link between citizenship and national origins. In her appeal to the fugue Kristeva nuances this further. She does this first by associating the technique of analysis with the stratagems of Western *musical* composition—itself a pointed rerouting of self-reflection through aesthetics (playing) rather than reason (saying)—and then, in a subsequent maneuver, she links an aestheticized analytical technique (saying *as* playing) to a public critique of nationalism. This is as astonishing as it is enigmatic: astonishing, because who would have thought that analysis—precisely in order to engage the foreigner in/and ourselves with curative force—would have to articulate itself as a performance; enigmatic, because in spite of the structural rhyme that binds psychoanalysis to nationalism, it remains difficult to conceptualize the form through which such an analytical technique might participate in the public sphere without thereby losing everything that marks it as distinctive. Put differently, can we imagine a form of technical intervention within the debate about homelands that does not undercut the dissonant logic of the uncanny?

At the risk of invoking a cliché, this would appear to be the moment to effect yet another return to Freud. Specifically, in turning to "Why War?"—perhaps the only other explicit discussion of nationalism in the Freudian corpus (depending on the vexed matter of whether the collaboration with Bullitt is to be included)—one discovers what I take to be a significant detail in the present context. I am referring to the fact that the title actually has come to designate an exchange of letters, in fact "open letters," between Albert Einstein (who initiated the correspondence) and Freud. Given what we have come to know about the "talking cure," one cannot help but be struck by the fact that Freud responds to Einstein by saying (implicitly), "well, of course, you've already said everything that can be said, but since you asked [...]." In effect, Freud proceeds to "analyze" Einstein, not by telling him what his question, "Why War?," *really means* but by repeating Einstein's own discourse with a difference—that difference being the frame of the psychoanalytical hermeneutic itself—a frame that Freud introduces in what are clearly pedagogical gestures: "Will you allow me to take this opportunity of putting before you a portion of the theory of the instincts [...]" (Freud 2001, 22, 209). I emphasize this for two reasons. First, it suggests that Freud to some degree recognized the "translatability" of his own analytical technique from the consulting room to the postal system; and second, these observations direct us immediately to the second chapter of *Nations* where we find what is titled, "An Open Letter to Harlem Désir."

Though there are many things about this letter that deserve comment, I will restrict myself to raising three issues: (1) the distinction drawn there between the nation and *l'ésprit général*, (2) the stress placed upon education both formal and informal (notably through the media) and (3) of course, the formal technique of the intervention itself, that is, the open letter.

Since the letter opens by grounding its categories in the analysis of foreigners in *Strangers*, its propositions can be interpreted either as elaborations or repetitions of the earlier text. This includes, of course, the matter of technique that I have so belabored. Unlike Freud's letter to Einstein however, Kristeva does not appear to analyze Harlem Désir, although when she insists in the letter that immigrant communities have an obligation to answer the question, "what do they expect from [the] *national spirit*," she clearly verges on broaching the Lacanian "*che vuoi?*" Instead, she presents herself as clarifying a misunderstanding of her own making. The open letter thus becomes a way to place before the public—in fact, details of this exchange circulated on the pages of *Libération*—an exchange in which the "subject supposed to know" is made subject to the other's demand. Although this position might well be construed as an analytical one indeed, it more typically comes at the end, not at the beginning of analysis. This is not then a short session, but nor is it a quick fix. Kristeva has, in effect, rushed—perhaps even brushed—past the foreigner: the one who has touched her and the one she wishes to touch back. As if to render this effect as conspicuous as possible, Kristeva pointedly drops psychoanalysis early on saying, "we have no choice here but to abandon psychoanalytic references and turn to political sociology" (Kristeva 1993, 53). While at one level this clearly motivates her turn to Montesquieu, at another it draws attention to the sequence and rate of technical modulations that define the letter, modulations which culminate with the form of the open letter giving way to official graffiti: "I should like to suggest that the following statement be engraved on the walls of all schools and political institutions; commented and elaborated upon, it could become a touchstone for anyone wishing to participate in the French nation understood as an *ésprit général*" (Kristeva 1993, 63). She then proceeds to quote from Montesquieu's *Mes Pensées*. Before coming back to articulate what this permits us to conclude about Kristeva's perception of the relation between psychoanalysis and the public sphere, let us first attend to the themes of education and *l'ésprit général*.

In my discussion of Habermas I suggested that Kristeva did not share his convictions about the broadly pedagogical function of self-reflection. In the open letter this would appear to be contradicted by her numerous invocations of the importance of *education* to the process of transcending nationalist racism (and note that she is writing prior to *L' Affaire du foulard*). Indeed, I have perhaps overstated the distinction here. However, it is important to acknowledge that the references to education take place *after* psychoanalysis has given way to political sociology, and—more to the point—Kristeva remains more concerned about the *means* of educating than does Habermas. This is not to say that she is unconcerned with principles and ends. On the contrary. For in the preceding citation, she makes an understanding of *l'ésprit général* the clear aim of public education. What is striking though is how she links this understanding with the technical modulations traced, in effect, performed by the open letter, modulations that eventually include the commentaries and elaborations that embroider Montesquieu's "thoughts." The associating of these registers, their echoing—writing within psychoanalysis, writing within political sociology, writing on walls—*is* the realization of *l'ésprit general*. This implies that in spite of the announced withdrawal of psychoanalysis, its unique attentiveness to the technique of engaging foreigners survives—if nowhere else—in the very form of the open letter, a letter which, much like an official graffiti, is posted where others can write on it. Strangers like me.

But what—despite Kristeva's explicit evocation of *Strangers* in the opening of the open letter—is to be made of the fading out of music here? To respond by insisting upon the constraining brevity of a letter will not do, because, after all, the fugue, when compared to a symphony, is itself a short piece. Instead, let us recall the function of the nation within psychoanalysis sketched earlier. My point was that beyond the issue of susceptibility, that is, beyond psychoanalysis' confidence in its ability to comprehend (hence affect) national identifications, the nation functions at the metapsychological level to ground the analysis of the ego in collectivity; to, in effect, provide psychoanalysis with "public access." In my citation from the open letter what one sees is a deft displacement of the nation by *l'ésprit général*. This displacement is motivated within the letter by Kristeva's recognition that, in the long run, the nation too—however strategically important it may remain within the maelstrom of Americanization—will go the way of all flesh. In anticipation of this she introduces Montesquieu's concept, and does so by openly dropping psychoanalysis. While, at one level, this can be read as a confirmation of the metapsychological status of the nation for psychoanalysis, it must also be understood to bear upon the musical question. That is, if psychoanalysis, the nation and the formal technique of performing all drop out together, then perhaps we are to conclude that music—despite (or because of?) Freud's insistence that he knew nothing about it—is in some way essential to a specifically *psychoanalytical* intervention in and on the national problematic. And indeed, it may well be. For, as I have already argued, performing has everything to do with the matter of touch, that is, *how* one compromises with the myth of origins, at once respecting and rejecting the drive to belong, to be somewhere or, as Heidegger might have said in the 1950s, to dwell. Thus, if music drops out it is perhaps because psychoanalysis itself is understood to be at risk in the critique of nationalism, an insight that might well guide us in our assessment of the technical strategy embodied in the open letter. Where to turn?

In *Nations* one finds an interview with Kristeva in which she is asked to comment upon "her shift to fiction." Her response contains two interesting observations: (1) that France is plunged into a "national depression" (she is speaking in 1990) which has manifested itself in the opening of a chasm between intellectuals and the masses and (2) that in order to write fiction (as opposed to Theory) she needed to gain "sufficient distance from [her]self." The rhetoric here is unmistakable. Not only is this a psychoanalytical explanation of the shift to the technique of fiction, but it is an acknowledgment of the political urgency motivating such a shift. The volatility of this insight repeats in many ways a point made ten years earlier about psychoanalytic interpretation in "Psychoanalysis and the Polis," where analysis is characterized as giving expression to the insight that "desire and the desire to know are not *strangers to each other*" (Kristeva, 308, my emphasis). If I emphasize the theme of volatility here it is with an eye toward stressing the degree to which the status of psychoanalysis and the political status of the talking cure are not only caught up in a reflection upon the idioms and genres of technique (Theory vs fiction) but are so in a manner that registers a profound ambivalence. The question here is not whether one should write novels or counsel patients, but rather whether psychoanalysis can, strictly speaking, *touch* the public discourse within which the nation's depression is inscribed. Can it abandon itself and yet cure the affliction of nationalism? Ultimately, is it through the open letter—presumably no longer strictly psychoanalytical but not yet fictional technique—that psychoanalysis touches the nation, a nation already therefore becoming *l'ésprit général*? If Kristeva's thought hesitates here—where music and literature, nations and nationalism, hang in the balance—it may well be due to the fact that although the open letter clearly invites one to reconceptualize the clinical dimension of analytical technique, the consequences for both psychoanalysis and the national public sphere of what I wish to designate "an open session," that is, a manipulation of "consultation" that is decidedly less temporal than spatial, are unfathomable. One thing, however, is clear. Like the open letter, the open session would necessarily be uncanny—it would have no final destination, no home (not "shelter," but home)—qualities that might account for the dislodging of musical technique which, in Kristeva's hands, seemed bent upon constructing the familiar destiny that the analysis was otherwise dispossessing.

No doubt, one's reservations here (and I will admit to sharing them) are partly spurred by the initiatives taken by the likes of Žižek who, in reconceptualizing the conditions of analytic training, has been driven to regard the cinema—and specifically the *oeuvre* of Alfred Hitchcock—as the as yet unrecognized purveyor of Lacan's teachings, a state of affairs that—in spite of all that Žižek himself has taught us about nationalism and the phantasmatic theft of *jouissance*—might well lead the less charitable among us to conclude that he was analyzed by Ménie Grégoire instead of Jacques Alain-Miller.[5] Obviously, the problem of the institutions and technologies of the mass media, particularly as these bear upon the organization—or as Habermas might still insist, "disintegration"—of the public sphere is a pressing one indeed. The analysis in *Strangers* is eloquent about the menace they represent. Nevertheless, if something like an "open session" is to be possible it will perforce engage the space wherein nationalism circulates not simply as a mythic fantasy, but as an ensemble of institutions like, for example, Radio France or, for that matter, NBC. The question, to my mind, is not whether psychoanalysis should touch this space—its curative ambitions leave it no alternative—rather, the question is *how* will psychoanalysis touch this space, how will it brush past its strangeness or, to invoke a formulation of Walter Benjamin's, how will psychoanalysis brush this space against its grain?

Regardless of whether the conceit of "an open session" is helpful as a way to pose and begin exploring such matters, it strikes me that, at some point, academic intellectuals will nevertheless have to decide where to stand on the postcolonial question: nationalism versus internationalism. Kristeva herself—as she separates nations from nationalism only to later displace nations with *l'ésprit général*—seems inclined to preserve the nation chiefly for strategic purposes. It represents both a historicopolitical reality and a metapsychological function that makes possible the transcendence of nationalism. Does this commit her, and implicitly those of us touched by her analysis, to an internationalism that is fast becoming indistinguishable from multinational capitalism? I think not, but given that psychoanalysis continues—in spite of all her meta-critical precautions—to set the terms of her engagement with these issues, and given that *l'ésprit général* is conceived as displacing the very concept—the nation—that had otherwise functioned to separate psychoanalysis from nationalism while nonetheless providing psychoanalysis with its broad healing powers, perhaps it would be wise to remain open to the alternative glimpsed in the uncanny slogan: nationalism without nations. Frankly speaking, it *sounds* strange, but it should.

Two chapters are then dedicated to Theory as framed within the diffuse tradition of psychoanalysis, first in its Freudian iteration, then in its French, specifically, Kristevan, reiteration. In each case, my reading has sought to bring out some of the diverse, certainly various, forms of the where and when of Theory. In Chapter 2 this took the form of tracking the stumble, the misstep, that both structured Freud's encounter with the urban space of his clinical practice and that then echoed in this thinking about the inscription of "everyday life" in the metapsychological frame of psychoanalysis. My proposition is not that Freud "is" psychoanalysis, whence my general lack of interest in doctrine, but that reading Freud's texts draws attention to the surprising when and where of Theory as it plays out in psychoanalysis.

In this chapter my reading developed this notion of the urban inscription to consider its national articulation, and more particularly to consider the situation of the "foreigner" (both as theorist, Kristeva the alienist, and as an instance of what Simmel would have called "mental life" or, more pointedly, what Houria Bouteldja calls the "*indigene*") within this inscription. Teasing out and isolating the plane of expression, the distinctive enunciative gestures, of Kristeva's theorization of the stranger urged sustained consideration of the place of music in her thinking of the contact between Theory and what Habermas has called the public sphere. Again, this set of gestures allows one to amplify the resonance of the when and where of Theory: when and where does it arise? How is this manifest as Theory, that is, in Theory as where Theory responds to what it treats as the call to theorize? Implicit here, clearly enough, is the problem of context and it is the challenge of thinking this anew that will consume much of what remains to be written in this text.

Equally implicit, especially in the wake of these chapters, is the matter of the reading to which Theory is to be offered, sacrificed. It is not enough to stress, as has been done, that the chiasmus of Reading/Theory pushes reading past sheer literacy, alphabetization or simply a rhyme word, the first, in the formula of the three "r's."

Ultimately, it strikes me as important to think about reading as a form of listening, but to justify this, and however counterintuitively, it matters that we remember what Derrida offered us about writing, an act, even an event, that had to be differentiated from its alphabetical incarnation. As the passages concerning the "*grammē*" of grammatology are as thorny as they are overcited, I turn elsewhere.

> To write is to produce a mark that will constitute a kind of machine that is in turn productive, that my future disappearance in principle will not prevent it from functioning and from yielding, and yielding itself to, reading and rewriting. [...] For the written to be the written, it must continue to "act" and to be legible even if what is called the author of the writing no longer answers for what he has written, for what he seems to have signed, whether he is provisionally absent, or if he is dead [...].
> (Derrida 1982, 316)

This is the "generalized" and "displaced" concept of writing that includes within the purview of the machine that constitutes the written mark, the principles of action and legibility. He earlier has specified that the mark might be "pictographic, hieroglyphic, ideographic, phonetic, alphabetic," but as productive machines marks must be capable of agency in the absence of their producers, and agency here implies that they must provoke, even sustain, reading. The written mark is radically legible whether addressed to anyone or not.

Bernard Stiegler, in passim but very bluntly in the interviews that comprise *Echographies of Television* (2002), is not the first to discern the narrow range of "signs" affiliated with grammatological writing. Put differently, the mark may be a machine, but a machine—even if not installed in a penal colony—marks on and in media whose grammatological properties Derrida generally avoids elaborating. Stiegler draws the hasty conclusion that the theory of the supplement thus falls out of step with the present and requires a mediological supplement, but he is correct to stress that Derrida is read "as if" such a supplement is called for. Readers will not be surprised to read that I take this to be a symptom of the concept of legibility that I wish to rewrite. What is called for is a Reading/Theory that races ahead in mis-step with grammatological writing understood to be a mark that is a machine operating in the potential absence of an operator and in and on any medium whatsoever, manifesting in any conceivable semiotic profile: icon, index, symbol and so on.

How then to conceive the "generalized and displaced" concept of reading? Drawing on a richly debated motif from sound studies I will invoke the event of listening as a means by which to handle this concept properly. In sound studies, now rampantly ambient in the precincts of higher education, it is common to distinguish between hearing (largely deemed physiological) and listening (accordingly deemed psychological). To deploy a convenient but therefore compromised formula: one can hear without listening, but one cannot listen without hearing. Listening is, in effect, parasitic upon hearing, a relation I have, in the introductory pages to *Sounds: the Ambient Humanities*, examined under the heading of the audit (modeled loosely on the concept of the gaze). This staggered dynamic invites the misunderstanding that listening is receptive, it receives what hearing perceives, but even in its active attention to the heard, its "harkening" (as Heidegger might have intoned), it exhibits a reactive passivity. There are two related ways in which this is a misunderstanding.

The first of these can be specified by thinking about Jean-Luc Nancy's ruminations on listening, ruminations that include the proposition that his discipline, philosophy, cannot listen (Nancy 2007, 1). Exploiting semantic intricacies no doubt brought to his attention by Derrida's early writings on Husserl, Nancy proposes that philosophy is wedded to the verb, *entendre*, that is, it hears in order to understand, the problem here being the hermeneutic presumption of meaning arising in hearing oneself speak whether aloud or not. To listen is to enter into a reflexive structure wherein sound produces the agent of its reception. In effect, listening calls for a subject that cannot hear itself speak, that arises as an echo of the sound it is. It is in this sense nonphilosophical. It is thus akin to what I am calling here Theory. Theory listens and its listening manifests in a reading shaped by the fact that it is reflexive, that its effects loop back on a reader who does not and cannot hear itself speak, even when reading "silently." Reflexivity folds productivity and receptivity back over upon each other, making the distinction effectively moot.

An even more provocative questioning of the receptivity, the passivity of listening arises in a source with special pertinence to these chapters on psychoanalysis. I am thinking here of "Listening," a lecture written by Barthes and an analyst, Roland Havas. Apparently recycling Pierre Scaheffer's typological cataloguing of listening, this lecture settles down on what it calls "the third type of listening," a listening that takes the voice of the other as its proper object. Clearly linked to analytical listening—the figure of the silent dummy hovering over a session, its third ear perked—the third type of listening is also called modern, and it is brought into direct connection with certain expressive practices of modernism (Cage is mentioned). What seems important to stress here is that this is a "transferential" listening. This is a listening that *acts upon* the analysand's speech so as to produce there what s/he wants to say, but cannot. More colloquially perhaps, this is a type of listening carried out by a "good listener," not necessarily a "sympathetic ear," but someone whose listening compels a speaker to produce that which needs to be said. In David Scott's recent book, *Stuart Hall's Voice*, he characterizes Hall's listening as capable of "clarifying one's own thoughts," putting a somewhat more philosophical, perhaps even forensic, spin on the concept of transference. Regardless, what emerges is a way of thinking about how listening, of a certain sort ("third" might be as good as any designation for it) is at least as active as speech, and perhaps even more active than a hearing so attentive to what is meant, that it cannot listen to what is said.

Whether this has resolved all misunderstandings that might arise regarding the passivity of listening is not the point. What *is* the point is that perception of the reflexive productivity of listening helps clarify features, perhaps even decisive features of a "general and displaced" concept of reading. Specifically, such a reading must be recognized as an activity that produces something like what a text says whether the writer means to say this or not. In effect, the text succumbs to the force of the reading to which it is offered. We call Theory the system of that force, and for a long time have organized that system around the identity of a patronym. Precisely what is meant when we say that X is a Freudian reading of Hamlet, and those who affiliate in relation to such readings swear allegiance to this patronym. They are "Freudians." Although not typically emphasized all this actually says is that they read in a certain way. If "Freud" is stenography for a certain type of Theory, then is this not also a certain type of reading?

But what of the so-called "founders of discursivity," the theorists, surely they are something else. Perhaps. But surely they are first and foremost readers. Just to stick with Freud. He was clearly conversant with an immense body of writing, everything from Greek classical drama to Darwin and Einstein. He was routinely involved in the loop of listening and writing down to later read and later still to write up the speech of his analysands (or even of analysands he never met, Haizmann or Wilson) and, as the correspondence with Fliess makes perfectly clear, he wrote and read letters on a regular basis. All this and we haven't even got to watching his grandchildren play, his traversals of Vienna and visit to the acropolis, his encounters with sundry *objets d'art*, colleagues, friends, rivals and enemies. The mode of attention he brought to all this, and especially that within it that escaped his attention, this listening articulated itself in the reading that produced the discourse of psychoanalysis, its

Theory. Although I would be hard-pressed to find a formulation like "the when and where" of Theory in Freud (he wrote comparatively few English words, although he speaks them in his one on camera role), I would argue that this designates precisely what attentive listening listens for: the where—at which points in the mark/machine, on which grounds—and the when—under what circumstances, on which occasion—of what a reading can do. What this invites are precisely those characterizations of literacy to be found in Spivak ("transnational literacy") or Wlad Godzich ("critical literacy"), characterizations that in adding more to literacy than sheer comprehension point exactly at what reading can and should be. To read a text is to listen to and thus bring out its difficulties. It is to sacrifice those difficulties to a reading that "makes sense" of them. What results can be and often is written down, and what is written down is at once (*pace* Barthes) readable and writable. It is Theory.

Notes

1   In what might reasonably be characterized as a tightening of her autobiographical turn, Kristeva just prior to the onset of the new century began speaking and writing about her identity as a Bulgarian exile. In "Bulgarie, ma souffrance" from the fall 1995 issue of *L'Infini* she broaches the issue of her strangeness by exploring her relation to her two tongues: Bulgarian and French. One is not therefore surprised when—in characterizing the twisted tongue that emerges from these "communicating vessels" (her citation)—she not only characterizes it as *"une parole étrange"* but she explicitly cites her own prior discussion of the foreigner (in French, *Etrangers à nous-mêmes*) by adding, "*étangère à elle-même*" (Kristeva 1991, 43). Though it anticipates my argument, this text is also rife with musical allusions, notably one where, in delineating what is at stake in her category of maternal memory (explicitly contrasted to Proust's voluntary and involuntary memories), she encrypts the mother's body in her own and then figures their relation as one *"qui vibre à l'unisson"* (ibid., 44), an effect which—I will argue—plays itself out discordantly in *Strangers*. On this theme one might also consult the interview Kristeva gave to *Magazine Littéraire* concerning the publication of *Sens et non-sens de la révolte* (Kristeva 1996b). Concerning the general problematic of the foreigner and subjectivity see also the interview with Suzanne Clark and Kathleen Hulley, "Cultural Strangeness and the Subject in Crisis," now reprinted in *Julia Kristeva: Interviews* (Kristeva 1996a).
2   It is worth recalling here that many of those opposed to the racist initiatives that prompted the formation of *S.O.S Racisme* sported buttons that read *"Ne touches pas à mon pote"* (Don't touch—in the sense of hassle or bug—my buddy), buttons which thus drew attention to the way foreigners were being singled out and harassed, notably by the police and immigration service. In insisting that the foreigner *be* touched, Kristeva's position might be interpreted as aligning itself with the confused and defensive policies of the Mitterand regime. Though, as we shall see, there is an ambivalence to Kristeva's position, I would argue that here—the discerning reader of Louis Dumont—she is seeking to distance herself both from those for whom the foreigner is the "untouchable" and from those who, when push came to shove, would no doubt proclaim, "Some of my closest friends are Arabs!"

3   I note here that in Sarah Ahmed's far more recent pass over the question of the stranger (see *Strange Encounters*) she faults Kristeva (whose position she compares to Bülent Diken's) for paying insufficient attention to the political histories that render some strangers stranger than others. Of course, this is right, but it is worth noting that Ahmed soon, literally within a scant three pages, turns to probe the very concept of history that supports this criticism, a development that appears to acknowledge that the psychoanalytical problematization of the distinction between ontology and epistemology is one that Ahmed may be closer to than she thinks.

4   Earlier I drew attention to the function of "unison" in Kristeva's articulation of the maternal memory. Though the uncanny remains unthematized in "Bulgarie, ma souffrance," the encrypted mother returns here in national guise. I am thinking, obviously, of the pun that unsettles her title, where Bulgaria is not only where she suffers a delay, a site of pain, but also her beneath or under France. Bulgaria is thus memory itself, that is, something that comes-to-one-from-below (*souvenir*). In the fantasy of bearing her own mother, Kristeva returns us to the gestational scene of "Stabat Mater" which is now reversed.

5   Ménie Grégoire, in addition to being an author of numerous "popular" psychoanalytical studies (e.g., *Les Cris de la vie*), was the longtime host of a radio show where callers could be "analyzed" on the air. The general issue of the relation between psychoanalysis and popular culture has been discussed, albeit without much theoretical sophistication, in Sherry Turkle's *Psychoanalytic Politics*. Of course, Kristeva herself has "appeared" on numerous radio talk shows (in fact, one of Lacan's more provocative statements, "*Radiophonie*" was conceived to be delivered "on the air"), and though my disparagement of Ms. Grégoire might lead one to assume that I have some principled beef against radio, I do not. In fact, a more thorough fleshing out of the "open session" would have to take account of the early investments of Brecht and Benjamin in the pedagogical potential of radio technology. I have taken these matters up in *Radio: Essays in Bad Reception* where, among other things, Lacan makes an encore appearance.

Chapter 4
"JAMMING"

So perhaps Theory takes place when and where we least expect it. For example, in a musical performance. If so, what then are the challenges of reading it? Slavoj Žižek and his collaborators in the "remake" of Allen's *Everything You Always Wanted to Know About Sex** (itself "based" on David Reuben's best seller), more precisely in their staging of a reading of Lacan through the films of Alfred Hitchcock, have taken bold steps down this path, a path that has since culminated in Alain Badiou's proposition, "cinema basically consists in creating new ideas about what an idea is" (Badiou 2010, 202). This chapter will pursue this gambit, not by refining what it might mean to argue that the cinema thinks theoretically about ideas but by tracing how a piece of music, specifically Bob Marley's recording of "Jamming," can be shown to offer a theory of improvisation. As this formulation suggests, offering (whether Theory and anything else) involves jamming, not, as my reading will argue, just making it up but by seizing up and releasing, that is, enunciating the rhythm of thought.

As many readers will know, the fortunes of "the object" are changing. Long neglected or disparaged (perhaps nowhere more vociferously than in a humanities devoted to subjectivity), the object, especially in the hands of those committed to what is marketed as "object oriented ontology," has now formally filed for recognition. In what follows I will be entertaining a certain strand of this trend, notably that moment within it when the ontology of the object is understood to withdraw from human attention. My orientation, however, will be different, and this for at least two reasons. First, as intimated above, the object at issue here is a recorded song and, as a rather obvious instance of "expression" (what Marx following Hegel called "externalization"), it might on those grounds be excluded as an object worthy of ontologically oriented attention. And second, while I will agree that this object exists, as it were, on its own terms, I will turn toward it to listen, not so much to what it refuses to say but to what its taciturnity offers as a form of theoretical pedagogy. Having earlier brought listening and reading into practical and theoretical proximity, I hope it is clear that my concern here focuses more directly on Theory than on the object, assuming provisionally that they can be kept apart. To retrieve, for an instant, my earlier engagement with Cavell and Adorno, at issue here is not whether one means what one plays, but how playing says something "meaningful" about its relation to meaning. So yes, among the several points I will be concerned to make, one will bear on the relation between art and whatever it is thought not to be, including—and the argument will require some patience—the humanities as a field of academic inquiry.

If I may be indulged an anecdotal opening gambit. The research chair I now hold at the University of Leeds—the Leadership Chair in the Critical Humanities—takes its name from an initiative begun at the University of Minnesota prior to my departure in 2012. Tasked with rethinking curricular offerings in the College of Liberal Arts, a study group of which I was a member confected the term "critical humanities" as an abbreviation for a far more cumbersome, because still inchoate, formulation about that area of the curriculum not to be immediately conflated with either the fine arts or the social sciences. The phrase was a placeholder that stayed in place. While at Leeds I have entertained two other formulations, formulations similar in concept but less immediately concerned with curricular design. In 2014 I published *Sounds*, a text that bore the portentous subtitle, "the ambient humanities." The following year I presented a lecture at an event convened by the Noötechnics Collective at Kent University, titled, "Left Leaning: Toward a Sinister Humanities." The point here is not to presumptuously narrate highpoints from my CV. At least it is not merely that. Instead, I wish to draw attention to the adjectival series—critical, ambient, sinister (CAS)—and do so in order to further elaborate my broad aim in the reading that follows. Put in the form of a question: What must the humanities be if it (and I will treat it as a plural singular), can be modified or, more precisely, inflected, by this adjectival series, CAS? Of course, framed in this insistently personal way, such an opening gambit may strike some readers as inauspicious, so let me, in the spirit of Roland Barthes who insisted that after the *Elements of Semiology* he *only* wrote for occasion, stress that pursuing the question I have posed will require sustained engagement with the concept and practice of improvisation.[1] So, to abruptly show all the cards in my hand: if the humanities can be or is in *some sense* improvised it is because it can be inflected by the adjectives critical, ambient and sinister. Obviously enough I mean something rather particular by the concept and practice of improvisation, especially if understood to be "offered" by "Jamming."

One way to initiate this tarrying with improvisation is to trace certain events that led me to it. In March of 2015 the Austrian guitarist Christian Fennesz played the Howard Assembly Room in Leeds. Billed as a performance exploring the music of Mahler, notably his second symphony (the "Resurrection Symphony"), Fennesz took the stage with an accompanist, the graphic artist Lillevan. Exploiting the miscegenational capacity of computing, the two performers began—and this is what grabbed my attention—to "play" together. In fact, they jammed. Despite the fact that much of what the performers worked with existed as prerecorded files, the strategies of assemblage were not prerehearsed: sounds summoned images, images summoned sounds as both unfolded in so-called real time. Although not presented directly as "call and response," the musicality of the encounter was framed so as to foreground the indistinct, hard to pinpoint site of the mix as such.

In July of 2016, in the Factory of the Arts in Cape Town, a "quintet" led by the Centre for Humanities Research resident scholar Reza Khota with Dathini Mzayiya, Thokozani Mthiyane, Daniel Grey and Brydon Bolton set up what deserves to be called "an instrument." It consisted of an electric guitar (played through a pedal board and amp), an upright bass (also amped and at times bowed), a sampler and mixer, a large cloth canvas and the various implements used to apply oil paint to it (brushes, sponges, palette knives, etc.). Tying the canvas and the musical instruments together were contact mics applied to the recto of the canvas, mics that amplified the sounds made between the painters and the canvas. Although rather traditional musical instruments comprised aspects of "the instrument" the performance, titled, "People You May Know" (and the preemptive phenomenon of algorithmic community is far from irrelevant here), was precisely the improvised cocreation of a painting and a musical composition. Literally, as Khota and Bolton played, Mzayiya and Mthiyane painted, and they worked together as two duos: the painters would take turns at the canvas, then step back, observe, sometimes crossing from left to right, sometimes extending, sometimes breaking off what the other had been doing, but just as insistently they would paint *ensemble*, together. Precisely the same patterns of engagement could be discerned among the musicians. Even Daniel Grey, the "*bricoleur*/engineer," who was otherwise coaxing and shaping the sonic encounter between the canvas and the amps, jammed his way into the event, at times content to mix for shear audibility, other times generating sampled loops that would produce sonic gestures to which both musicians and painters would respond. The resulting work, the painted "recording," was left for all to see. Something was happening here both to the relation between sounds and images, and to the concept and practice of improvisation itself.

Both of these encounters (and I will return to give this term its due) might be thought to give the bizarre event of the "jam" between Ornette Coleman and Jacques Derrida that occurred at La Villete in 2002 a more profound, less wacky, character, a performance that might otherwise simply be tucked into the comparatively long series of encounters between jazz and something like "the spoken word." Consider the scene in *The Subterraneans* (the 1960 film adaptation of Jack Kerouac's novel) where we see and hear Gerry Mulligan's quartet enunciated in a left to right pan that shows a painter painting *while* the quartet is playing. As this might suggest, were it not for the decisive fact that the quartet is essentially ignoring the painter, that the gambit of "People You May Know" is also old news, that is, history.

But here's the point. In the now voluminous writing about improvisation (Duke University Press now has a series, "Improvisation, Community and Social Practice"), it is commonplace to stress how the practice transforms the relations among those participating. For people like Fred Moten this means recognizing how improvisation operates as the space out of which emerges the "black radical tradition, whereas for David Toop and Derek Bailey improvisation transforms non-musicians into musicians and non-instruments into instruments. Less common, and this will explain my cumbersome insistence on the formulation the "concept and practice of improvisation," is emphasis placed on how the very concept of improvisation is re: worked in the event of its exercise.[2] This is what I find so striking about the encounters whose details I have sketched, and it is precisely this re: working of improvisation that bears so immediately on the humanities, both in the sense of it serving as a locus for this re: working and also in the sense of the humanities fostering this re: working by improvising with the arts and the social sciences. In this, the humanities, as an enduring if endangered institutional project, emerges as a means by which to conceive the when and where of Theory.

To return then to Marley, the alas Dead Black Man who has so much to teach those willing to read. Of specific interest here is "Jamming" that he recorded with The Wailers on their LP *Exodus* from 1977, a song written after the attempt on his life that obliged him to decamp to the UK. Although in Jamaican patois, "jamming" connotes getting together or gathering, it is a word that exhibits the lexical qualities of what Freud sought to capture in his essay, "The Antithetical Sense of Primal Words." Of particular interest to me is the fact that the word means to break down, to seize up and to let go, to relax or, in a musical context, to improvise. This lexical polyvocality operates in both the verb (to jam) and the noun (a jam) forms. Precisely why this is of interest in the context I am weaving here is illuminated by a series of formulations that appear in Jacques Lacan's seminar from 1954 to 1955, *The Ego in Freud's Theory and in the Technique of Psychoanalysis*. Since it is from this source that I will tease out what this helps us think about the concept and practice of improvisation, especially as it bears on the humanities, drawing out what in its several formulations matter to Marley is called for.

Those familiar with what Lacan insists on calling his "teaching" will know that the activities gathered together in Seminar II include a series of talks held under the auspices of the Société Française de Psychanalyse on the theme of "Psychoanalysis and the Human Sciences." I stress this both to reassure the reader that I have not, in fact, strayed far from the question of the humanities and also to draw attention to Lacan's own contribution, a paper titled "Psychoanalysis and Cybernetics, or, On the Nature of Language." Even if one knows little about Lacan, received wisdom has it that he took language seriously, indeed the brilliant linguist and comparative philologist Emile Benveniste presented a paper in the "Psychoanalysis and the Human Sciences" series. Less known, except perhaps for Anthony Wilden, is Lacan's fascination with cybernetics, a fascination given fresh impetus by scholars like Antoinette Rouvroy and her examination of what she calls, in more direct dialogue with Michel Foucault, "algorithmic governmentality" and its pastoralism of the digital. Much could be said here, but what will matter to my reading is the fact that for Lacan, cybernetics in illuminating *the nature of language* also posited a notion of "the machine," that might otherwise seem ill-suited to a discussion of what Lacan called, "the speaking subject," that is, the human being. Instead of opposing the human and the machine, as a certain Eurocentric humanism was and is inclined to do—disparagement, now routine, of "instrumental reason" stings for this reason—Lacan wanted to embrace a certain machinic materialism as a way to theorize the human freed of the optimistic suspicion he and others of his generation associated with Maurice Merleau-Ponty and existential phenomenology. Frantz Fanon, not typically mentioned in the same breath as Lacan, emphasized in his own reading of Lacan's essay on the family complexes from the *Encyclopédie française* the provocation of his critical gambit, writing in a footnote to *Black Skins, White Masks*: "When one has grasped the *mechanism* described by Lacan one can have no further doubt that the real Other for the white man is and will continue to be the black man. And conversely" (Fanon 1967, 161).[3]

But let us turn directly to what is going to matter in my effort to listen to, to read Marley's song. In the discussion that follows the session devoted to Claude Lévi-Strauss's presentation on the exchange mechanism of kinship (formulated five years after *The Elementary Structures* and 16 years after Lacan's encyclopedia entry), we find the following in the Tomaselli translation:

> The philosophical criticisms made of strictly mechanistic research assume the machine to be deprived of freedom. It would be very easy to prove to you that the machine is much freer than the animal.

And then:

> The animal is a jammed machine. It is a machine with certain parameters that are no longer capable of variation. And why? Because the external environment determines the animal, and turns it into a fixed type.

> It is in as much as, compared to the animal, we are machines, that is to say something decomposed, that we possess greater freedom. (Lacan 1988, 31)

As the reader will have guessed, given my title, the formulation that caught my ear is the sentence: "The animal is a jammed machine." Striking indeed, but obviously Lacan wrote in French, so what is "jammed" a translation of? It is a translation of the French "*bloquée*," perhaps more typically rendered "blocked." The animal is a blocked machine, and this because, on Lacan's account, its environment operates on it to turn it into a fixed type. A sea bass becomes a sea bass (now *despite* its environment). Suspending for a moment our rush, in the spirit of animal studies, to shield the animal from such microaggressions, let me observe that, in fact, Tomaselli is not here taking unwarranted liberties. In fact, what she has done is to remind us that a text object often instructs us how it is to be translated by listening carefully to a later moment as it says the following when discussing the history of telephonic communication:

> The quantity of information then began to be codified. This doesn't mean that fundamental things happen between human beings. It concerns what goes down the wires, and what can be measured. Except, when one begins to wonder whether it does go, or whether it doesn't, when it deteriorates, when it is no longer communication. This is what is called, in psychology, the jam [in English], an American word. (Lacan 1988, 83)

In effect, what Tomaselli does—and, of course, one cannot entirely escape the classic convergence between translation and betrayal—is that she takes this code switch between French and English as an instruction about all prior instances of the use, in French, of *bloquée* insisting to Anglophone ears that the connotative resonance of jam, jammed, jamming, be heard everywhere Lacan appeals to what might otherwise simply be rendered as blockage. I note, in passing, that Lacan might also have had recourse to the French *coincée*, or "kinked," but he does not. At least not here.

If these remarks have led one to think that the familiar Lacanian formula—the Unconscious is structured like a language—is here formulated as "the Unconscious is *machined* like a language" one would not be entirely wrong, but it is essential, given the presence of Lévi-Strauss, that one also hear "elementary structures of kinship" in the word machine. For Lacan, the distinctly human arises in this circulation of goods, women and words. Be that as it may, if "jam" translates "block," is not Lacan potentially factoring *out* the antithetical character of "jamming" as put to work by Marley, the letting go, as opposed to the getting together? I think not, but since clarifying *why* helps us pose the question of what is designated by the expression, "the sinister humanities," it is worth lingering over.

In the passage where the "Anglish" word "jam" sounds, and it is in a session called "Circuit," Lacan is tracing how a certain medium of communication fails. When the information being transmitted on the wire is not communicated, we have a jam. Now, unless he is assuming that nonhuman animals use telephones—and we know, of course, they have been depicted playing poker—but unless they are also using phones, then here the earlier proposition about the *animal* as a jammed machine has either been contradicted or rather deftly displaced. The latter option is encouraged when one turns to the other moments in the seminar when "jammed" translates "blocked."

Thus, in the session titled "Homeostasis and Insistence" what are we to make of the following formulations regarding the unity of the human subject:

> The subject is no one. It is decomposed (*décomposé*), in pieces (*morcelé*). And it is jammed, sucked in (*aspiré*, so in fact, aspirated) by the image, the deceiving and realized image, of the other, or equally, by its own specular image. That is where it finds its unity. (Lacan 1988, 54)

Clearly, Lacan is here diddling with the very mechanism that arrested Fanon, the encounter with the Other on the aptly named "mirror stage," but it is hard to overlook the fact that he is also clearly situating "the jam" *not* in the nonhuman animal, but in the human-machine, a machine jammed by its imaginary capture in the Other. *Or*, and the hypothesis seems invited, is he acknowledging here, however implicitly, the commonplace that, when all is said and done, the human subject *is* an animal, that it shares with the animal a jam that ties both to an environment that strips their development of contingency? Lacan never *quite* says this, but in not doing so he lets something even more interesting slip.

When in the session on the relation between Freud's "Project for a Scientific Psychology" and *The Interpretation of Dreams* Lacan takes up the theme of what he calls "thinking machines," in effect, AI, he makes the following observations:

> Why has the paradoxical expression "thinking machine" been created? I who say that men think only very rarely, I'm not going to speak of thinking machines—but all the same, what happens in a thinking machine is on average on an infinitely higher level than what happens in a scientific society. If you give a thinking machine different elements, it, at least, answers something different. From the point of view of language, these little machines purr (*ronronne*) something new for us, perhaps an echo, and approximation let us say. (Lacan 1988, 119)

He then turns[4] directly to a consideration of the status of language in the human sciences. Since we know that throughout Seminar II Lacan is committed to thinking about the human as a machine, what this rattling of AI is meant to underscore is the reduction of the human to what Descartes called the cogito. In ridiculing the thought that takes place within a scientific society, Lacan reintroduces the figure of the animal in a colloquialism, significantly *shared* with English, of the machine that, precisely when operating smoothly, "purrs." In this translingual onomatopoeia, I will propose, the nonhuman animal figures not as a jammed machine but as the sign (indeed a sonic sign) of a machine that runs without a glitch. Thus, as the sessions of Seminar II concatenate, we move from the nonhuman animal as a jammed machine to the nonhuman animal as the sound of the flawless machine, flawless less because it is perfect than because it is demonstrative. It *shows* repeatedly that thinking and speaking, or communicating are not the same.

The point. On the one hand, what can be traced here is how jam—the "American" word—designates both function and malfunction. In effect, Lacan grasps perfectly Marley's proposition that to jam means to lock up, to seize and to release, to flow. But on the other hand, this discussion situates jamming precisely at the vexed join between what Jacques Derrida called long ago, "the traditional opposition of the life form called human, and the life form called animal" (Derrida 2001, 51). Indeed, it is here, I will propose, that the enormous ambition of thinking the chance encounter between improvisation and humanistic inquiry really starts to fall within range. Improvisation, what I am here exploring through the notion of "jamming," bears not merely on those activities (whether mental or manual) we would be inclined to call humanistic, but even more to the point it bears on the matter, that is, the embodied concept of the human that such activities have long been thought to give expression to.

It is here that the issue of the "sinister humanities" demands its due. "Sinister" especially as part of the phrase "sinister resonance" (initially to be found in Joseph Conrad) has been taken up by David Toop and Julie Beth Napolin to designate the ephemeral and distinctly haunting character of sound itself. And while I have no particular quarrel with this work, in bringing "sinister" into conjunction with the humanities I wish rather to emphasize its contrast with "dexterous," that is, right-handedness. The warrant for this derives from the enormous paleontological import attached to the hand by Friedrich Engels in his fragment, "The Part Played by Labor in the Becoming Human of the Ape," an argument developed with extraordinary rigor by André Leroi-Gourhan in *Gesture and Speech* and more recently by both Colin McGinn in *Prehension* and Darian Leader in *Hands*. On a more strictly philosophical register the hand figures cortically in Derrida's critique of Martin Heidegger's use of the distinctly human hand to grasp (literally) *Dasein*, that is, the signature being-there of humanity. Although Derrida is keen to underscore the fact that Heidegger refers to the hand only in the singular (preferring, e.g., writing with a pen, to writing with a typewriter), what he does not tease out is what Robert Hertz obliges us to face in his extraordinary essay on right-handedness, that is, the culturally enforced bilateral asymmetry of the human being. So, if one takes the hand as a way to think the distinctly embodied concept of the human, and recognize this life form as the ground of the humanities, then to emphasize the "sinister" element here is to draw attention to how a massive political theology favoring "dexterity" (and remember, ambidexterity simply means having two right hands) is woven deep into the embodied concept of the human. For Kant, human spatial orientation—whether toward objects or subjects—rests upon the left/right distinction, reminding us that there is no human without embodiment, and that there is no embodiment without power.

A "sinister," that is, "Left leaning" humanities, then is a project based within the increasingly troubled space of the university committed to a materialism, neither dialectical nor new, that resists reducing the human of humanism to a matter of spirit, a concept (decidedly Eurocentric), but one responsive to the pressure Lacan has placed upon the notion of determination through his re: working of the machine. As noted before this reappropriation has essential recourse to jamming, but—and this is crucial—so as not to lose touch with the jam at the level of matter, I will further urge that we consider Louis Althusser's late essay, "The Underground Current of the Materialism of the Encounter" as the, if not proper then certainly pertinent, means by which to hang onto a *matter of the Left*, a sinister matter. Written in the wake of the horrifying psychotic episode that left his wife Hélène strangled, this text restates Althusser's argument that the so-called mature Marx had little if anything to do with Hegel. It is, as others have noted, an effort to work out a philosophy consistent with the break earlier thought to have separated Marx from the impasses of German transcendental idealism. In a gesture that has become less remarkable in the wake of the Spinoza revival it heralded (see the subsequent chapter), Althusser begins his hydrological genealogy in the falling rain. Specifically, he returns to Lucretius and the ontological proposition that "in a beginning that will have always already begun," all matter was falling vertically through the void. At a certain unreconstructable point, a swerve (technically the so-called *clinamen*) takes place causing one falling particle to "encounter" another. This triggers a process of structuration that over millennia results in the material world as it presents itself to humans as an "object" of both cognition and labor. This "encounter" (earlier I said I would essay to give this word its due) is self-causing in the sense that it happens by chance. Nothing *rationalizes* it. As this might suggest, the materialism of the encounter is also, and Althusser says as much, a properly *aleatory materialism*, that is, a materialism whose vibrancy, whose dynamism, is essentially derived from a certain game of chance, the Lucretian swerve, constituting matter as such. Worked out hydrologically, this traces an underground current that rushes through Spinoza and Pascal, to Rousseau and Marx. In affiliating with this current Althusser is proposing that a materialism consistent with the radicality of Marx's mature thought (not, it is worth emphasizing, what Lenin thought he was securing in the contrast with "empirio-criticism") is distinctly aleatory, that is, non-dialectical, dialectical reasoning here thought to have illegitimate recourse to *laws* of historical development, in effect, to non-contingent necessity, or the metaphysics of a chronological orientation that survives every so-called synthesis. Thus, a "sinister humanities," precisely to the extent that it is Left leaning, embraces an aleatory materialism in which "right-handedness" is a lucky accident, an utterly contingent necessity inscribed in the very founding of the human, in its orientation on the earth. That such a humanities is also committed to "jamming" as an engagement with the aleatory that works and re: works the human, the nonhuman animal and the machine also follows even if accidentally.

Implicit here is the broaching of a line of flight, a vanishing point, that will eventually draw us back to the problem of a humanities neither merely *engaged with* nor simply *based on* improvisation, but since this is also the proper context within which to pose the problem of ambience, why avoid it?

Readers will not be surprised to hear that "ambience" has emerged as a problem within sound studies. Notables such as Christopher Cox, Timothy Morton and most recently Seth Kim-Cohen have all tugged and warred over the concept of ambience. Kim-Cohen, doubtless the most suspicious of ambience, frames the matter in a way useful to this discussion. Responding to a series of exhibitions on the East Coast earlier in this decade, he bemoans, audibly, the fetish of immersive anticonceptualism that he finds summoned up in the term "ambient." In effect, Kim-Cohen repudiates the effect ambience has had on a globalized field of art practices committed in various ways to the gambit of conceptual art. In a recent interview given to Ear Room, Kim-Cohen softens his critique, not by suddenly embracing immersion but by noting that ambience—and he happens to be an unrepentant fan of Brian Eno—might take *alternative* forms, forms that would extend and complicate the place of the conceptual in both art and art theory. While I appreciate the polemical impulse of his unsoftened view, it is his, but also Morton's affirmation of an aleatory, delocalized agency of the ambient that matters to my confection of the "ambient humanities."

This formulation appears in *Sounds* where it is deployed to caution sound studies about the confidence animating its emergence as a field of inquiry, a confidence rooted in its eager advocacy on behalf of sound, as if its partisans were certain what sound is. Ambience is thus not about immersion or anti-intellectualism (whence the conflict with conceptual art), but it is about the distinctly theoretical problem of thinking when and where *what is called* sound takes place. More recently I have pursued this line of questioning under the heading of the "Ding in Itself" where the question of sound sounds within and as Kant's concept of the noumenon, that is, the thing that, like Lacan's concept of "the real," resists symbolization, in failing to present itself to human consciousness. Teased out more programmatically and in more direct engagement with the context being woven here, ambience then might be said to involve three elements.

First, it involves the notion that the humanities is taking place well outside its traditional institutional settings, indeed, anywhere and everywhere that the human is in play/at stake. In the essay cited earlier by Derrida on the "New Humanities" he specifies in addition to law and jurisprudence, that is, fields where "human rights" and "crimes against humanity" figure prominently: "departments of genetics, natural science, medicine and even mathematics" (Derrida 2001, 50). This invites the speculation that, in a certain sense, ambience and the humanities might be two ways of saying the "same thing."

Second, ambience involves recognizing that this redistribution of the humanities changes the way workers in the university work, especially when they work on what they take to be most their own. At one level what this illuminates is the fact that what just two decades ago would have been named, "the Crisis of the Humanities," can be, and is now named, "the Crisis of the University." As the logic of neoliberal austerity infuses its preoccupation with measure (the measurable and the measured) throughout the university, it clarifies how broadly the terrain of intellectual labor fans over practices that resist measure, practices that can be methodologically captured, if at all, only through terse and thus hopelessly vague recipes like, "read, think, write, repeat." The hum or buzz, perhaps even purr, generated by this immeasurable work feels like it is coming from everywhere at once. Lawrence Kramer's recent *The Hum of the World* is written in a similar vein.

Third, ambience, especially when used to modify a humanities it might otherwise simply restate, invites us to consider that a distinctly ambient humanities, like Lucretian rain, has always been underway, that is, that the encounter animating it, its aleatory swerve, has been happening for as long as any life form considered human can remember. In fact, and I will not have time to defend this proposition in detail, instead of imagining that the humanities grounds itself in a humanism thought to have emerged in Europe, perhaps what is implied by the ambient humanities is that this humanism, that its concept of the human was a reaction formation, based in a "becoming-Europe" and seeking to give definition to an event whose mere outline can be traced, if at all, through the open series of pairings beginning with human-gods, but extending through human-savage, human-animal, human-machine and so on. Ambience in this sense designates the event horizon along which the university as a "spiritual" (*geistlich*) project carried out by beings self-identified as human teeters between appearing and disappearing.

What specifically is posited here about the *encounter* between improvisation and the humanities is now audibly just outside the gates of these remarks. Certainly, the proposition I am most blatantly advancing is the one that in troubling the embodied concept of the human, and situating this event in a space of ambience, effectively grounds (and surely that is not the right word) the humanities in the very condition of improvisation, that is, what Althusser means by the aleatory encounter. Improvisation is thus not something done in practices studied *by* the humanities; improvisation is what the humanities does. Fair enough, but what might this offer us regarding improvisation as a form of practice? How does this bear on the questions posed by the work of Fennezs and Khota (just to pick out the guitarists) summoned in the opening pages of this chapter?

In earlier stressing that these performances confronted me with a surprising and challenging engagement with improvisation, I avoided the matter that now seems paramount, namely, if improvisation is in some sense what the humanities does, does it do it differently than it is done within the so-called arts? More particularly, if what Fennesz and Khota put in play/at stake is the question—how does improvisation re: work the tools and conditions of its exercise?—then does this question resonate differently, and if so how, within the humanities and the arts? In formulating such a question I am obviously distinguishing, at least in principle, *between* the humanities and the arts despite their routine and insistent pairing. On what grounds and to what effect? In posing such a question I am broaching the urgent practical matter of how to think tactically about the present of higher education and its funding. While this cannot be resolved here (in this moment and in an academic publication), it can be put in play.

I will play this out along two fronts.

In the context of British higher education one is routinely called upon to give an account of oneself. Not in the spirit of what Judith Butler means by this phrase, that is, the piecing together of the stories through which one is told to/shared with others, but in the rather more austere form of a report on activities. As is characteristic of all austere exercises this one appeals remorselessly to metrics such as outputs and, rather more rebarbatively, "impacts" (earlier "benefits"). Again in the British context, what distinguishes these metrics is the notion that while "output" might be translated as "result," "impact" is properly translated as a "public good," and not just any public. Specifically, an impact is an effect that occurs in and with a public that is, by definition, extramural, that is, nonacademic. I am sharing this not merely to limn the depravity of those few fortunate to be engaged in academic labor in the UK, but to point to one of the ways, within the context of a neoliberalism in decline, that the humanities and the arts are sociopolitically differentiated: the humanities can produce outputs, but they cannot, at least not typically, produce impact. In this calculation the arts have impact and in this they join the so-called applied sciences in producing a familiar crenellation in the outer wall of the university. There is an economic manifestation of this distinction whose delineation I will leave for another day.

In the lecture of Derrida's on the new humanities referred to earlier he takes up this issue in decidedly less austere terms, even as he too entertains a distinction between the humanities and the arts by proposing that it can be captured under the heading of work, or as he prefers, "*travail*." From this vantage point, the work of the humanities is said *not* to result in works, in *oeuvres*, a result he reserves for the arts. One might certainly want to object that if anyone working in the humanities might be thought to have produced "works," it is Derrida himself, but this misses his distinctive emphasis on the link drawn insistently by both Michel Foucault and Roland Barthes between works and authors. Texts in the humanities are not signed by "authors," and this despite the contractual language those of us who publish books today are very familiar with. In fact, if you buy books on Amazon—shame on you—then you will know that Derrida, along with many others, has an "Authors Page." But one might reasonably propose that this is a practice designed precisely to absorb the critical force of an argument like Derrida's. In this it resembles the *Schadenfreude* to be discerned in Derrida's obituaries: you see, he *is* a subject after all, and now, like all subjects worthy of the characterization, he has died.

Second front. There is, however, another perhaps even more provocative account of the difference between the humanities and the arts in Derrida's essay. He tries to render it by inflecting his concept of work with J. L. Austin's distinction between constative and performative utterances. As some readers will know, this distinction figures prominently in the opening pages of Austin's series of lectures from 1955 titled, *How to Do Things with Words*, a text that figured cortically in the heated, even ugly, exchange between Derrida and John Searle in the 1970s. In this text Austin draws attention to a type of language use he characterizes as largely ignored by the logical positivists around him, this is what he nominates with some hesitation as "the performative." He contrasts it with the type of language use that logicians concentrate on, namely utterances that make statements that purport to be either true or false. This type of utterance he calls the constative. What then distinguishes the performative and thus recommends it for our attention is that it is an utterance that, as his title says, *does things* with words, the canonical example being the response, "I do," in the context of an Anglophone, Christian marriage ceremony. There is much more to be said about this fabulous little text, but here let me simply observe that Derrida deploys this distinction in a quite particular way. He uses it to align the humanities with constative utterances, and the arts with performative utterances, implying in doing so that works signed by "authors" are, in some sense, the results of performances, indeed performances of the sort invoked earlier in this essay. Somewhat surprisingly, Derrida insists upon this distinction even as he notes that the act of professing, teaching, is performative while "the doctrine is not" (Derrida 2001, 39).

That said, my quarrel here is not really with the perceived desire to distinguish, with whatever degree of rigor, the humanities and the arts. I actually agree that they are different—indeed denying this I think does more harm than good—but what becomes crucial is what arises within what I will insist upon calling their *encounter*, an encounter that allows these domains to touch while remaining apart. If, as I have argued, the humanities committed to an aleatory materialism is doing little more than improvising, how does this touch particular acts of improvisation without reducing them to statements and what happens to improvisation as a result?

To make headway here it is useful to recall a distinction made by the distinguished Afro-American musicologist and trombone player George E. Lewis. In his essay, "Improvised Music after 1950: Afrological and Eurological Perspectives," he sets out to explore a deep structural distinction between Euro-American and African and Afro-American experimental music between, not to put too fine a point on it, John Cage and John Coltrane. To formulate this distinction Lewis draws a contrast between two types of improvisation: the spontaneous and the indeterminate. That one is more authentic than the other does not concern him. Instead, he wants both to understand the performative principles at work in the two modes of improvisation, and on that basis make sense of a certain disdain among Euro-American experimentalists for jazz. Crucial here is Lewis's observation that the indeterminate or aleatory—and he is thinking of Cage's use of the *I Ching* or the principle of durational structures—engages improvisation in the form of planned accidents, *determined* indeterminacy. By contrast, spontaneity of the sort to be found, say, in The Art Ensemble of Chicago, is not planned, it is provoked, summoned out of the constraints that set the terms for any given "musical" performance. All other things aside, what emerges here is a difference in temporality, that is, the matter of when improvisation takes place, a difference that cannot help but pose a question of the sort I have been asking about the humanities, that is, at what level and when does it improvise?

The temptation here is to consider that the aleatory by which I have already characterized encounters of the humanities kind is the means by which we might contrast *its* commitment to improvisation with the improvised acts to be found in the arts. While this racializes the humanities as Euro-American in a way that is not entirely false, it Afro-Americanizes the arts in a way that plainly is. To resist then what is clearly a stale option, let me, in the guise of some concluding remarks, swing back around to the Wailers and suggest that "jamming"—precisely to the extent that it is itself formed by the encounter between the spontaneous and the indeterminate—that "jamming" is the concept and practice needed to think the touch between the humanities and the arts that keeps them apart. To be clear: if the song and this essay have the same title, it is because they are, as is said in the musical world, "covers" of each other. Note, however, that cover here has less to do with "version" or "rendition" with their oblique reference to translation, than with the singular relation, described by Borges, between *Don Quixote* as written by Pierre Menard and Miguel de Cervantes.

I have already drawn attention to Marley's prescient attraction to the antithetical senses of "jamming," but what more does the song teach us about "jamming" as a model, even a prototype, of the Left leaning aleatory encounter? The lessons here are at once lyrical and musical. Lyrically, one needs to look no further than the opening chorus:

We're jamming. I want to jam it with you. We're jamming, jamming; and I hope you like jamming too. Ain't no rules, ain't no vow, we can do it anyhow; and I & I know we'll see it through. 'Cos everyday we pay the price with a loving sacrifice, jamming 'til the jam is through.

There is an enormous amount to fuss over here: the internal rhymes (vow and how; price and sacrifice; etc.); the rhyme words (you, too, through, etc.); the grammatical drift of gerund (jamming), noun (the jam), verb (jam it), not to mention the dreaded braid of personal and impersonal pronouns (we, I, you, it) and the double negatives placing both rules and vows under erasure and this in a song that nevertheless *vows* that jamming will continue until the jam is through, a vow that then becomes either utopic or merely technical, that is, subject to the lead out groove. But let me concentrate on one detail, namely the evocation of jah. The line reads: "Ain't no rules, ain't no vow, we can do it anyhow; and I & I know we'll see it through." In Iyaric, the Rastafarian creolization of English, the I & I is the pronoun (and it is *not* the plural we) by which one states one's unity with jah. I am jah; jah is I (never "me"). Having commented on the double negatives, let me simply note that while this evocation of jah, especially as it is later taken up in the bridge, is doctrinal, it is also subtly sonic bringing the Rastafarian evocation of Spinoza's "intellectual love of god" into contact with the word "jamming." I & I echoes here as jah, resounding the title as "jah man," drawing our attention to the theoretical, yes theoretical, proposition that situates the human–god relation, and this is vital, *within* the jam. Reggae thus presents itself as one of those places where the problem of the human is in play/at stake, indeed it demonstrates that the jam, the improv, *purrs* at the heart of the human-machine. Fans may bristle at the suggestion that Marley is doing anything more than singing about god, but in plainly singing about singing, playing about playing, he is insistently gesturing at a feature of god—its structural operation—there is no good reason to ignore.

Similar intricacies abound in the music. Of course, strictly speaking, the song is not improvised. It is rehearsed, even if, as we know, it was written quickly and immediately in the wake of an attempt on Marley's life, whence the line, "No bullet can stop us now" (not "me," but "us") in the first verse. Nevertheless, not only does the song establish a steady rhythmic pulse, a "groove," it is a groove that, as the various live recordings attest, facilitates a cadenza-like jam as the outro. Crucial to this pulse is the subtle tension it establishes between the strong 4/4 feel of the guitar, bass and keyboards as they move through the chord pattern—Bm/ E 7th/ G/ F# m 7th—and the signature trap set pattern—here played by Carly Barrett—which stealthily deploys the one-drop pattern heard nearly everywhere in Reggae. Typical of the one-drop rhythm is the way it brushes most rock or pop drumming (also typically in 4/4) against the grain by dropping out or suppressing the downbeat on one, and shifting the snare strokes typically found on two and four, all onto three. In its more emphatic iterations, even the kick drum beats are condensed into the three with the high hat serving to locate most of the percussive activity of the part. Crucial to "Jamming" is Marley's strum pattern, a steady up/down that in accenting the rhythmic force of the up strum produces a groove in which the downbeat of each bar gets lost in the count. In effect, the strum pattern contours the entire track, almost as if one is listening to a strip of film played backward. Almost. In "Jamming'" this groove is further embellished with all manner of inventive fills and supplemental percussion, but the overall effect is that what musicians call a "pocket," that is, the lived or felt time of the performance, forms allowing the piece to advance by simultaneously reversing, or, by stalling and advancing flow. By, if I may, jamming.

But there is more. The faint percussive stress on three within a 4/4/ pulse, through a sort of topographic projection, draws a different kind of attention to the I & I/jah man matrix, by reminding us that the female vocalists (Marcia Griffiths, Rita Marley and Judy Mowatt) who execute the call and response pattern that implicitly folds all auditors into the piece are known as the *I Threes* (sometimes just Threes). As with the "I & I" gesture, this "name" with its blatant trinitarianism is also an instance of Spinoza-like immanence, that is, of the radical horizontality of a sacred that is no longer simply sacred. "Three" is thus an alternative spelling of jah. But here, quite pointedly, the response that gives the call its orientation, and thus its sense, is decidedly not man but woman, reminding us that feminism, whether international or not, has long been one of the sites around which the embodied concept of the human has been in play/at stake. Let me then propose that this is yet another way in which the musical detail—here the three-part women's harmony (three singing as one)—of "Jamming'" invites us to hear within it not simply a jam, but a jam reflexively engaged in performing, *but also* constating a "theory," of improvisation. This, as earlier intimated, is the object of the song. This is what it offers.

But what precisely does this tell us about the encounter, the touch, between the humanities and the arts? Crucial here is my quiet but insistent appeal to Theory. If we abandon the devotional account of Theory that grasps it as a canon of textual sources that derive from certain geographies and date from certain times, to think about it in the spirit of Alain Badiou when he enables us to situate Theory at the point where philosophy *avoids* the encounter, then I think we are onto something. If Theory is exactly what happens when the philosophy machine jams, then Theory's very existence underscores the role jamming must play in carrying on, without rules, without vows as the humanities touches on what most provokes it. Significantly, this situation, this aleatory encounter is precisely echoed in the arts, a field of practice that eschews the provocations of "Theory" at the risk of lapsing into a cult of personalities, the trauma of creation and ineffable consolations. How the humanities and the arts can *theorize* together, touch each other deeply while remaining apart is the critical question before us. It is *the* defining question of a *critical* humanities. Because, as those of us active in the humanities are well aware, the hour is growing late, *this* question calls upon us to respond not, I should think, by trying to find new beauty in ruins (I'm looking at you Bill Readings), but in jamming machines that should be put out of their misery, while simultaneously jamming our way into alternative shelters, fresh conditions for the work that Theory tells us is too important to carry on without. Among the things on offer in such shelters might well be the reading of improvisation that Marley obliges us to listen for. Have we then the warrant to expect Theory to take place here? We do not, but this is no argument against preparing to read as though it could. And in what consists its potential? Reading is how we encounter the text we offer to it. It's the jam.

Notes

1 The kernel of this chapter was presented at an event hosted by the Centre for Humanities Research at the University of Western Cape and the Mellon-funded annual meeting of the Consortium of Humanities Centers and Institutes. Our topic: "The Humanities Improvised." I was, and am, grateful for the chance, but I wish also to acknowledge the special counsel I received from the following: Qadri Ismail, Reza Khota, Anaïs Nony, Eric Prenowitz, Wilton Schereka and Marcel Swiboda. The chapter would be very different without them, and they may have preferred that.
2 The idiosyncratic spelling of "reworked" derives from my translation of Bertolt Brecht's concept of "*Umfunktionerung*" (more typically, refunctioning or repurposing with a hyphen). See, *Radio: Essays in Bad Reception* footnote 2, page 207 for a justification of this translation and spelling.
3 With the recent publication of *Alienation and Freedom* edited by Jean Kalifa and Robert Young the available Fanon/Lacan dossier has thickened considerably. See in particular Fanon's extended commentary on section two of Lacan's postwar lecture, "Presentation on Psychical Causality," keeping in mind that cause and mechanism are never far.
4 An EP version of this argument is to be found in my "On the One Hand, and the Other," in *College Literature* 42:2 (2015). Its distinctly sinister character is foregrounded in the unpublished lecture, "Left Leaning: Toward a Sinister Humanities," referred to in the chapter.

Chapter 5
WWJD?

When in 1994, 30 years after its initial publication, MIT republished Marshall McLuhan's *Understanding Media: The Extensions of Man* (later *reissued* by Gingko Press), it was clear that, in a quasi-Lazarean gesture, the great Canadian thinker of media ontology was back. Setting aside the symptom of which this return gives expression, I wish here to point to the discussion in this text that might be taken, at least in the Western scholarly world, as the birth of cool. I am thinking here of the distinction drawn by McLuhan between hot and cool media. Crucial to this distinction is the problem of speed. Hot media are those whose messages (in a pre-semiotic sense as Eco and others objected) are consumed, as it were, in a flash. Cool media, by contrast, are ones whose messages take time. Although television is famously characterized as a hot medium, it is often overlooked that on his list of cool media McLuhan includes the academic ritual of the seminar. It takes time. Indeed, if you have offered one, you will know that its design is approached as if modeled on what Adorno called "structural listening," that is, the notion that patient retrospective scanning is how knowledge-effects are to be generated. Even one's introductory lecture, in flagrant violation of Hitchcock's dictum that one must never give away the beginning, does little more than establish the temporal parameters of this particular instance of "the long game." Regardless of one's ranking on RateMyProfessor.com, every seminar is thus cool, even, as Erving Goffman might stress, a cool "form of talk."

If this chapter begins here it is because in it the Theory/reading chiasmus is to be examined in relation to the medium of the graduate seminar, specifically Derrida's seminar on the encounter between Spinoza and Descartes, an encounter that, in Derrida's hands, makes much of the structural tension between a philosophical project that depended on its renunciation of teaching (about which more will be provided in due course) and one that argues, as if advancing a set of axioms about deconstructive philosophy as such, for the profound snarl of philosophical method and the work of educating. The force of such propositions will be elaborated in the pages that follow, but crucial to this exposition is McLuhan's prescient insight into, irrespective of its coolness, the *legibility* of the seminar as a text. It is a medium. It is comprised of widely divergent incarnations of significant details, details that while not merely linguistic are nevertheless legible instances of thought. While it makes persistent reference to things like pages on which are inscribed cited text matter, the seminar is off-the-page in a way that insistently reminds us that "off-screen" in the cinema is never simply "outside" the filmic text. The seminar is thus another "where or when" of Theory.

As is generally known, the acronym "WWJD?," circulated as a bumper sticker in the United States where it was understood to mean "what would Jesus do?," a condemnation, suffused with mourning for the absent god, of some current practice or policy. Its genealogy as a syntactic form has been traced by Daniel Shore in 2010 on the pages of *Critical Inquiry*.[1] Of course, J. D. is or are also the initials of Jacques Derrida, and while I have never been persuaded by Cixous's efforts at beatification (Derrida as a Jewish saint), I do want to deploy the acronym as a way to begin thinking about how Derrida might respond (what would Jacques do?) to the sustained resurgence of interest in Spinoza that has been so fundamental to a certain rethinking of Marxism in the last half-century. Even for Deleuze, at a certain point Spinoza usurped Nietzsche as his decisive philosophical enabler/precursor. Interestingly, and this is something that I will worry over directly, Derrida never published at length about or on Spinoza and this despite the fact that when he first went to the United States in the late 1950s, he spent considerable time translating Harry Austryn Wolfson's two-volume commentary on Spinoza into French.[2] However, consulting the Derrida papers in the Langson Library at UC-Irvine, one finds not only that he took courses in which Spinoza's work, notably *The Ethics*, was taught, but that he engaged with Spinoza extensively in several of his own seminars from the 1970s and 1980s, reading his two early essays on Descartes, "On the Improvement of the Understanding," and both *The Theologico-Political Treatise* as well as *The Ethics*, offering them up to a form of deconstructive pedagogical attention that I will propose is "instructive," both as readings of Spinoza and also as stagings of a distinctly theoretical pedagogy grasped as a form of "offering." As has been argued, I insist on this last term because I want to stress the ways that Derrida's pedagogical practice brings out forcefully the fraught dynamics of sacrifice in the work of instruction.

Among Derrida's unpublished papers there are two seminars of immediate relevance to sorting the matter of WWJD?. Eventually, of course, all of this material will be translated and published, but since Peggy Kamuf and Geoff Bennington have begun at the end with "The Beast and the Sovereign" seminars, it is likely to be some time before we have the Spinoza material available in English much less in circulation. The first of these dates from 1981 to 1982 and it is titled, "Language (*la langue*) and the Discourse on Method." The second dates from 1986 to 1987 and thus falls broadly within his sustained preoccupation with philosophy and the nation. It is titled, "Theological Politics: Nationality and Philosophical Nationalism." I will focus the analysis that follows on the first of these because in "Language and the Discourse on Method" he first concentrates attention on Spinoza's study of Descartes, a text Spinoza regards as nondoctrinal and thus devoted to the work of teaching, specifically, to the teaching of how to read Cartesian rationalism as embodied in "The Discourse on Method." Indeed, although Derrida's punctuation gives no indication, "the discourse on method" in the seminar's title is an explicit engagement with Descartes, the very thinker who had figured decisively in his vaguely Oedipal quarrel with Foucault. I will return to this.

A preliminary. As many will know Derrida has written voluminously on teaching, on high school curricula, on educational policy, on pupils, on chairs or heads, on Heidegger's notorious rector's address, on the very structure and essence of the university. So the obvious question presents itself: Why approach what he has to offer regarding pedagogy so, as it were, obliquely? Partly, this has to do with the distinctive role of Spinoza in Derrida's thinking. I will propose that, in the absence of an extended, dare I say book length, textual engagement with the corpus, Spinoza emerges as a distinctive site for engaging the work of pedagogy, as if offering him uniquely in a seminar responds to something important, perhaps even crucial, about his thought. By the same token, given the protocols of what Derrida was never afraid to call "deconstruction" (and this even in the wake of the term being applied to everything from suits to salads), what in *Of Grammatology* he describes using the notion of "surrounding," or framing (*entourer*) concepts, given this, I am tempted to conclude that precisely an oblique strategy is called for when working with Derrida's texts, especially those typed for the purpose of stirring oral improvisation and something resembling dialogue. In effect, my method—and the term will emerge here as decisive—is itself a realization, however fraught, however compromised, of WWJD?.

"Language and the Discourse on Method" is comprised of four lengthy lectures, three of them typed out on Derrida's mechanical Olivetti, and one written in what many, according to Benoît Peters, regard as his impenetrable scrawl. As those familiar with the Derridean corpus will recognize, the seminar dates from the same period during which Derrida was wrestling with Blanchot's *Madness of the Day* and, in particular, with the theme and problem of the "*récit*" or "account" as it figures in his lecture at the Strasbourg conference on genre, "The Law of Genre." Although it takes some time before the deep pertinence of this problem announces itself, one certainly glimpses it in the introductory lecture. Appealing both to Descartes' correspondence with Mersenne (specifically the letter from 1627 on the invention of a language whose concluding word is "novels")[3] and to the considerably later introduction to the French edition of *The Principles of Philosophy* (1644) Derrida underscores the vexed philosophical (and not merely "rationalist") status of literature. In the *Principles* the matter is put thus:

> I would also have added a word of advice about the way to read this book. I would like the reader first of all to go quickly through the whole book like a novel (*comme un roman*), without straining his attention too much or stopping at the difficulties that may be encountered. The aim should be merely to ascertain in a general way which matters I have dealt with. (*Principles*, 185)

Descartes goes on to urge that the book be read an additional two times, one with pen in hand, and the shift from reading to writing or marking—especially as it traces the difference between literature and philosophy—catches Derrida's attention. This is hardly surprising.

What is surprising—although perhaps not to the *careful* (neither "close" nor "distant") readers of the testy exchange with Foucault, "The Cogito and the History of Madness"—is that Derrida does not here pounce on Descartes to decry his logocentrism. Instead, he deploys the thematization of literature within and against philosophy to unfurl a reading of Spinoza's reading of Descartes, a reading that traces carefully in what ways Spinoza fails to engage what stubbornly remains, what resists, in Descartes' encounter with the novel. In "The Law of Genre," the force and significance of the novel is displaced onto the status of the *récit* where the language game board is reshuffled: Blanchot's question is not about the relation between literature and philosophy so much as it is about how and where in the *récit* something that is neither philosophy nor literature takes place. Derrida retrieves here, from "Living On: Borderlines" (his contribution to the Yale School "reading" of Shelley) the figure or motif of invagination, reminding us how profoundly gender and genre resonate in each other, but also then bear, however indirectly, on the encounter between Descartes and Spinoza.

Now that "the post-Cartesian subject" has become a clichéd metonymy for "deconstruction," it is hard to realize that Derrida, whether in disagreeing with Foucault or Spinoza, is actually pressing the case *for* Descartes as someone whose thought exceeds the frames set around it. In "The Cogito and the History of Madness" this point takes the form of showing that dreaming, precisely to the extent that it opens up a modality of radical doubt not exhausted in the concept of madness, questions the historicity of philosophy itself. In "Language and the Discourse on Method," this is done differently. How?

Tracing a line that runs from Spinoza's two early essays on Descartes—"The Principles of the Philosophy of René Descartes Demonstrated in the Geometrical Manner" and "Thoughts on Metaphysics"—through to *A Theologico-Political Treatise* and *The Ethics*, Derrida is keen to pressure Spinoza's account of method, specifically the well-known *more geometrico*, as it operates both to present and disfigure Descartes' own thinking of method. As we will learn, crucial here is Spinoza's own engagement with language in general (signs) and fiction more specifically. What makes this of immediate pertinence to the project of "Offering Theory" is the simple fact that Derrida's presentation of method ties it immediately and intimately with pedagogy, with, in effect, the cool medium of his seminar. The lecture reads (in my translation):

> The question of method, is, in general, inseparable from the question of teaching. Indeed, all teaching is unthinkable without a methodological doctrine. All teaching implies, even if it does not profess it, a methodological technique, an ordered path that is not pure "wandering" (*errance*); the transmission of tools, of instrumental forms that would not simply be reducible to content. This means that all teaching is methodical, also that all method, which is yet another thing, must be thought, transmitted according to regular procedures. What would a non-transmissible method even be? ("Language" 11, 4–5)

Situated where they are—at the head of the second session of the seminar—and resounding certain motifs from the first session, these formulations are reflexive, perhaps even apotropaic. That is, they are as much about the nature of teaching as they are about the teaching Derrida is engaged in the context of the seminar, etymologically, of course, a site of dissemination. As such they are also about method, and for this reason Derrida directly ties these rather general, theoretical propositions, to his reading of Spinoza, a reading that seeks to trace how the *more geometrico* reads a discourse on method. Unsurprisingly, the echo chamber of readings is instructive, both about Spinoza and Descartes, but even more importantly about WWJD?.

Because the source materials to which I am referring are not published indulge me as I summarize and trace the threads of the argument. In his reading of Spinoza's commentaries on Descartes, Derrida is intrigued by the fact that Spinoza's pedagogical use of the *more geometrico* first shows up in the only text of his that appears in his lifetime and under his own name. This coupled with the proposition that the commentary is simply that, commentary (i.e., *not* interpretation)—indeed a commentary required by the need to "offer" Descartes insights in a way accessible to the multitude—alerts Derrida to the methodological gesture of effacement: Spinoza has signed a text in which the expressed goal is to disappear within the words of another. Of course, and no reader of Spinoza misses this, Spinoza's commentary contains—perhaps within the very space and gesture of effacement—a critical *interpretation* of Descartes. Apart from rejecting any distinction between understanding and the will (another bone of contention), Spinoza is keen to demonstrate that skepticism, the method of radical doubt, is at once abstract and incoherent, for the god eventually discovered to limit doubt must have already secured the possibility of understanding in general. Otherwise, how can it be "true" that I doubt? How can I understand that I am in doubt? The idea of truth, Cartesian certainty, must, for Spinoza, give way to the true idea, but what, in the course of the seminar, returns for Derrida is the theme of doubt, now recast as an invocation of difference in general. For reasons that only become clear in a subsequent session, Derrida stresses the fact that Spinoza treats doubt as a rhetorical fiction, a device, a *method* for getting to truth, not the expression of a true idea. See *The Ethics*, Book Two, Prop. XLIII for a thorough, if later, articulation of this mode of argumentation.

Armed with the concept of the understanding and its relation to the true idea, Derrida then turns to Spinoza's treatise, *On the Improvement of the Understanding*, where the latter is concerned, on his reading, to establish both a decisive and enabling distinction between understanding and imagination and, in a more metacritical gesture, underscore repeatedly Spinoza's persistent recourse to the figure of the path, the *via*. The latter is made relevant because it picks up on one of the etymological resonances of "method" (the Greek, *hodos*, or way, as in "way of knowing"), and Derrida is keen to tease out the methodological implications of a method that insistently deploys a rhetoric of steps, or procedures, while simultaneously insisting that the procedures of geometry are so purely formal that they essentially vanish into the insights they enable. One is reminded of the dramaturgy of Plato's dialogue, "The Meno." If the distinction between the understanding and the imagination is likewise pertinent, this is because the priority of the understanding, to the extent that it clarifies in what way the imagination is, by definition, limited by its essential recourse to memory and representation, enters into a certain dependency on a method that is *expressly* not one. As might be assumed, this line of inquiry finds its fullest elaboration in a consideration of Spinoza's thinking about signs whether in the forms of omens or indications, pictures or paintings, or simply words, especially, as it turns out, Hebrew words. In effect, Derrida is, in a sort of signature/event/context gesture, puzzling over the entire problematic of the inscription of philosophy as it grips Spinoza's thought.

The question of method (to cite Sartre citing Descartes), which might otherwise appear to have receded into the background, returns in the opening of the third lecture. It does so in a way that points directly, if implicitly, at Pierre Macherey's *Hegel or Spinoza* and thus to the matter of how we might begin to situate Derrida's offerings in relation to the French return to Spinoza, a return initiated by Deleuze in *Expressionism in Philosophy: Spinoza*, from 1968, a text that dedicates a brief but important chapter to Spinoza's reading of Descartes.[4] The third lecture opens by asking the seminar to consider the philosophical implications of a method either coming before or coming after the ideas it legitimates, precisely the same sort of didactic device deployed by Macherey. For Macherey, this tells us something decisive about the *more geometrico*; for Derrida, this draws attention to the increasingly perplexing methodological gesture of repudiating Descartes—whose method comes *before*, that is, as a means by which to realize the idea, for example, of the cogito—a repudiation conducted in the name of a nonmethodical method that nevertheless exhibits, in the very sequence of its enunciation, an investment in an ordered, even Euclidean, *path* of inquiry. For Derrida it is far from irrelevant that *The Ethics* itself follows from and upon the preliminary commentary on Descartes. Again, as if directly engaging Macherey's study, Derrida notes that the matter of where method logically and temporally falls establishes a telling contrast between Spinoza and Hegel. Hegel joins Descartes in setting method *before* philosophical insight. And, to be clear, the seminar is following in the same footsteps.

Derrida's persistent underscoring of the Spinozian rhetoric of the path, of *via*, builds carefully through a consideration of the rhetoric of philosophical exposition to an examination of the status of fiction in Spinoza's thought. Triggered by a reading of the *strategy* of Spinoza's commentary where he insists upon merely presenting Descartes' thought only clarified by the method that is not a method—a reading in which it is clear that Spinoza's own thought, notably the repudiation of radical doubt as a starting point, is deftly interpolated into the Cartesian program—Derrida begins to probe this space that opens and cuts through Spinoza's corpus. This space is brought systematically into alignment with the motif of the *récit*, the account, such that the structure of repetition, the re, emerges as a mode of enunciation that Spinozian philosophy qua philosophy can neither live with, nor without.

Starting with the speculative refrain—who can sign for the *Ethics*, under what circumstances and in what language?—Derrida teases out Spinoza's comparatively scant thinking about language and signs placing special emphasis on *The Improvement*. Directly, words lead him to the imagination where two problems wait. Because, for Spinoza, many words are associated, even confused, in memory (a faculty traditionally tied to the imagination), words necessarily generate fictions. Only when grasped in the understanding can words be brought into a true relation to things and thus clarified. Prior to this, that is, prior to the work of the understanding on the imagination, words fall under the sway of the *vulgum*, the crowd, and adequacy, thus clarity, is elusive (Spinoza 1951, 33). If one builds philosophical ideas on words under circumstances such as these one is condemned to produce and proliferate fictions, here marking the point at which philosophy properly understood gets what traction it has. Enter, and the seminar here does what it says, the familiar Derridean motif of usurpation and the logic of the supplement. If one "begins" with the imagination, it always risks usurping the philosophical preeminence of the understanding, a preeminence that makes the proper beginning, not in method, but in the intuition of god.

As readers of the "Linguistics and Grammatology" chapter in *Of Grammatology* will know, "usurpation" is the lever by which Derrida inverts and displaces Saussure's account of speech, to wit, if the epistemic force of the latter *can* be usurped by writing, then this usurpation has always already been at work in the relation between speech and writing. The Saussurean sign, as the proper (correct but also unique) object of linguistic science, is thus rendered deeply problematical (a comment here on Saussure's teaching is in order, no?). In "Language and the Discourse on Method," fiction (or "the account"/récit) assumes the place of the sign in Derrida's argumentation and what he traces is how fiction (not only as an example but also as the *making* of philosophical discourse itself) usurps, destabilizes, the vital Spinozian distinction between the understanding and the imagination.

This manifests at several registers. As we have seen it plays itself out in the status of words within the imagination. Derrida puts emphasis on an important passage in *The Improvement* where Spinoza describes how otherwise affirmative ideas are retained in the understanding using negative verbal constructions such as the in-finite, the im-mortal, the in-dependent, all evidence of the way imaginary (here "negated") things usurp, through words, the understanding. But he also draws attention to an example Spinoza offers to illustrate how a word is easier to retain in memory when it is inserted into an "account," fusing the latter and the word in a way that prepares for a much later discussion of the problem, agitated in the *Treatise*, of the near impossibility of changing the meaning of a word compared to the relative ease of changing the meaning of a passage in scripture. However, Derrida also acutely accents the following passage in *The Improvement*:

> The memory is also strengthened without the aid of the understanding by means of the power wherewith the imagination or the sense called common is affected by a particular physical object. [...] If we read, for instance, a single romantic comedy, we shall remember it very well, so long as we do not read many others of the same kind, for it will reign alone in the memory. If, however, we read several others of the same kind, we shall think of them together, and easily confuse one with the other. (Spinoza 1951, 31)

Crucial here, for Derrida, is the way the novel (here as "romantic comedy") is put to work as the example that elucidates the ontological distinction between the understanding (Spinoza's privileged because rigorously philosophical category) and memory, here the avatar of the imagination, a point fully fleshed in the seminar in a reading of *The Ethics* where Spinoza is maneuvering to subordinate the power of the imagination to the understanding, while simultaneously conceding that the matter is worthy of urgent philosophical attention because the imagination has powers of its own, powers that allow it to usurp the authority of the understanding and thereby empower fictions.

If earlier I compared the broad contours of this argument to the one found in Derrida's reading of Blanchot's *The Madness of the Day*, it is because the series: word, imagination, fiction, culminates in a discussion of the *récit* or account that designates the philosophical cost of mediation, or to use Derrida's early vocabulary, writing. However, if these propositions are to cast some light on WWJD? as concerns the Spinoza resurgence, then we need to insistently separate the matter of the *récit* or even fiction more generally from the question of truth. In other words, what concerns Derrida here is not the epistemological question of whether and how the truth can be known—and this contrary to received opinion—but rather with the means by and through which philosophy is made (practiced, as Althusser might insist); both through what sort of cognitive procedures and also, and even more importantly, with which media, shaped by which languages and which models or genres of expression. In short, what concerns Derrida here is philosophical method and especially, as we have seen, the method—whether it comes before or after—that is not one. Bernard Stiegler, of course, has insisted that the Derridean concept of writing is not yet a concept of what he, Stiegler, calls "tertiary retention," but I think that in his stress on the event of mediation, on his attention to Spinoza's concern about the potential usurpation of understanding by a memory too receptive to or taken by physical things, Derrida at the very least identifies the principle and risk of "tertiary retention." Be that as it may, what is also clarified in Derrida's preoccupation with method is his keen interest—early in the "Language and the Discourse on Method" seminar—in Spinoza's famous letter to the elector Charles Lewis, in which Spinoza declines an invitation to teach, in favor of developing his philosophy, thus mobilizing a distinction between teaching and philosophy that, for Derrida, conceptually prepares the move to advocate on behalf of a method that is not one, a method, if characterized in terms of Spinoza's three types of knowledge, that is im-*mediate*, that is, intuitive.

Fiction, especially in the Latin, takes one quickly to *fictio*, to making. Doubt, whether radical or not, implies that one turns to fiction, to making, in the context of uncertainty, to, in effect, making up or improvising. Spinoza himself, in a remarkable footnote to *The Improvement* (see Spinoza 1951, 24) brings dream and fiction into alignment. Making or improvising are acts that weave the practical tissue between method and teaching where philosophy enters into contact with the practice of everyday life, a way of living. While it seems evident that Derrida thinks there is something here in Descartes' method whose import escapes Spinoza, what this foregrounds is the task that the seminar places before us, namely, the teasing out of how the thinking through doubt, especially radical doubt, might be said to bear on, to invoke the title of a hugely important volume, the *new* Spinoza.

In Macherey's study, to which reference has already been made, the political valences of the stand-off between Hegel and Spinoza are left understated. Although Spinoza figures only in passing in Judith Butler's account of the French Hegel (she is concerned to track the subject of desire, a subject decisive to the influential reading of Hegel pursued by Kojève), Macherey, while not framing his intervention in precisely these terms, likewise seeks to intervene in a certain political reception of Hegel in France. What this prompts him to say is (and these are actually the concluding words of the text): "To read Spinoza following Hegel, but not according to Hegel, allows us to pose the question of a non-Hegelian dialectic, but we must also admit, and this is also a way of being Spinozist, that it does not enable us at the same time to answer it" (Macherey 2011, 213). Earlier in the same paragraph Macherey had tied the urgency of this very question to the task of identifying and neutralizing the idealism that Marx recognized in his own inheritance of the dialectic, making it clear that Spinoza mattered, in part, because of the way his thought brought new and important energy to the reading of Marx and Lenin initiated by Althusser in the early 1960s.[5] This was a reading conducted in intermittent dialogue with the French Communist Party (PCF) and, as such, very concerned with setting forth the terms of a practical and theoretical commitment to both materialism and communism in the post-Stalinist era. As if having anticipated the entire business, Charles Sanders Peirce once observed that, "Faith requires us to be materialists without flinching" (167).[6]

Derrida's seminar, convened at the EHESS, does not pose the political problem of dialectical reasoning, it does however dwell on and in the doubt that animates Macherey's conclusions. This is hardly the last political word. While not precisely seeking to answer the unanswerable question posed by Spinoza to Hegelian Marxism, Antonio Negri, on the pages of *The Savage Anomaly*, nevertheless sets out systematically to think the politics of Spinoza's project. Written while in prison and published in 1981, Negri argues in this text that in the distinction between *potestas* and *potentia* (rendered as Power and power in the Hardt translation), Spinoza works out a political ontology in which *potentia* as "productive constitution" structurally and dynamically antagonizes *potestas* understood as monarchic, economic or religious power. Although the philological dimension of this argument has been challenged, Negri is entirely compelling in producing the conceptual profile that overrides such hesitations. Indeed, in the closing formulations of the text Negri, who has previously signaled his admiration for Macherey's study, brings his perspective into line with the critique of dialectical reason writing:

> The subjective nexus of the objective complexity of being constitutes the most specific determination of Spinoza's thought, considered in its historical context—and considered as a metaphysical proposal. Now, in this sense, the production-constitution relationship represents the fulcrum of Spinozian projectivity. It is the surpassing of any possibility of logic, both classical and dialectical. And it is perhaps, still, the contemporary meaning of his thought. (Negri 1991, 229)

Of course, at this point the meaning of the word "contemporary" has shifted, but the move executed earlier in his argument to bring *potentia* into alignment with the multitude's relentless drive toward radically democratic social relations makes the critique of dialectical reason into an alternate version of the project first rolled out by Negri and Guattari in *Communists Like Us* (originally, *Nouvelles espaces de liberté*) but taken up as a cudgel by Negri and Hardt in *Empire*, *Multitude* and *Commonwealth*.

On the face of it, and Negri glances occasionally into this face, the relation between Power and power reads like a restatement of the *dialectic* between power and resistance, except that resistance precedes power. This is important, nay crucial, because it clarifies that the critique of dialectical reason makes essential reference to time: not the time of becoming but time as a spatialized duration through which what is productively constituted relentlessly passes. Indeed, Power assumes the institutional shape it has because it devises means by which to meter, to measure this passing. This subordination of time to a constitutive spacing will remind many of Derrida's arguments in *Voice and Phenomenon* from 1967 where he deploys it to articulate what Husserl avoids in trying to grasp the temporal punctuality of the living present. And while this might suggest an obvious way to bring out WWJD?, I wish instead to puzzle briefly over Negri's treatment of the imagination in Spinoza, a faculty, as we have seen, near to the core of Derrida's reading of the latter's corpus in his seminar.

As if sensitive to the difficulties posed by linking imagination, memory and the word, Negri, in turning his attention to the *Theologico-Political Treatise*, emphasizes what he perceives to be two types of imagination. He writes: "In the first place, there is the differentiation of the negative imagination, which becomes superstition, from the imagination as positivity, which becomes obedience. Next, obedience is presented as the positive form of the imagination because its content is peace; it is the possibility of establishing a contract-consensus among men" (Negri 1991, 106). The challenge this distinction might otherwise pose to Derrida's reading in the seminar is then compromised as Negri ties peace to reason, concluding: "Reason traverses the imagination, liberating the truth it contains, and meanwhile the imagination constructs the positivity of the existent and, therefore, of reason itself" (ibid). In effect, the distinction between superstition and obedience repeats in the distinction—one Derrida's reading has familiarized us with—between imagination and reason. Negri himself is aware that Spinoza is struggling here, but since his own reading is designed to trace precisely how Spinoza overcomes the limits of his own thought, he lurches forward to prepare his readers for the claim, "Human intelligence is the articulation of nature" (Negri 1991, 222) where intelligence subsumes both reason and the imagination, and "articulation" becomes a way to state the ontology of productive constitution that defines the core of Negri's reading. In effect, Negri's treatment of the two imaginations is designed to shift attention to the political character of Spinoza's ontology, an ontology meant to ground the proposition that all of being is nothing but an expression of the desire for the liberation of the multitude. The politics of anthropocentrism, though urgently relevant, is not on the table.

Those familiar with the conversation between Deleuze and Foucault from 1972, "The Intellectuals and Power" in which they propose that the masses—free from intellectual mediation—represent their interests directly in their political practice, might reasonably conclude that Negri in *The Savage Anomaly* has carefully elaborated the Spinozian provenance of this set of assertions about intellectuals. Moreover, if one concedes that Deleuze and Foucault are developing a set of formulations meant to challenge the response of the PCF, in the person of Georges Marchais, to the student uprisings of May 1968; and if Negri—in his several invocations of what he calls "autonomasia"—is likewise concerned to think the necessity of revisiting the philosophical foundations of the Italian Left (from prison, no less); then, the matter of WWJD? must be thought to bear directly on the question of to what extent Spinoza is either crucial or even helpful to this conjunctural task. Can the corpus bear the weight of the reading placed upon it?

In *The Praise of the Commons*, Negri's probing and wide-ranging "conversations" with Cesare Casarino, he somewhat testily distances himself from Derrida's thought and this despite formulations in *The Savage Anomaly* such as: "Spinozian logic does not know the hypothesis, it knows only the trace, the symptom. The versatility of being, which it accounts for, is within a woven fabric of material acts that, in diverse compositions and figures, experience a process of combination and self-formation" (Negri 1991, 213). A footnote here leads us to a text by Carlo Ginzberg from 1979 and this despite the massive reencounter with the Freudian corpus in France well underway since the 1950s. Tellingly, in the exchange with Casarino, Negri, as if from within the seminar, protests that what annoys him about Derrida is the excessive preoccupation with "fiction" in his work. Specifically, he says: "I would want to make also a further differentiation between, on the one hand, Nancy and Agamben, and, on the other, Derrida. The latter has worn himself out in the attempt to articulate an intellectual project that has never been able to exit the stage of literature, to move beyond the literary domain" (Casarino and Negri 2008, 88). Of course, a great deal would need to be said here both about Negri's precise formulation and also its blunt solicitation of WWJD?. Thus, to isolate a few threads from the woven fabric, I will observe that "fiction," and specifically in Derrida's reading of Spinoza, does not signify falsity. It is put to work so as precisely to underscore the labor, the practice of philosophizing insofar as that practice is woven into a social text where beings read and write under the constraints of medium, language and geopolitics. From this perspective Derrida might be seen as reading Spinoza so as precisely to chime in with Negri on the notion that productive force emanates from and radiates through the endlessness of being. As his call for an "open Marxism" already in 1980 might suggest, this chiming is aimed so as to strike a blow against a certain Sartrean incarnation of dialectical reason deemed at odds with the task of emancipation. WWJD? He might well read Spinoza so as to align with various Western European voices engaged in a teasing apart of the legacies of Marx and Hegel.

However, if earlier I compared the tone (whether apocalyptic or not) of Derrida's reading of Descartes in "Language and the Discourse on Method," with his reading of Descartes in the dispute with Foucault, I did so to draw attention to the critical fold in his text, a fold one also detects in the seminar on Spinoza whose propositions I have been tracing. Put differently, despite the common ground between "fiction" or "the account" and what Negri calls the "the world as *production*" (Negri 1991, 225), what insists in Derrida's reading is a certain, perhaps even a (mis-)calculated, doubt. Doubt about the actual status of fiction—whether as genre or as event—in Spinoza, and doubt as a reading of "fiction" that probes the very openness of Spinoza's destruction of philosophical rationalism. When Negri writes: "If difference founds the future, then here the future ontologically grounds difference. This reciprocal relationship is the fabric of construction" (Negri 1991, 228), one imagines Derrida wondering aloud, "fabric" (both weaving and making or even factoring, *fabbricare*)? Is the fabric of textuality woven of relata that stand in relations of reciprocity? Is "reciprocity," as a rewording of nondialectical opposition, not the sign of precisely how difficult it is to break with Hegel and the Marxism elaborated in his name? As Negri will have known, "reciprocity" is the term that Kojève (and later Sartre) stressed in his effort to existentialize the "recognition" of the slave in the master and the master in the slave. The persistent recourse to "phenomenology" throughout *The Savage Anomaly* entitles one to assume this with some confidence.

So as not to belabor things: although Negri takes up the question of methodology repeatedly—indeed he proposes that Spinoza is not only following a path that proceeds in fits and starts, but that this method *precedes* its formalization in the *more geometrico* of the *Ethics*—he does not take up the problem of teaching, of offering Spinoza. The lecture theater is only *like* a prison. By contrast, as we have noted, Derrida tenaciously reads Spinoza as an articulation of the method that is not one, of a method that vanishes into its teaching or, and this is the more provocative formulation, a method that cannot be taught without sacrificing the adequate ideas it might otherwise be thought to legitimate. In effect, Spinoza avoids offering. His corpus is thus shielded from doubt in the name of living in accord with a teaching that cannot, or should not, be taught. It would seem that folding this very wrinkle into his own teaching, of offering to offer Spinoza, is what Jacques Derrida would do. Indeed it is what he did. Although it would take us far afield, Derrida's hesitation here regarding the force, the *potentia* of Spinoza's difference with onto-theology, mimics closely his doubt regarding Levinas' critique of metaphysics. Both Levinas and Spinoza pass in and out of the political through ethics.[7] Derrida instructs that our moment asks that something else be offered and that our theoretical offerings take this matter up as the very madness of method.

"Language and the Discourse on Method," the seminar, ends on an improvisation. The final lecture, as I have noted, is not typed. It is written by hand, as if to draw to attention the handling that has proceeded. Importantly, it does not summarize. It suspends or, better, it releases, aware that if teaching and method are twisted together then no last step can, nor should be taken. *Pas encore*, the sound of no seminar clapping. Cool indeed.

Notes

1   See Daniel Shore, "WWJD?: The Genealogy of a Syntactic Form," *Critical Inquiry* 37:1 (Autumn 2010), 1–25. Tracing what Shore calls "parodic spin offs" (e.g., What Would Jesus Bomb?) he notes John Caputo's "What Would Jesus Deconstruct?" a formulation with certain obvious resonances with my own. His sustained attention to the notion of "doing," the doing about which one knows not, is usefully heard in the background of these remarks. Somewhat more remotely one might also recognize the sonic profile of my title in the special issue of *Discourse* from 2008, " 'Who?' or 'What?'—Jacques Derrida."

2   One might note here, for example, the passing reference Derrida makes to Spinoza in Part One of *Of Grammatology*, where a discussion of the theological character of the sublimation of the trace prompts a footnote to Wolfson's translation of Spinoza's *Short Treatise on God, Man and His Well Being* (Derrida 1976, 71).

3   In the letter Descartes insists that the adequate invention of an Esperanto-like language through which all other languages might be understood would require enormous changes in the "order of things." The earth would have to become a terrestrial paradise, the sort of change one might risk proposing in the world of the novel. Jonathan Bennett's translation of the correspondence, conspicuously edited with an eye toward isolating and highlighting only its philosophically interesting elements, introduces an ellipsis in the text at precisely the beginning of the phrase that invokes the world of the novel. Derrida's interest in the passage could not be more emphatically confirmed.

4   In "Spinoza Against Descartes" (chapter 10), Deleuze zeroes in immediately on the vexed question of method. Contrasting clear and distinct ideas from adequate ideas, Deleuze shows how in processing differently the Aristotelian understanding of the relation between cause and effect Spinoza is led to favor synthesis over analysis. Method is not here connected to teaching, but there appears to be a foundational gesture at work: Spinoza cannot be engaged without teasing out the seam that joins philosophy and the *more geometrico*.

5   In "The Only Materialist Tradition: Part One, Spinoza," Althusser aligns with those who insist upon a fissure or discrepancy between Spinoza's thought and his method, the *more geometrico*. Specifically, he underscores the tension between what he perceives as the "dogmatism" (4) of the method in contrast to the freedom instilled and inspired by Spinoza's thought. As this would suggest, Althusser and his former pupil and collaborator, Macherey, do not see eye to eye here. It is also important to note that when Althusser mentions Derrida in this essay, he draws particular attention to the latter's principled alertness to "strategy," as if predicting the approach Derrida was himself to take to the Spinozian corpus.

6   This formulation appears in an outline of an unfinished and unpublished project that the editors of the chronological compendium of Peirce's writings place under the heading, "A Guess at the Riddle." Others, notably Stephanie Dea and Rocco Gangle, have been exploring the entwinement of Peirce and Spinoza, and since the matter of the relation, Althusser even risks the term "parallel," between thought and method recurs throughout this discussion, it is worth stressing that in his review of Hale White's then recent translation of *The Ethics* for *The Nation*, Peirce heaps unmitigated scorn on the "*more geometrico*," first emphasizing the logical flaws of Euclid, but then dismissing the method as a mere "veil" over a philosophical project that somewhat ironically he later sought to enlist in the "pragmaticist" cause. Although it would take us far afield, it is not without significance that Peirce is read in a far more compelling way by Derrida—he is invoked powerfully against the phonecentric impasses of Saussure in *Of Grammatology*—than by Deleuze who, in the cinema books, appropriates precisely what is most tedious and categorical about Peirce (the semiotic typology), and this despite the widely held perception that Deleuze, and not Derrida, is the more faithful, thus serious, reader of Spinoza.

7   It is important to signal here that in the exchange with Casarino cited above, Negri explicitly attacks not only the alignment between Derrida and Levinas but also wonders aloud whether Levinas's thought is "truly open" (Casarino and Negri 2008, 88). In light of Derrida's call for an "open Marxism," and his later sustained attention to the

Rilkean motif of the "the open" in Heidegger, there is a matter here that calls for more attention than can be given now, especially since my reading is suggesting that Derrida's own critique of Levinas anticipates his offering of/engagement with Spinoza. To invoke a formulation put in play by the late Stuart Hall the crucial theoretical and political question is whether there can be an open Marxism *with* guarantees, that is, a materialist ontology in which radical doubt can only appear as an index of an eternity that humanity has only *yet* to fully intuit instead of the difference that repeats in everything. No less a figure than Althusser has weighed in the matter when late in "Ideology and Ideological State Apparatuses," while summarizing the findings of his "investigation," he introduces the following footnote:

> Hegel is (unknowingly) an admirable "theoretician" of ideology insofar as he is a "theoretician" of Universal Recognition who unfortunately ends up in the ideology of Absolute Knowledge. Feuerbach is an astonishing "theoretician" of the mirror connection, who unfortunately ends up in the ideology of the Human Essence. To find material with which to construct a theory of the guarantee [the ideological effect of the "So be it"], we must turn to Spinoza. (Althusser 1971, 181)

Left unspoken here is the status of the guarantee *in* its Spinozian theorization, the truth force of true ideas.

Chapter 6

WHAT SAID SAID

As noted, the when and where of Theory cannot evade the question of context. If, as has been posited, the "sociographic" is to serve as the means by which to designate a re:worked concept of context, then the issue of how it figures in the reading that is Theory calls for clarification, perhaps even justification. To open this line of reflection I turn to another theoretical occasion. Read on.

In 1986 at the Institute for Education in London the trajectory mapped in Edward Said's "Traveling Theory" reached if not its terminus then certainly its re-culmination. It did so because at the Institute Said and Raymond Williams, long fellow traveling companions, appeared together to comment on two films—one by Mike Dibbs, *The Country and the City*, the other by Geoff Dunlap, *The Shadow of the West*—inspired by their works. The transcript of this encounter appears as the final chapter of *The Politics of Modernism*, a book published a year after Williams's death in 1988. If I reinvoke "Traveling Theory" it is not simply because Said situates Williams's project there in a provocative, indeed telling way, but because the book in which it appears, *The World, the Text, and the Critic* (*WTC*), from 1983 served as the context for the exchange between Williams and Said.[1] Because the theoretical problem of the relation between what both men refer to as representation and history figures centrally in their remarks, the matter of context imposes itself on the event of this exchange and asks to be read. The relation between representation and history is thus both the object and the very medium of this exchange. As such, it directs initial attention to the matter of historical context, especially since, as I will argue, what Said said about it is more subtle than has yet been acknowledged, especially by those who find in his work a justification for their own need to vulgarize the relation between representation and history. Indeed, the matter may have been more subtle than Said himself realized, suggesting that in pondering his legacy and the legacy of the discursivity he helped found, postcolonial studies (referring here back to Iser's propositions), the matter of history-as-context has a special claim to urgency as it was left, as it were, unsaid.

The opening statements of both writers in "Media, Margins and Modernity" are at once important and resonant, but the angle of Said's "further expansion" (Williams 1989, 179) deserves special emphasis. In commenting upon Dibbs's film Williams had stressed the way it clarified the relation between Theory (the broadly "Marxian" one at the heart of *The Country and the City*) and history in a way that established how such a relation could be made accessible or, in the end, teachable. In further clarifying the importance of teaching, Williams relates an anecdote from the classroom, an anecdote in which he is challenged about his commitment to history by a postgraduate student. In mock dismay at being hailed as an "old foggy" (Williams later stresses how the student came to recognize the error of his ways), Williams defends himself by presenting a view, largely formalist, of representation that Dibbs's film corrects in a pedagogically useful way. The notion of history thereby rescued, that of the "material past" (ibid., 178) is then placed at the core of a "method of analysis" (presumed to be shared with Said), a method whose verification is to be derived from its being productively applied to "two very different geographical and historical locations" (ibid., 179).

Said "expands" this by introducing the problem of "compartmentalization" (ibid., 179), which he explains by elaborating how his Middle Eastern background had to be abandoned in order to professionalize himself within the discipline of English. The representation/history theme enters when he continues: "and that in turn led [...] to a general understanding of my background and the background of many like me whose lives had become in fact compartmentalized by—to borrow a phrase from Raymond's film—processes that took place elsewhere" (ibid., 180). As if to hit every note, Said then rephrases compartmentalization as "separation," allowing him to draw a connection between images that present themselves as just images and those aspects of his background that his emerging professional identity obliged him to jettison. What this says about representation—that it bears on both image and self-image—is frankly not as interesting as how history makes its appearance on this "stage" (a figure to which Said has frequent recourse). It does not enter here simply as that to which representation is to be "connected," but as an elsewhere in space through which the connection or lack of connection is mediated and thereby made. What Said does not do here (nor in the course of the remaining dialogue nor, for that matter, in the course of *The World, the Text, the Critic*), is to rethink, to re:work the very concept of history in play in this discussion, a discussion that makes explicit reference to Orientalism without thereby asking whether and how the distinction drawn between representation and history by both him and Williams belongs to an Orientalist discourse.

I am not saying, and it should be obvious were it not for the fact that so little is or ever was, that Said—all appearances to the contrary notwithstanding—does not, in fact, take history seriously. Rather, I am saying that in his discussion of history he gestures insistently to the limits of the concept, and while during his distinguished tenure as the presiding officer of the Modern Language Association he was known to strike out at the rebarbative excesses of Theory, this gesturing registers a properly theoretical drive in Said's writing, one that he was not always able to handle. This gesturing expresses itself in fullest form in the collision between history and geography that transpires in the opening section of *Culture and Imperialism*, a collision whose significance for a postorientalist or perhaps postcolonial conception of history, this chapter will be concerned to formulate.

Those suspicious of taking oral and largely improvised remarks too seriously may be reassured as my reading turns back now to engage in greater detail what earlier I referred to as the "re-culmination" of "Traveling Theory." As this essay has justly become one of the most cited bits in the postcolonial canon (assuming the existence of such a thing), I'll not rehearse its conclusions in detail. These are stated plainly enough when Said writes:

> I am arguing, however, that we distinguish theory from critical consciousness by saying that the latter is a sort of spatial sense, a sort of measuring faculty for locating or situating theory, and this means that theory has to be grasped in the place and the time out of which it emerges as part of that time, working in and for it, responding to it; then, consequently, that first place can be measured against subsequent places where the theory turns up for use. (Said 1991, 241–42)

This passage continues on to articulate an uncanny and ultimately startling convergence with Paul de Man's nearly contemporaneous "Resistance to Theory," but what I wish to emphasize is how economically this passage states the essentially cartographic logic of the essay in which it appears. As will be recalled, after a brief meditation on the then contemporary state of Theory enshrouded in, alternately, aimless pluralism or sulky gloom, Said charts the westward migration of a theory he grounds in Georg Lukács essay on reification from *History and Class Consciousness* from 1923. Setting aside how the theory of reification and totality got to Hungary, Said traces its steady "degradation" (he likens it to the fading of a color) as it travels from Paris (in the hands of Lucien Goldmann) to Cambridge (in the hands of Raymond Williams). By emphasizing the theme of degradation, I am suggesting that like Harold Bloom, Said shares the view that influence spreads through anxiety (an affect writ large over Williams's tribute to Goldmann, "Literature and Sociology"), although unlike Bloom Said resists reading this Oedipally, preferring instead to insist upon the influence of one's context upon one's theoretical allegiances.

Although Said later changes his mind about the axiomatic character of degradation (about which more in a bit), here it serves as a powerful example of what the Theory can show especially, one supposes, when this Theory is pressured by what Said cautiously refers to as "critical consciousness," "a sort of spatial sense […]."

Now, if it makes sense to characterize the encounter between Williams and Said described earlier as a "re-culmination," it is because in marking the encounter between them as taking place in Britain, it repeats the fact that "Traveling Theory" ended before it crossed the Atlantic. In other words, given the westward trajectory of the piece and given the broad but distinct theoretical allegiance between Said, Williams, Goldman and Lukács—not to mention the essay's opening engagement with the fate of Theory in the United States and its concluding excursus on the Dutch encounter between Foucault and Chomsky (Paris/Cambridge, MA)—the context not addressed in it is the context of Said himself. At the risk of again reinserting the pertinence of Oedipus, this might surely have to do with the implication, obvious enough once the theme of degradation is amplified, that Said's work, perhaps even the Theory of "traveling theory," is even *more* remote from the "fiery rebelliousness" (ibid., 240) of Lukács than that of Williams and hence *more* politically attenuated if not ultimately neutralized. Surely, some such anxiety spurs Said's defense of Williams's "distance" from the Budapest of the teens and 20s, arguing that this is precisely what protected him from a devotion to the theoretical articulation of reification and totality that would have rendered the critical character of Lukács's own project either unthinkable or incoherent. Although it is stated *sotto voce* this distance is what stands at the heart of the "analytical method"— indeed an analytical method obliged to test its powers of critical discernment by traveling from one place to another—shared by Williams and Said.

Such "autobiographical" or, better, "affiliative" considerations cast useful light on what happens when Said repeats this repetition in "Traveling Theory Reconsidered" from 1994. Sensing that business from "Traveling Theory" remained unfinished Said reanimates its concerns, not to address explicitly the question of its implications for his *own* critical consciousness, but to settle the matter in advance by arguing that careful consideration of the work of Adorno and Fanon could show that theory does not *necessarily* degrade as it travels from one place to another. To motivate his reconsideration Said accuses himself of too hastily placing an unjustified premium on originality and novelty, thereby desensitizing him to the way a theory can acquire new force and energy as it switches locations. Avoiding the more trenchant claims from the earlier piece about the very nature of Theory—that it *is* the possible non-reified consciousness of the proletariat—Said embarks on an arduous, even torturous journey to show that as Adorno migrated back and forth across the Atlantic (from Europe, to the United States and back) Lukács's theory recovered itself through its negation. In other words, that the radicality of Lukács's critique of the subject/object relation found new expression in Adorno's unreserved repudiation of the politics of *engagement*, a stance restated and thus exemplified in Schönberg's approach to musical composing (despite Schönberg's own misgivings). He prepares us for this link to the aesthetic by rehearsing Lukács's early work and especially its drive to aestheticize the logic of reconciliation, a logic found to be at work in the least politically attractive—for Said—aspects of *History and Class Consciousness*. Things become a great deal more tenuous, indeed Said frankly concedes that he is obliged to "speculate" (Said 2000, 445) when this line of argument is brought to bear on Fanon who also crossed and recrossed the Atlantic, returning to die not to Martinique but to the United States. What is tenuous about this reading is not only the slim evidence upon which its claims are based, but the rather obvious way in which it sets up a foil to what Said finds troubling in Lukács, namely, the fantasy of reconciliation. Through a rousing restatement of Sartre's defense of Fanon's position on redemptive violence, Said shows that the postcolonial world—especially, and perhaps even uniquely—is one in which reconciliation is just another pitfall of an emerging national consciousness. Thus, Fanon is the ultimate, one might also say "perfect," sublation of Lukács. "Fiery rebelliousness" comes back with a fresh, post-reconciliatory energy. Here, however, our own reading stumbles over Said's passing anxiety about where exactly the link between Fanon and Lukács takes place. The most precise account of this location is given in the verb, "to speculate." In other words, the location of this connection is to be found in Said's "critical consciousness," a critical consciousness situated in the same New York that could not be named in the first version of the essay, indeed at the same terminus of the westward traveling theory whose potentially degraded character is the immediate subject of redemption in "Traveling Theory Reconsidered." In short, as with all repetitions, many of the same issues haunting the earlier piece return in the latter one. Indeed, this very fact makes their presence in the earlier piece all the more important.

Because critical consciousness is clearly an avatar of what elsewhere in *WTC* is referred to as "the critic," or "criticism" and because it is characterized there, however tentatively as "a sort of spatial sense," it seems important to consider how the "distance" between Williams/Said and Lukács connects with or otherwise borders upon the "spatial sense" that articulates Theory and critical consciousness both with one another and, presumably, with their place, their "situation," to invoke the term Sartre rescued from Jaspers. Because Said, despite his reliance upon it, has virtually no *theoretical* interest in the concept of "consciousness" (critical or otherwise)—he tends in the *WTC* essays to equate it with "intention"—we would do well here to seek instruction from those moments where Said links the critic or criticism to distance or space. Perhaps the most dramatic (to use one of his own oft-repeated adjectives) instance of this appears in the overtly architectonic title, if not essay, "Criticism Between System and Culture" that falls immediately before "Traveling Theory" in the table of contents of *WTC*.

In situating his own project, as articulated in *Orientalism*, in relation to those of Jacques Derrida and Michel Foucault, this essay is certainly eligible for postcolonial canonization. This is especially true if one considers that both Gayatri Spivak and Homi Bhabha, important, if in the minds of some, derivative, cofounders of the discursivity known as postcolonial studies, have felt compelled to situate their projects in relation to the same two figures. And, although there is much to say about this piece, it can be read so as to weigh in immediately on the matter of distance by citing the following crystallization of its thesis: "Between the power of the dominant culture, on the one hand, and the impersonal system of disciplines and methods (*savoir*), on the other, stands the critic" (Said 1991, 220). As Said himself notes this formulation points back to the headboard of his essay, indeed to its very title (a title, by the way added to the essay when republished in *WTC*), but it also states clearly that the critic (and presumably criticism since for Said you do not have the one without the other) occupies the space of the between, what Derrida was to call, *l'entre*, implying, does it not, that criticism is the distance, the wedge, that separates culture and system. This then complicates the distance between Williams and Lukács by becoming decidedly less physical (or, for that matter temporal) and more structural. In other words, even if we say that Said is saying that the theory of the distinction between Theory and critical consciousness (it is not, after all, a bald assertion of fact) arose because of the distance traveled by the theory of reification and totality from Hungary, he is still also saying that the "between" wherein criticism faces off against both culture and system is not the result of theorizing (that would locate it within "system"), but is part of the structure of the geopolitically given relation between culture and system. In short, because there is distance between these two facets of structure, there is *space* for criticism. What is more, this distance, precisely to the extent that, as I have said, New York is absent from both its articulation and its rearticulation, this distance is distanced from itself. It is structured by a detour that, in a certain sense, culminates in London in 1986 on the stage of the Institute for Education. Said rejoins Williams where he left him in "Traveling Theory."

To clarify how this bears on the concept of history it will be important to consider how history operates in "Criticism Between Culture and System," how history engages or fails to engage the space of criticism. Because this belongs fundamentally to the comparative evaluation of Derrida and

Foucault, and because this relation anticipates the one drawn by Williams and Said between representation and history it will clarify the angle of my reading if we playback more of the anxiety surrounding the discussion of this relation in "Media, Margins and Modernity."

I have already repeated Williams's anecdote about the student who asked him about his commitment to history, but of perhaps greater consequence is the account of formalism that transpires just prior to the Q & A or, what once was called, discussion. It is important not only because within it Williams swears his allegiance to the theory of traveling theory (stressing how formalism underwent a theoretical transubstantiation in coming back to Britain after a 50-year lag), but there he also gropes toward the "between." As if in confirmation of Said's account of his "distance" from the "fiery rebelliousness" of Lukács, Williams opens this analysis by distancing himself from "crude sociologism" (Williams 1989, 183), that is, an approach to literary representation that rifles it for those elements that could simply be related to its "conditions of production" (ibid., 183). Williams builds on this anxious repudiation of, let's call it, vulgar Marxism by adducing the contribution to literary formalism made by figures like Bakhtin, that is, formalists who sought to capture the play of distinctly social forces in language and, by extension, within the literary text. At first glance this position appears to be advanced in order to rescue formalism, but in fact it is advanced in order to complicate the relation between history and representation. In short, Williams wants to have his form and eat it too. Although he does not say as much, he sees the history of formalism as the means by which to resist being buttonholed as an old fogey. In other words, precisely because he does not accept a reductive view of representation, he cannot therefore be accused of holding a reductive view of history. Speaking declaratively he characterizes history bluntly as the "material past" (ibid., 178) and describes the view he shares with Said as one in which representations "are part of history, contribute to the history, and are active elements in the way that history continues" (ibid., 178), thereby clarifying that much hangs on what is meant by the adjective "crude." Because this is a discussion that culminates in a cautionary tale about the excesses of Theory, no effort is made to clarify how being a part of the material past is to be rigorously distinguished from an account of historical belonging that is neither crude nor banal. If it is important to insist that representation is part of history, rather than, say, culture, or society, then this is because history is something to which representation belongs in some distinctive and significant way. In short, the concept of history cannot simply go without saying once "crudeness" (vulgarity, or the *vulgum*) is on the table, a fact that applies considerable pressure on Williams's continual recourse to the term "determination" when explaining the genesis of his own writing (whether Theory or fiction).

To say, as I have said, that such issues matter to the way Said thinks about the difference between Derrida and Foucault is to say little. So more. It is useful to recall that in "Criticism Between Culture and System" Said too has recourse to the theme of crudeness, or, as he prefers, the notion that things can be "in some vulgar way caused by extrinsic socioeconomic factors" (Said 1991, 194). Articulated in the context of a discussion of the history of narrative representation, and more specifically, Derrida's avoidance of same, this riff on the history/representation relation tells one that the subject matter of his latter conversation with Williams is, perhaps surprisingly, being deployed in his effort to make sense not simply of the exemplary positions on textuality represented by Derrida and Foucault, but even more importantly of the space, the where, of criticism itself.

Another important adumbration of the later discussion appears in the perfunctory way history is defined in Said's essay. In characterizing Derrida's lack of attentiveness to the matter (except, of course, in his reading of Foucault's *historical* treatment of *la folie*), Said glosses history by describing as properly historical texts, texts that are "committed to some thesis of consequentiality in their internal structure" (ibid., 193), a formulation that at once indicts his characterization of Derrida's work (one assumes he read the protracted discussion of "consequentiality" in virtually all of Derrida's early critiques of Husserl), while also positing, as history uncompromised by vulgarity, a concept of history that insists the sequence of events, and where one falls in that sequence, matters. Of course, and I would be mad to deny it, Said invokes history with great rhetorical vigor throughout the essay, but he also, precisely in establishing the grounds upon which one would embrace Foucault's dismissive characterization of Derrida's project as a "little pedagogy," puts us on guard against such rhetorical flourishes. Once so alerted, we are entitled to expect a more vigorous theorization of what makes history as "consequentiality" decisive. It is left unsaid.

Perhaps the most direct way to situate the history/representation problem in this essay is to draw attention to the stress Said places on the "internal structure" of properly historical texts (wherein arises the thesis of consequentiality) and observe that this implicit spatiality is fundamental to his evaluation of Derrida and Foucault when he writes in tidy summary, "Derrida's criticism moves us *into* the text, Foucault's *in* and *out*" (Said 1991, 183). Or, to put the matter bluntly, history—that outside of which representation is a part—is decisively at stake in Said's evaluation of these critics. As such, this evaluation serves as the primary setting in which history is defined, as it were, in "Criticism Between System and Culture." In emphasizing Derrida's movement or voyage in (to anticipate my reading of *Culture and Imperialism*), Said, who otherwise shows considerable admiration for Derrida's skills as a reader, motivates his judgment that Derrida is, when all is said and done, a formalist of the non-Bakhtinian sort. While this certainly spares Derrida of the charge of "vulgar" historicism, it does stick him with the more damning charge of having abandoned the thesis of consequentiality altogether. By contrast, Foucault's double movement, both in and out, reveals awareness on his part of the global position of history, that is, its location squarely outside representation. One goes into the text from history and one comes back out into history, as though history were simply a place name writ large on the traveling theorist's map. This becomes most vivid as Said adjudicates the dispute at the heart of Derrida and Foucault's quarrel over Descartes. Impressed with Foucault's charge that Derrida has read the wrong text (the French rather than the original, read "consequentially prior," Latin—but let us not forget that Descartes wrote them both and even confesses to a special pride in writing in French to his countrymen, the vulgate) and that Derrida is ignorant of the juridical and medical discourses that furnish Descartes with his concept of madness, Said files an amicus curiae on behalf of Foucault. This implies, clearly, that Said identifies (not without reservations as we will see) with the round trip taken by Foucault, not because it is double, but because the doubling signals one's awareness of the outside of representation. It apportions representation and in doing so locates history.

However, what this forecloses is precisely what should matter to Said. Remember, Derrida and Foucault are not simply arguing about whether any philosophy can articulate the silence, the absence of work, that is, madness in relation to reason, they are also arguing about the role of historical contextualization in the work of philosophical interpretation. In aligning with Foucault, Said repeats the former's own silence with regard to one of Derrida's more important charges (and recall that Foucault initially wrote Derrida in praise of "Cogito and History"), namely, that what Foucault is trying hard to locate as belonging decisively to the seventeenth century, is, in fact, already present in 500 BCE. Although typically read as a point about the discourse of philosophy as such, Derrida is also clearly asking after Foucault's concept of history and the attendant notion of historical determination. In other words—to accept, for the sake of argument, the premise of consequentiality—if something referred to in a text is demonstrably present much earlier in a sequence of intellectual developments than is claimed, what explanatory power is then to be granted a rather dubious claim about the originality or distinctiveness of some event in the sequence? In this Derrida is not staying "in" the text so much as he is asking about the precise explanatory force of an outside that cannot be punctually indexed to a text's publication date. Surprisingly, this is not altogether unlike Said's own criticism of Foucault when, late in the essay, he repeats, almost verbatim, Sartre's defensive accusation that Foucault cannot really account for historical change. Although Derrida is not, as Said correctly observes, worried here about "intention," he is worried about the problem of how we read the difference that gives sequence its consequence, or put in terms of the debate over Descartes, he is concerned to probe the matter of to which outside of representation are the representations that comprise *The Mediations* decisively but not *crudely* connected? This cannot be a matter of indifference to the thesis of consequentiality.

Unquestionably, Said prefers Foucault's construal of the relation, the connection, between history and representation to that of Derrida, but, as Tim Brennan (2000) has insisted this is not because he is satisfied with Foucault's project. In this regard the matters of accounting for historical change, of intention and therefore responsibility have already been raised. However, because Said's siding with Foucault in the quarrel over Descartes authorizes him to defer the task of theorizing history once it has been separated from "vulgar" socioeconomic reductionism, history remains theoretically neglected when, toward the end of the essay, Said aligns himself with figures like Gramsci, who on a certain reading would appear to be committed to precisely the sort of systematic determinism both Said and Williams decry (hegemony, in complicating domination, does not thereby complicate the vulgar subordination of representation to history). This said, I do not wish to suggest that Said is either unaware or reconciled to this dilemma. In fact, I think that already here he is groping for a theoretical articulation of history up to the task he has set for it, and this becomes visible once we set the "vulgar" theme of determination alongside the theme of distance, and especially the distance traversed by criticism as wedged between culture and system. Doubtless it is fair to say that determination is vulgar because it subordinates criticism to system, in effect, closing the space of the between altogether. With the closure of this space criticism itself is closed out, a point made crystal clear in the opening essay of *WTC*, "Secular Criticism," where Said writes that criticism that is properly secular is criticism that is "constitutively opposed to the production of massive, hermetic systems" (Said 1991, 26).

It is hard, if not impossible to resist aligning with Said's stand on the importance of criticism, and for that reason it is crucial to be more attentive to those features of his account of history that would appear not to surrender it to either system or culture. This might well mean recognizing that even in as banal a formulation as "the situation I attempt to describe in modern criticism (not excluding 'Left' criticism) has occurred *in parallel* with the ascendancy of Reaganism" (Said 1991, 25) (my emphasis, for, what sort of determinant link is he envisioning between two lines that, by definition, never meet?) Said is theoretically invested in space. Indeed, was he not already saying as much when I cited him earlier as adding to Williams's account of the teachability of

Theory, the matter of his compartmentalization having been administered by "processes that took place elsewhere"? Let me suggest that it is precisely such gestures toward a rhetoric of spatiality (as opposed to "consequentiality," the sequence of cause and effect) that culminate in the following remarkable discussion from *Culture and Imperialism*.

In elaborating what is at stake in connecting empire to secular interpretation (a close relative, one assumes, of secular criticism), Said turns again to Lukács comparing him this time with neither Goldmann nor Williams, but to Gramsci. Both the terms and the aim of this comparison are extremely important. Said says:

> Lukács belongs to the Hegelian tradition of Marxism, Gramsci to a Vichian, Crocean departure from it. For Lukács the central problematic in his major work through *History and Class Consciousness* (1923) is temporality; for Gramsci, as even a cursory examination of his conceptual vocabulary immediately reveals, social history and actuality are grasped in geographical terms—such words as "terrain," "territory," "blocks," and "region" predominate. (Said 1994, 49)

These remarks—further elaborated two years later in "History, Literature and Geography"—give more and stronger teeth to an earlier point Said makes about a certain "idea of history" that predominates in the precincts of Western literary criticism and Theory. It does so not by measuring how far Theory has traveled from the "fiery rebelliousness" of Lukács, but by teasing out of the theory of reification and totality (Said is again focusing on *HCC*) its deep-seated commitment to temporality, and a Hegelian temporality of historical sublation at that. Because only a few pages into this text Said makes a point of confessing to his lack of a systematic temperament, thus again putting back on the proverbial table the central categories and concepts of *WTC*, we are prompted here to read temporality as an expression of precisely the sort of system (here called Hegelian Marxism) that forecloses upon the space of criticism. Whether we agree with Said's characterization of *HCC* or not (Lukács's own account of his "intentions" famously stress the problems of nature, the object and science), it is clear that for Said, Lukács's investment in temporality makes his perspective less attractive than Gramsci's. However, in light of the issues teased out of Said's reading of Foucault and Derrida, such a view obliges one to think and to think carefully about what happens to the thesis of consequentiality once temporality itself is set aside as tainted by the excesses of systematicity or, when reconsidered, reconciliatory sublation, that is, the teleological mechanism (system?) whereby everything works out in the end.

What is it then that makes Gramsci, and the Gramsci of "Some Aspects of the Southern Question" more attractive to Said? To answer one needs to read the phrase "social history and actuality are grasped in geographical terms" carefully. Doing so prompts one to recognize first that history, precisely in being contrasted with actuality, is still being conceived under the broad heading of consequentiality (history is the past, what comes *before* the actual, the living present), and at the same time, so to speak, both history and actuality are being subsumed within, if not the discipline of geography, then certainly within a vocabulary, a *rhetoric* of geography. In other words, if Gramsci is preferable to Lukács this is because the space between culture and system, the space or physical condition of secular criticism is better attended to by someone who makes geography matter as much if not more than history in his or her analysis of, say, representation. Or, as this point is succinctly put in "History, Literature and Geography": "History therefore derives from a discontinuous geography" (Said 2000 466). How this helps one think about the crucial thesis of consequentiality is hard to discern without thinking back to an earlier moment in the essay.

Shortly after the characterization of his temperament, Said, in introducing the project of *Culture and Imperialism*, says:

> What I have tried to do is a kind of geographical inquiry into historical experience, and I have kept in mind the idea that the earth is in effect one world, in which empty, uninhabited spaces virtually do not exist. Just as none of us is outside or beyond geography, none of us is completely free from the struggle over geography. (Said 1994, 7)

As with the "sort of spatial sense" underscored earlier, Said again desystematizes, de-dogmatizes his appeal to geography by describing his project as "a kind of" geographical inquiry, anticipating here Bertrand Westphal and the emergence of "geocriticism." By further specifying that historical experience will be the object of this inquiry he keeps apart what in the discussion of Gramsci he twists, or intertwines, namely geography and history. However, the prudence of these first steps is then abandoned as he offers his recasting of Derrida's still inflammatory assertion—there is nothing before the text (reading *hors texte* as a calque on *hors d'oeuvre*)—as, there is nothing before/outside of geography. Including, unless Said intends something rather private by "none of us," those who might otherwise be said to have historical experiences of the sort one might share—at/on some stage—with Raymond Williams. If we read this in the spirit of his remarks about Gramsci, where vocabulary or representation clearly counts as evidence, this implies not only that historical events take place in spaces, but that history (indeed, the idea, or might we say, discipline of history) is overwritten by geography (again the concept, or discipline of geography). Isn't this what is being alluded to when Said refers to "spatial consciousness," a term clearly resonant with "critical consciousness," but one considerably more reflexive in underscoring the space of criticism that, presumably, is more rigorously grasped, even secured in a geographical displacement of history?

But precisely what amplitude does this bring to the thesis of consequentiality? To put the matter succinctly, it tells us what it means to say things like "overlapping territories, intertwined histories" (Said 1994, 48), or even more bluntly, it tells us what it means to pluralize (perhaps the real opposite of capitalize) the noun history. In other words, because contact and contiguity in a certain sense trump sequence and continuity, it is possible in and among spaces—let's say countries or continents—for multiple sequences or accounts of sequence to coexist. Histories can intertwine because they are ultimately not subject to a general temporality (homogeneous empty time), but because there are as many times as there are spaces in which the struggle to mark off time's intervals and episodes takes place. This means, does it not, that the thesis of consequentiality is likewise subject to a geographical rhetoric wherein any claim to an absolute explanatory ordering of events and their consequences is rendered if not obsolete then feckless. In fact, the suspension of this thesis represents the final blow against historical determinism (whether vulgar or not), for if sequence cannot be absolutely and therefore systematically determined, then nor can temporal coincidence be secured, and without coincidence it becomes very hard to show that something outside but merely coincident with a representation *caused* that representation to assume a certain form or content. The geometric rhetoric of "parallels" is all that is left and lines that do not meet lack a certain explanatory force, indeed, they lack precisely the force necessary to turn a line into the party line.

Although it may seem odd to say so, and all protestations to the contrary notwithstanding, there is something very Foucauldian about this. I say this not primarily because Said was among the first to recognize the importance of Foucault's mid-1970s exchange with the journal *Herodote*, but because the unsettled and unsettling relation between geography and history mimics the relation between genealogy and history in Foucault's "Nietzsche, Genealogy and History," his homage to one of his former mentors and teachers, Jean Hyppolite (c.f., Chapter 1). Toward the end of his career Foucault labored to "systematize" the distinction between genealogy and archaeology, suggesting that history—even the history that appeared in the title of his chair at the Collège de France—had, in effect, dropped out, a fate perhaps sealed when in the final pages of *Discipline and Punish* the present itself became history. In the early 1970s, however, Foucault was less clear, by which I mean that the conceptual relation between genealogy and history was quite unstable. In the course of "Nietzsche, Genealogy, History" Foucault variously contrasts the two terms, subordinates one to the other (part six of the essay is a "genealogy *of* history"), proliferates distinctions (genealogy helps open up the space of "effective history" *within* history) and so on. At the essay's close, as Foucault rewrites Nietzsche's modalities of history, it is altogether unclear whether genealogy occupies the meta-historical position it is otherwise characterized as having rejected, or whether genealogy *is* what history becomes once Nietzsche's monumental mode becomes the parodic, the antiquarian becomes dissociative and the critical becomes the sacrificial (although the inspiration is Bataille, this transposition resonates deeply with "offering").

It is precisely this hesitancy, perhaps even ambivalence, that I discern in Said's discussion of geography. In other words, although it is clear that the project is framed as a "geographical inquiry into historical experience" where geography is deployed as something like an extra-disciplinary perspective *on* history, the unqualified praise for Gramsci's recourse to "geographical terms" and, perhaps most telling of all, Said's own invocation of the practice of contrapuntal reading (a nod to Ortiz?) suggest that history is not simply the object of geography, but that history has succumbed to itself as that which has been superseded by geography. What makes the contrapuntal so important here is the way it is glossed by Said who argues, in an uncharacteristic echo of Lévi-Strauss's musicological account of the structure of myth, that the texts that ought to concern critics are best treated as polyphonic themes in a Western tonal composition. Although this discussion ends on a surprising formalist note—Said insists upon the radically *immanent* character of the tensions arising within the contrapuntal reading—in explaining how it is that different histories can be put into contact with each other, it is clear that what is vital about counterpoint is the distribution of themes in space, that is, the way notes can be sounded at the same time but in productively different places on the stave, including I suppose, the stave of the world.

The tendency to "geographize" history expressed here perhaps finds its deepest expression in the tension between the pluralization of history and the, for lack of a better term, singularization of geography. As noted, there is no outside/before to geography, a view which while coming dangerously close to the panoptic Western "super subject" (Said 1994, 35) Said deplores does imply that unlike histories which can be multiplied through intertwining and overlapping, geography cannot be so multiplied. In other words, Said pointedly does not turn the disciplinary corner and explore whether geographies, presumably experiences of displacements, contacts and contiguities, can intertwine and overlap within and across themselves. This further implies that while geography designates the space of history it does not itself have either one or several. One might attribute this to shortsightedness, but better I think is to consider that in Said's reading geography—as if utterly separated from disciplinary reason—applies an important pressure on the discipline of history, a pressure that, when the sun finally sets, seeks to establish the Orientalist provenance and character of the thesis of consequentiality. It is not for nothing that Said cites Johannes Fabian's study of the Western denial of the coevalness of the non-Western other with untinctured approval. Or that, again in "History, Literature and Geography," he insists upon the recursive availability of historical experiences (plural) in "the post-Eurocentric world" (Said 2001, 470). In short, Said would appear to be chaffing under if not directly challenging the ontological and epistemological preeminence of time in Western hermeneutics and cultural criticism.[2]

In this he can be said to have anticipated Benedict Anderson's now dated meditation on the imagined community of synchronicity and homogeneous empty time. More importantly (since the value of preemption has fallen precipitously in the course of these remarks), as the phrase "rhetoric of spatiality" suggests, Said is also swimming against the current of both the Benjaminian and de Manian account of allegory, arguing that the signification of the symbol is not immanently disrupted by temporality, but by space, precisely the space that is articulated, however impossibly, at the joint, the ding that hinges the two scenes (the scene and its other) that structure the allegorical sign. In fact, contrapuntal reading is deeply allegorical, but in a way that suspends or at least complicates the nationalism that Fredric Jameson found difficult to dislodge from allegory. What is nevertheless foreclosed here is an effort to think through the production of the fraught relation between space and time in more straightforwardly theoretical terms, a foreclosure that no abhorrence of system ought to be allowed to justify, for such abhorrence then simply becomes the alibi for reinstalling Theory in a space outside geography, that is, somewhere that everyday materialities (whether past or present) fail to reach. Just because the child effectively shields his or her own eyes does not mean that s/he is in fact invisible to others.

To follow the path in then out of geography, the path left untaken by Said is to return, as if through a wormhole, to the Foucault/Derrida quarrel but from, or on, the other side. If earlier it was important to underscore Said's contention that Derrida favored theater over narrative it was not in order now to question Said's having overlooked the contentious exchange that took place between Derrida and Lacan around Poe's "The Purloined Letter." Rather, this gesture mattered because it prepares us to reread sentences such as this one from "Criticism Between Culture and System": "Many of Derrida's essays employ not only spatial metaphors, but more specifically theatrical ones" (Said 1991, 202). In the analytical con-text generated by Said's essay recourse to spatial metaphors is a defect not simply because it prompts one to ignore narrative, but because in ignoring narrative one fails to see, as de Man had already said about Rousseau, that texts, especially those unable to disarm or otherwise suspend the force of narrativity, deconstruct themselves. More than a challenge to Derrida's novelty, this point, especially as twinned with the claim that both Foucault and Derrida have abandoned the concept of intention and therefore responsibility, this point is more directly about Derrida's unconscious. That is, his inability to recognize that what he is really doing is nothing more than theorizing, and theorizing belatedly or derivatively the logic of narrativity.

But, under the capacious heading of "if the shoe fits wear it," given the later emphasis placed by Said on what he was to call "spatial rhetoric," might we not wonder here about Said's unconscious, that is, to reverse the pronunciation of my title, what said Said? Having already observed that Said has not worked out a theory of what "consciousness" means in the phrase "critical consciousness," any effort to think his unconscious is lured immediately into the cul-de-sac of denial. It is also uninteresting. More interesting though is if we follow his citation of Derrida's third major treatment of Husserl, *Voice and Phenomenon* (note that *la voix* in the French picks up voice, but also, the homonym *voie* or way, path, rendered untraceable by Allison's "speech"), follow it to the following passage from Chapter 6 of that study, "The Voice That Keeps Silence."

> Since the trace is the intimate relation of the living present with its outside, the openness upon exteriority in general, upon the sphere of what is not "one's own," etc. *the temporalization of sense is from the outset, a "spacing."* As soon as we admit the outside, there can no longer be any absolute inside, for the "outside" has insinuated itself into the movement by which the inside of the nonspatial, which is called "time," appears, is constituted, is "presented." Space is "in" time; it is time's pure leaving-itself; it is the "outside itself" as the self-relation of time. The externality of space, externality as space does not overtake time, rather, it opens as pure "outside" "within" the movement of temporalization. [...] Time cannot be an "absolute subjectivity" precisely because it cannot be conceived on the basis of a present and the self-presence of a present being. Like everything thought under this heading, and like all that is excluded by the most rigorous transcendental reduction, the "world" is primordially implied in the movement of temporalization. [...] Hearing oneself speak is not the inwardness of an inside that is closed upon itself; it is the irreducible openness in the inside; it is the eye and the world within speech. *Phenomenological reduction is a scene, a theater stage.* (Derrida 1972, 86, emphasis in original)

I cite this lengthy passage because it offers much to ruminate. In particular, the final italicized phrase should have given Said pause as it clearly complicates any attribution to Derrida of some unconscious investment in, or simple preference for theater, as Derrida here explicitly draws attention to the way the thematics of spacing (whether as rhetoric or as metaphor) opens up within the purity of phenomenology's "staging" of the voice, a purity thereby forever deprived of its transcendental shelter from the outside, maybe even the world. Even a cursory reading of Derrida's essay on "The Origin of Geometry" (doubtless inspired by Merleau-Ponty's earlier lectures on this very text) would recognize that the argument for placing the world within the spacing that is time is precisely the means by which Derrida seeks to problematize Husserl's account of history. And while the general and now quite familiar discussion of the troubled relation between the inside and outside might invite a return to the history/representation debate animated by Williams and Said, more pertinent is recognition that in the theory of consciousness evoked here by Derrida (a theory worked out in detail in the nearly contemporaneous essays, "*Différance*" and "Freud and the Scene of Writing") there is an account of the relation between space and time that essentially thinks the grounds, and if one insists, the existential grounds, of Said's preference for Gramsci over Lukács, not to mention his pronounced if unresolved investment in the rhetoric of spatiality made available by geography in its putative confrontation with history.

But there is more. This passage also reiterates the problem of the "between," that is, the space—between culture and system—of critical consciousness as such. It does so not by theorizing how consciousness can identify and then assume critical tasks, but how within the very material structure, the event of consciousness, the "between" that secures a foothold for criticism by driving a shunt between system and culture, arises. This is important because it fleshes out, as it were, Said's reiterated but unelaborated appeal to consciousness, but even more importantly it helps us recognize the daylight that shines between Said's position and those we have come to associate with identity politics, a perspective taken to task at length in "Literature, History and Geography."

The airing of differences between Williams and Said that a questioner sought to provoke at the event in London assumes its fully belated character in *CI* where Said, after conceding the importance of Williams's insight into the topography of the country and the city, not to mention the *structure* of feeling, proceeds to criticize Williams, his spatial consciousness notwithstanding, for "feeling that English literature is mainly about England" (Said 1994, 14). Said goes on to attribute such a view to precisely the notion both he and Williams had been disputing in London, namely the notion that literature was somehow, even when rooted in a national structure of feeling, "autonomous" (ibid., 14). The adumbration of this bone of contention appears in the opening statements where, as has been pointed out, Said "extends" Williams by invoking his distinctive encounter with "compartmentalization," a term whose spatial resonance should sound differently this time around. In effect, what Said is saying is that beyond the pedagogical and political problem of history and representation, there is the question of identity, that is, the fact that Said experienced his relation to English literature as one marked by "processes that took place elsewhere" (Williams 1989, 180). If Derrida's account of spacing and world is relevant here, it is because it provides one with a way to read Said's "extension" as something other than a request for recognition. In other words, one might easily conclude that Said is insisting either on the uniqueness of his personal encounter with the overlapping and intertwined spaces of England, Western literature, empire and the Middle East (not likely, however, given the explicit emphasis placed on his relation to "many like me") or on his belated identification with the Palestinian diaspora. Against this, and against all systematic identitarianisms, stands the notion that the very ground of identity is, as it were, spaced out. If we can take up critical positions against processes that take place elsewhere, it is because we can take up a critical relation to ourselves. Critical consciousness starts at home, that is, in the capacity for the seat of identity to be at odds with itself. In this, despite his impatience with rebarbative abstraction, Said is a Theory partisan.

Contrary to the oft-repeated assertion that Derridean spacing is devoid of particularity and therefore purely abstract, I think a more consistent reading of this figure is one in which it accounts for how we are deeply open—indeed open all the way down, as we say—to any and all the particular spatial overlappings that position us in what Said and Derrida are willing to call "the world." We are open here in a way that extends well beyond the vulnerability of identity, indeed we are emptied into the space of criticism, not at the level of stance but at the level of materialization itself. By the same token, the Derridean appeal to spacing, no more or less prone to becoming orthodoxy than any other academic category, say, for example, Eurocentrism, is systematic without being a system. In fact, in linking spacing to the "openness on exteriority in general," Derrida provides Said with the very theoretical principle that systematically frustrates system building, a goal, as we have seen, vital, even indispensable, to Said's effort to secularize criticism. Holding open the space of criticism cannot be accomplished by transcendental assertion or by empirical demonstration. In fact, if it appeals to either it effectively disqualifies itself as criticism whether secular or not, whence, one might argue, the intrigue of immanence that has insistently gripped the critical humanities in recent decades.

It is in this sense that we have returned to "Criticism Between Culture and System" from the other side, that is, from Derrida's side. I am arguing, perhaps scandalously, that beneath or before (in the logical sense of prior)

Said's favoring of Foucault in this quarrel there is, buried in the problem of history and the meaning of the critic's commitment to a certain idea of it ("the impossibly vague notion that all things take place in time"), an unsaid affinity with Derrida's problematization of the concept of temporality and the attendant thesis of consequentiality. Not surprisingly, this muted gap, this unsaid, appears in the essay as part of its enunciation, not as part of its statement. It is nevertheless tempting, perhaps irresistible, to consider that *Hamlet* serves as the setting in which this unsaid is, strictly speaking, staged. I am thinking, of course, of Said's appeal to the staging of the play (whose name, as Said reminds us, is unmentioned) that occurs in Dickens's *Great Expectations*, and the fact that *Hamlet* is the portal through which, ten years later, Derrida initiates his probing, if belated, meditation on "the spirit of Marxism." Said's point is to motivate and justify the charge that Derrida's theory of representation is at once "complex" and "tautological" and, most damning of all, derivative, that is, already articulated in *Great Expectations*. In this the charge of preemption is meant to sting as badly as that of theatricality (i.e., antinarrativity), an odd gambit given what implacably happens to the thesis of consequentiality in Said's essay.

For his part, Derrida, studiously avoiding any direct reference to Said's critique, revisits *Hamlet* and makes what for the post-1970s Derrida is a beeline for the joint in time, the ding haunted by, among others, the ghosts of Marx. To avoid exhuming a well-exhumed corpus, let me simply observe that Derrida gives every appearance of replying to Said by querying, "and *where* precisely does anyone stand on the history of historical materialism today?" Not only does he make much of Marx's interest in theater in general and Shakespeare in particular, locating it, for example, in the very secret of the commodity, but Derrida closes Chapter 2 with a trenchant extended parenthesis where, among other things, he restates the difference between Francis Fukayama's "end of history" and a deconstructive challenge to a concept of history, "historicity" (Derrida 1994, 74) that otherwise forecloses or shuts down the "openness" of the event, that is, the fact that its taking place is disseminated in and as the world. Precisely to the extent that Derrida associates this challenge with a certain inheritance of Marxism, to a sustained openness to the spirit of Marxism, he brushes aside the notion that somehow the claims of historical materialism are settled by repudiating either the vulgarity of "determinism" or the general movement toward totalization, toward systematicity. In this Derrida moves to the left of Said, finding in the openness, the immanent spacing, of the event (say, the assassination of Chris Hani to whom the book is dedicated) a principled if not systematic politics—articulated in theoretical terms to be sure—that Said is reluctant to claim in his geographically Oriented inquiry into historical experience.

The general proposition that beneath or behind Said's adjudication of the quarrel between Foucault and Derrida stands an unsaid solidarity with Derrida finds perhaps its most material and concrete confirmation in the procedures of Said's reading. In characterizing Derrida's deconstructive reading practice Said, and in this he is not alone, stresses the importance of the former's discovery of an author's "ambiguous innocence about a detail" (Said 1991, 188). Whether this insistence on the singularity of detail is a compelling account of Derrida's reading practice is not really as important as the fact that Said both thinks so *and*, while holding such a view, *reads this way himself*. In tracking the rhetorical gestures of "Criticism Between Culture and System," one cannot but be struck by Said's insistent recourse to the "one word" (ibid., 184), the "one aspect" (ibid., 186), the "only once" (ibid., 188), the "one important thing" (ibid., 192) and so on, strung like buoys along the expository wake of his text. Although much could be said about this—does it reveal Said's anxious need to beat "Jacky" at his own game? His command of the rigors of immanent critique? etc.—I will settle for the observation that it is in *reading as such* that the unsaid solidarity between Said and Derrida leaves its indelible mark. Now, before the scandal of such a counterintuitive assertion becomes simply a distraction, consider the importance it attaches to reading as a practice within which the space of criticism is staked out. In drawing attention to the uncanny effect of Derrida's readings, that in representing texts he "rereads and rewrites them" (Said 1991, 201), Said avows that he shares, not Derrida's reputedly tautological economy, but a view of criticism that when articulated as a theory of reading embraces the work of both reading and writing. Barthes, as we have seen, tried to index these functions to a textual typology—the *lisible* and the *scriptible*—in which primarily modernist texts were readable as writable, but Derrida proceeds as though there are only "modernist" texts. As if vulnerable to hypnotic suggestion, Said, in reading Derrida's readings in accord with the technique promoted within them, invites us to consider whether his own rereading is also a rewriting. As a matter of intellectual honesty or the lack thereof, this is uninteresting. More interesting is the suggestive alignment here, and the fact that it moves Said to summarize (however "baldly") Derrida's project in the following highly charged terms: "These ideas have a special interest for critics today who may wish to place themselves skeptically between culture as a massive body of self congratulatory ideas and system or method, anything resembling a sovereign technique that claims to be free of history, subjectivity or circumstance" (ibid., 202). Aside from the important glosses adduced here for the titular concepts of the essay (is Said theorizing or mimicking textuality here?), this establishes the immediate relevance of Derrida to the space of the between, a space cleared through the reading writing underway within it.[3] The, or a, space for Theory.

Some time ago Said's colleague at Columbia, Gayatri Spivak, argued, in her debate with the Subaltern Historians (Guja, Chatterjee, Chakrabarty et al.) for the advantages of a grammatological project committed to the proposition that logocentrism is the founding ethnocentrism in prosecuting the critique (she invokes deconstruction as such) of nationalist historiography. As I do not wish to be read as merely repeating this argument, let me clarify this by taking up the challenge that has been put before postcoloniality by Goethe's concept of *Weltliteratur*, rephrased now as "the world republic of letters" (Casanova) or simply, "world literature." This turn is recommended by the simple fact that, as has been noted, "world," and more specifically "worldliness," is a deeply enabling concept for Said, one that remained so long after *WTC* in 1983. In the later, worldliness is invoked as both extending beyond mere "circumstantial reality" and as exhibiting greater precision than history. It is something that characterizes all texts and all acts of reading. In light of the recent work by Aamir Mufti (*Forget English!*), Siraj Ahmed (*The Archaeology of Babel*), even Werner Hamacher ("95 Thesis on Philology"), the maneuvering that characterizes the final chapters of *WTC*, wherein "world" is provocatively indexed to the philological articulation of Sanskrit, Latin and Hebrew, strikes one as destining "world literature," or even "global humanities" to a fateful compromise, one that fails politically and theoretically to unsettle "postcoloniality" even in the act of, purportedly, doing so. Put differently, if philology—as both hermeneutic and bureaucracy—is the enabling condition of empire, then the world put to work within "world literature" and made philologically legible is an imperial projection. All the post- or trans- or antinational literary encounters facilitated by this projection, while certainly "worldly" and delectable in their own ways, sacrifice their criticality to the dubious principle of accumulation (perhaps even a new enclosure). Here "world" degenerates into a purely geographic site, where the politics of spacing crucial both to deconstruction and to postcoloniality is reduced to a surreal GPS location: Europe. Advanced in the name of a definitive, perhaps even decolonial repudiation of Theory, "world literature" aligns itself only with what Said said, not with what said Said, an equally decisive aspect of his legacy, but one typically obscured by our devotion to it.

Notes

1   At one point in the exchange Said refers to a passage from this text read by Bob Catterall (*WTC* 1991, 29) that was read, into the record, earlier that day. Said uses this episode to show how an appeal to the "life enhancing" power of criticism can be translated as "kill all the Jews" by the teletechnologies of the media, a point that underscores the general thesis advanced not just in "Media, Margins and Modernity" but in "Traveling Theory," namely, that location, indeed con-text, conditions meaning

and mutatis mutandis politics. The immediate stress Said lays on the matter of the two sides of his professional existence (his affection for both Fanon and Trilling) is far from insignificant. So much so, in fact, that when Said revisits his essay ten years on, he expressly retrieves the "Fanonian" thread, without however being any more forthcoming about the undisclosed location from which he does so.

2   Certainly, one way of thinking about the profundity of Said's commitment to the Palestinian cause is in terms of the relation between the process put in place and initiated by the Oslo Accords, a process which in the long run led to Said's embrace of the single state, binational solution, and his principled if vexed abandonment of the thesis of consequentiality. Instead of quarreling endlessly about who occupied the disputed territories first, as though political authority followed from temporal priority, the suspension of temporality fields a different argument, one about the geographic facts of contact (displacement, Diaspora, war and occupation) and contiguity. While no less fraught this argument nevertheless moves to produce conviviality out of the hybrid and overlapping histories of the region, essentially suspending the priority of priority. While an historian might wish to stress the coincidence of the Accords and the publication of *Culture and Imperialism* (both in 1993), I think such stress would be, as it were, misplaced.

3   At the risk of appearing to appeal to a higher authority and thus conceding the outlandish (interesting word, no?) nature of the thesis advanced here, I observe that in Julia Kristeva's *roman à clef*, *The Samourai*, the character rather obviously standing in for Derrida is named "Saïda." As there would be any number of ways to mark Derrida's "foreignness," something led her to this option. I believe that I have sketched in aspects of the "something."

Chapter 7

APART FROM THEORY

The matter this chapter seeks to agitate is evocatively miniaturized in the following line from George Eliot's *The Lifted Veil*: "I was no sooner in Bertha's society again, then I was as completely under her sway as before" (Eliot 1999, 20). Although I have long wondered about the idiomatic expression "under one's sway," it is the apparent substitution of "society" for "company" that caught my ear. Put this way, of course, it sounds like what concerns me bears on the work of metaphorization, or perhaps English usage in Britain during the nineteenth century, but in fact what is at once striking and suggestive in this sentence is something else. Namely, the way the substitutability of "society" for "company" prompts one to probe "company" for insight into the specifically social character of society. The productivity of such a gesture will become clearer in the course of these considerations, but for now it will suffice to stress that my curiosity regarding the friction within Edward Said's work between history and geography, a friction initiated by the theoretical impact of the concept of the text on that of context, concerns itself with a disciplinary displacement that, if it has a corollary in the sociology of literature (or culture more broadly), may well be figured in what I am here proposing to call sociography. Such, in any case, is the argument that matters most in what follows.

If, has been proposed, the sacrificial character of Theory has something fundamental to do with its having outlived its moment, its context (see the Introduction), then one of the founding gestures of the institutional thought experiment that is cultural studies, namely, the gesture of "contextualization," calls out for consideration in any effort to think the when and where of Theory. What makes "contextualization" a topic of common concern is that cultural studies from its very inception—and I'll have more to say about this shortly— has distinguished itself from the mere study of culture, whether anthropological or philosophical, by insisting upon an essential relation between what Marx memorably called *das Leben* (life) and *das Bewusstsein* (consciousness). Put differently, contextualization, the analytical gesture of situating a text in its sociological or historical context so as to determine its sense, is not simply something cultural studies does, it is implicated in what it *means* to do cultural studies. Perhaps inevitably what follows then is both about context and cultural studies, neither of which is particularly secure here and now. As many readers will know the Centre for Contemporary Cultural Studies at the University of Birmingham was closed in the early 2000s, its project scattered in an institutional diaspora and its intellectual influence on the wane. David Scott's recent book on Stuart Hall is suffused with a poignant, and genuinely touching, nostalgia for his voice (Scott 2017).

My tone suggests that we are here confronting a matter of some urgency, even a problem, so what is, or might be construed as, the "problem" of contextualization? At the risk of appearing to avoid the challenge of my own question let me sketch simply the outer limits of what I have called the problem. On the one hand, the philosophical foundations of what has long gone by the designation "reflection theory" have crumbled and washed away. Given that from Marx and Engels, to Lukács, to Goldmann, to Williams to Jameson and Said, cultural expression (both form and content—although, truth be told, Engels was a bit more modest than others) has been understood to *reflect* the ideas thought to inhere homologically in a social class's "world view" (to use Goldmann's incisive formulation), the complications introduced into this model by the theory of language that, at a certain point, partitioned the work and the text, have, as it were, thrown the baby of reflection out with the bathwater of representation. If language does not represent, or represents with difficulty, then cultural expressions that derive from or are otherwise mediated by language do not reflect. How could they? Why then do we, the partisans of cultural study, persist in attempting to contextualize cultural expression? Put differently, are cultural studies partisans committed, by virtue of some interdisciplinary *conatus*, to, as Marx put it in *Capital I*, know not what they do, but do it just the same?

On the other hand, and here I am steering this discussion toward my specific concern with *sociological* contextualization, or, to crib the title from Rita Felski's special issue of *New Literary History* 2010, "new sociologies of literature," do we not now face the dilemma given expression in the following quotation from Tiqqun's *Introduction to Civil War*.

> Society no longer exists, at least in the sense of a differentiated whole. There is only a tangle of norms and mechanisms through which THEY hold together the scattered tatters of the global bio-political fabric, through which THEY prevent its violent disintegration. Empire is the administrator of this desolation, the supreme manager of a process of listless implosion. (Tiqqun 2010, ii)

One is entitled, of course, to balk at this eerie echo of Thatcherism, or to quarrel with such formulations on the grounds that they "reflect" a distinct, social alienation of "intellectual labor" (Tiqqun is a French collective of writers and other activists), but to do so is to gainsay precisely the matter in dispute. The *passe partout* of dialectical reason must be invoked here to demonstrate how the contention that society does not exist is, *in fact*, an expression of a reified social consciousness of first-world intellectuals. Conveniently and paradoxically, the social condition of possibility for this very criticism is rarely specified, and when it is, it is typically done so in a language deemed transparent to its users or otherwise inexplicably dematerialized. It purports to speak directly, immediately about objects, objects that in turn validate such speech. Marx, of course, set the standard here when as Fred Moten has detailed in *Capital* I he eavesdropped on commodities only to hear them giving voice to his theory about them.

This then is the hyperbolic formulation of the problem: the philosophical resources of reflection theory have been seriously depleted and the society thought to be reflected in reflection theory has disintegrated. How does cultural studies propose to sustain itself under such circumstances? Fortunately, the situation, our moment, is perhaps not as grim as it seems, and one way to get at this is to begin thinking carefully about the way the sociology of literature came to problematize itself. It is instructive that a version of said problematization coincided with the very founding of the Centre for Contemporary Cultural Studies at Birmingham.

As many readers will know, the center was founded in 1963. Richard Hoggart, the center's first director, gave the inaugural lecture titled, "Schools of English and Contemporary Society." There would be much to say about this brief perhaps even historic text, and I have said some of those things in *Radio: Essays in Bad Reception* (see "Birmingham Calling"). Here instead, I will highlight those moments in Hoggart's remarks that bear directly on the sociology of literature. The lecture opens by observing that there may well be a contradiction between English literature and contemporary society. His point is the familiar one: literary value is enduring while the concerns of contemporary society are, as a matter of principle, ephemeral. Aware that this insight would risk founding the center on a contradiction, Hoggart then goes on to stress that what constitutes the enduring character of literature is its care for the "life of a language," a construal of literature that then allows him to pose a more manageable question: What are the conditions of the life of language in contemporary British society? Those familiar with Hoggart's signature preoccupations recognize them in this question. However, what formulating it allows is the following characterization of the founding concerns of the center. "The field for possible work in Contemporary Cultural Studies can be divided into three parts: one is, roughly, historical and philosophical; another is, again roughly, sociological; the third—which will be the most important—is the literary critical" (Hoggart 1970, 255). Now what justifies the distinct privilege assigned to the literary critical part of cultural studies? Hoggart makes two important points. First, because the literary critical concerns itself directly with the life of language it has a vital role to play in restoring its use, its capacity to define the terms of the "cultural debate" more carefully. Second, the pressure placed on philosophy and sociology by the literary critical part of cultural studies prevents its partisans from engaging in what Hoggart calls "bad history and bad sociology and bad philosophy" (ibid., 259). It is precisely this appeal to "bad sociology" that not only links and links intimately the project of the sociology of literature and the disciplinary formation of cultural studies, but does so by underscoring the decisive way that literature confronts sociology with the challenge of not going bad, of not forgetting what he calls, following Friedrich Schiller one assumes, the "'playful' element" (ibid., 259) in literature. Cultural studies as a midcentury iteration of an aesthetic education?

I would argue that it is precisely the various connotative elaborations of "bad"—notably "mechanistic," "reductive" and "vulgar"—that are the watchwords of literary sociology and they are so precisely because they touch directly on the problem of contextualization. An instructive encounter in the unfolding of literary sociology can be invoked to elaborate this point. The matter has been touched upon in the exchange between Said and Williams as discussed in the preceding chapter (the latter's repudiation of "crude sociologism"), but other examples are not hard to come by.

Consider the Q&A that unfolds between Fredric Jameson and Nancy Fraser in the wake of his "Cognitive Mapping" paper presented at the Unit for Criticism and Interpretive Theory event in the summer of 1983 whose proceedings appeared at the end of the decade as *Marxism and the Interpretation of Culture*. Responding initially to Jameson's then characteristic even routine disparagement of theorists critical of the Sartrean/Lukácian concept of "totalization," Fraser begins her intervention by drawing attention to his conflation of often quite nuanced articulations of this critique, but then immediately turns to the burning issue, saying, "Thus, I wonder why you assume that cognitive mapping is the task of the aesthetic? Why wouldn't that be a task for critical social science? Or, are two different kinds of tasks conflated in your paper" (Grossberg and Nelson 1988, 358). As printed, the tone of this intervention is missing, but clearly the mention of "conflation" is provocative, as if to tease out its implicit relation to "totalization" (can one have the latter in the absence of some version of the former?) and thus to impute to Jameson a version of the problem his paper is attempting to redress.

Aware that the question is "unfriendly," Jameson responds in some detail and in ways that speak to the relation between art and society as implied within the concept of "cognitive mapping." His first gambit is to rephrase Fraser's query, drawing on Althusser's distinction between science and ideology to ask through which discourses can the structure of the world system be meaningfully explored. To downplay the risk of his implicit alignment of the aesthetic and ideology, he quickly then emphasizes the status of the subject in this invocation of Althusser: ideology is where one maps his or her relation to "global capitalism" as an individual subject; science is where this relation is mapped in the absence of a subject. He then turns to "the real problem" (ibid., 358), which "is that it is increasingly hard for people to put that [science's mapping of the world system] together with their own experience as individual psychological subjects, in daily life" (ibid., 358). Observing that "the social sciences can rarely do that," he concludes: "Aesthetics is something that addresses individual experience rather than something that conceptualizes the real in a more abstract way" (ibid., 358). For what it is worth a fuller, more carefully argued version of this position is presented in the "Culture" chapter of *Postmodernism, or, the Cultural Logic of Late Capitalism* (see pp. 51–54).

An unfriendly response to an unfriendly question. Although it would have been tough to "hear" it at the time, Jameson justifies the priority given to the aesthetic in "cognitive mapping," by invoking precisely the same concept indispensable to the sociology of literature from Lukács to Williams, namely that of subjective experience (here reaching back to the ancient sense of *aesthesis* as individual perception), arguing that the social sciences are far too abstract to make any meaningful appeal to subjective experience. They cannot properly ground what he means by "cognitive mapping," and cannot because they are too "vulgar," too "crude," here "abstract." Although Jameson appears to avoid the accusation of unwittingly engaging in conflation, it is not uninteresting that in his response he offers three quite *different* conceptions of the totality, namely, "world system," "global capitalism" and "the real" with the last, Lacan's most challenging structuring instance of the speaking subject, plainly situating psychoanalysis on the brow thread between science and ideology.

Of course, this is far from Jameson's last word on "cognitive mapping." As noted, it figures in the big text on postmodernism, nuancing what might be more than "logical" about a cultural logic of a particular phase in the history of capitalism, but also in several chapters of *The Geopolitical Aesthetic* (see pp. 188–89 in particular), as well as in the very recent collection of his writings on Raymond Chandler where it is deployed to think what the Situationists might have called the "psycho-geography" of the city of Los Angeles as it informs Chandler's novels (Hammett's San Francisco awaits). It is by far one of the most sophisticated recent innovations in the sociology of culture, but it is also plainly a theory of contextualization, and as such, of relevance to what is at stake in my production of the concept of sociography.

Perhaps, given my persistent engagements with Eagleton and Said, one of the more immediately pertinent invocations of cognitive mapping occurs in Jameson's contribution to The Field Day Theatre Company's pamphlets, "Modernism and Imperialism," an essay published together with Eagleton's "Nationalism: Irony and Commitment" and Said's "Yeats and Decolonization" in 1990. Jameson's contribution falls between his "Cognitive Mapping" paper and its refrain in *Postmodernism*. It exhibits no explicit engagements with his collaborators (both Eagleton and Said address themselves to their host Seamus Deane), but the theme of the difficulty one faces in situating him or herself in relation to one account or another of "the totality" is further nuanced here by adding "imperialism" (Said's great theme in *Culture and Imperialism*) to his conflation-resistant list of totalizations in the reply to Fraser. In terms of the "sociology of culture" Jameson frames the invocation of imperialism by stressing that he wants to pursue the "historiographic decision" (Eagleton et al. 1990, 45) that would tease out how the formal innovations of literary modernism (notably E. M. Forster and Joyce) respond to the spatial perceptions of subjects living in and under imperialism, not imperialism in its classic Marxist-Leninist dispensation, but imperialism as a vicious and tenacious logic of underdevelopment. That said, and Jameson goes out of his way to separate "cognitive mapping" from the puzzle of Alfred Korzybsky's "map versus territory" distinction, what asserts itself is precisely *space*, adorned with all the geographic force given to it by Said. I will suggest therefore that in this formulation of "cognitive mapping" the practice of sociological contextualization would appear, in principle, to be subject to the same sorts of theoretical challenges teased out of Said's critical reading of history in the preceding chapter. Moreover, as if inviting the turn to the sociographic that I am attempting here, Jameson writes the following with regard to the aesthetic mapping of the "new imperial world system":

> It is in this situation that modernist representation emerges, and this is indeed in general the relationship of formal and cultural change to what we have called its social "determinants," which present a radically altered situation [...] to which a fresh and unprecedented aesthetic response is demanded. (Eagleton et al. 1990, 50)

If read aloud, the word "determinants" would be accompanied with air quotes, drawing conspicuous attention to Jameson's desire to have his cake and eat it too, that is, to situate modernism *in* its social context, but to fudge the question of the effect *of* contextualization. Does the context (however nuanced) "determine" the text? Apparently the matter is subject to doubt. Extending Jameson's passion for space one might propose that sociography ought be produced so as to hold open, if not a space between society and sociology, then certainly something *like* a space between sociology and sociography, or, put differently, between the discourse (*legein*) on society and the writing (*graphein*) of that discourse. Where, after all, is mapping (cognitive or otherwise) inscribed?

This reinvocation of Said invites clarification about the status of the postcolonial in this discussion, both because the preceding "What Said Said" said precious little about it and also because Said's relation to the postcolonial has emerged as a contentious issue in recent literary scholarship.[1] To be blunt, the issue has less to do with the matters of affiliation or solidarity and more to do with sorting the matter of to what extent the critique of what even Said will call "Eurocentrism" bears on a theory of context. And in two senses: first, what is theoretically required to think the context evoked by the protest, "We are here (now), because you were there (then)" and also, which accents are recommended by the problem of the postcolonial in formulating the where and when of Theory. Said's contribution to *Nationalism, Colonialism and Literature* (the Field Day pamphlets) has the virtue of sounding the theme of Theory explicitly.

To be sure, "Yeats and Decolonization" is not first and foremost a theoretical intervention. It is, however, a reading. Specifically, it is a provocative argument for situating the great Irish poet and playwright within an aesthetic tradition more normally associated with Césaire and Neruda. To justify this maneuver Said has to produce, if obliquely, the concept of "decolonization." He does not make reference either to Ngugi's still pressing *Decolonizing the Mind* from two years earlier or to the existence of the United Nations Special Committee on Decolonization founded in 1961. Instead, he invokes what he calls "the age of decolonization" (Eagleton et al. 1990, 70) as a name for a wide variety of struggles indexed to the global event of imperialism. While one might then expect "decolonization," as an age, to assume a distinctive historical profile, Said turns to complicate the historical character of imperialism—insisting that it is older than the nineteenth century, even in its "modern" profile—and grounding this last in the more directly geographical concept of land, specifically its occupation, exploitation/degradation and later romanticization. His appeal to Theory arises as he traces two moments in the process of decolonization: the moment of independence and the moment of liberation. Crucial to the latter is the role Theory can play in delineating the shortcomings of both nationalism and nativism; nationalism, because it compromises too quickly with the politics of independence, and nativism because in refusing to compromise at all it capitulates without hesitation to the banalities of cultural diversity. Describing the means by which the "idea of liberation" is brought forward as the name for a distinct moment, Said writes that this sometime requires "the propulsive infusion of theory" (op. cit., 76), thus pairing theory with "insurrectionary militancy" in a manner that suggests Fanon might be the "proper name" of Theory in this context.

Might he also then be suggesting—given the role Fanon plays in "Traveling Theory Revisited"—that more is at stake here than delineating the leading role Theory might play in decolonization? Is Fanon's reading of, for example, the fifth year of the Algerian revolution a decolonization of Theory as such? What might that mean, and more particularly, what is the context of such a theory, and what does "context" mean when theoretically decolonized? The institutional drift from postcoloniality (and here Natalie Melas's stress on its impact on the *concept* of comparativism is instructive), to world literature, to the broad-based contemporary initiative to "decolonize" knowledge has not helped accentuate what is nevertheless critically latent in Said's reading of Yeats.

To abbreviate, let me simply propose that still today one might deploy the concept of "postcoloniality," as the designation of a problematic rather than as a development. As a problematic, an echo chamber of questions and answers (none of them satisfying), postcoloniality helps us hold on to the fact that the colonial articulation of the relation between the colonizer and the colonized (to use Albert Memmi's categories) organized this relation around a general apartness, a relation-of-separation that development can neither think through nor overcome. Indeed, it is precisely in this way that development— whether as concept or policy—necessarily fails. This does not mean that the colony and the metropole live this nonrelation in the same way, or that decolonization is pointless. Not at all. But what bears emphasis is that knowledge, especially disciplinary knowledge of the sort Said sought to capture in the enabling term "Orientalism," was itself implicated in and structured by this colonially inflected relation-of-separation. This includes, among many things, the disciplinary projects of say, history, anthropology or political science, that is, all disciplines within which some account of "relations" figures prominently in their objects. Sociography can then be understood as a concept risked in the context of a sociology whose understanding of social relations, or the relation between society and culture, has been affected by the critical force of postcoloniality. It enables precisely that sort of reading to which Theory is offered and one in which the context of said offering is in question.

However, before turning to the matter of what sociography might do, it is important to acknowledge that "sociography" is not my coinage. In fact, the concept was put in theoretical circulation by the Dutch scholar Rudolf Steinmetz. The qualities that make it attractive for my purposes, however, were given to it by the distinguished German social theorist Ferdinand Tönnies, author of the still influential study, *Community and Society*. Tönnies turned to Steinmetz's concept *Soziographie* in his debate with Georg von Mayr over the significance of statistics in social research (see "Statistics and Sociography" from 1928). At issue was the question of whether statistics constituted a mere methodology, or a unique *form* (and I am deliberately emphasizing the Jamesonian resonance of the term) of social science. Tönnies took the latter view arguing that statistics, precisely by virtue of its powers of formalization, obliged statisticians to recognize as their object an entire country, its natural features, its population, the economy, political and military organization, indeed *any* social institution or practice whose statistical description might be useful to what Tönnies called "statesmen." To avoid merely retrieving an earlier meaning of the German word, *Statistik*, Tönnies substituted "sociography" as the name for the new kind of social science he thought statistics ought to become. The substitution stuck. In 1933, prior to his departure to the United States, Paul Lazarsfeld coauthored a text titled *Marienthal: a Sociography of an Unemployed Community*, a text that sought to deploy Tönnies's concept to comprehend the lived destitution of a working-class community in southern Austria. What enters the foreground of this study, as its focus might suggest, is a Left politics of the sort Lazarsfeld and his colleagues located in Engels's study, *The Condition of the Working Classes in England*, or in W. E. B. DuBois's *The Philadelphia Negro*.

Michel Foucault, in his lectures on "governmentality," has stressed the political and epistemological ironies of these developments, urging one to think long and hard about the redeployment of sociography once it is clear that even its productive complication of the domain of the social (its singularization of Durkheim's "total social fact") arises as the modern European state staggers to its feet out of the swarm of practices it authorizes itself to administer precisely through recourse to state-istics. Such precautions noted, two subsidiary issues bear emphasis. First, as Tönnies's situation makes clear, sociography emerged as a disciplinary displacement of another concept, that of statistics (*Statistik*) in its more strictly positivist character. It bears the mark and charge of this displacement even if it does so within the dominant logic of governmentality. As such, it stresses the need to think it in relation to that which it stands opposite. Second, unless we are to assume that the production of sociographic knowledge is referred to in what Tönnies means by the omnibus formulation "other relevant social institutions," it not only stands opposite a term it displaces, but it stands opposite the very discursive practice it names. In other words, Tönnies, in accentuating the tension between statistics and sociography, effectively writes the *writing*, the producing of sociography out of sociography. He does so perhaps inattentively or inadvertently but he does so, and it is Derrida, not Foucault, who has shown us how to read this symptom of the writing out of writing especially when the verb to write, *graphein*, is written into the very name of sociography. The implications of this for the concept and practice of governmentality must be left for another occasion.

Rather than dwelling here on the complications that might well up in the redeployment of sociography, let me suggest some ways we might begin to think about its immanent relation to what I have been calling disciplinary displacement. To approach this, one is tempted to make the obvious explicit, namely, the fact that sociography, as a term, as a morphemic composite, bears a direct resemblance to the term "historiography." Indeed, by virtue of this resemblance, sociography calls up, albeit in a different rhetorical gesture, the rich theoretical material that has emanated from the debates often simply summarized under the heading, "the critique of history." We are familiar, I think, with the way this critique has culminated in two powerful tendencies, that of subalternity (a pluralization of history that rewrites it from below, or at least at odds with a nationalist project) and that of textuality (a discursification of history that grasps it meta-historically, as a scriptural, not to say rhetorical, practice.) Less familiar, I think, is the emergence—and I will add instructive emergence—of the *distinction* between history and historiography.

Consulting historians on this matter, and my native informant is the distinguished Princeton historian Tony Grafton, one is pointed immediately to Jean Bodin, a sixteenth-century jurist and theorist of sovereignty who in *Method for the Easy Comprehension of History* not only calls for a methodological distinction between history and historiography, but also leans the two terms upon each other in such a way that the distinction threatens to give way at every moment. Precisely what he wants to secure—ready comprehension of what truly happened in the past—is mocked by the fact that access to the truth of the past is only one of two necessary outcomes of the collapse of the distinction between history and historiography. The other, obviously, is that truth cannot be disentangled from a certain accessible way of writing about it. This particular conundrum is one that Bodin inherits from two slightly earlier sources, the work of Francesco Patrizzi and Francis Badouin, both of whom, as Beatrice Reynolds has argued, were essentially recycling positions staked out by the Greek historian Polybius in his modestly titled, *The Histories*. To her credit, Reynolds simply sets aside the old quarrel about the Herodotian versus the Thucydian "origins" of history.

Now, before panic besets the reader, I am not proposing here to work my way through the 40 surviving "books" of Polybius's text. Instead, I wish to concentrate my reading on certain formulations contained in Book 12, where he mounts his critique of a rival, a certain Timaeus (not, by the way, Socrates' interlocutor in the eponymous dialogue).

> Nature has bestowed upon us two instruments of inquiry and research, hearing and sight. Of these sight is, according to Heraclitus, by far the truer; for the eyes are surer witnesses than the ears. And of those channels of learning Timaeus has chosen the pleasanter and the worse; for he entirely refrained from looking at things with his own eyes, and devoted

himself to learning by hearsay. But even the ear may be instructed in two ways, reading and answers to personal inquiries: and in the latter of these he was very indolent as I have shown. The reason of his preference for the other is easy to divine. Study of documents involves no danger or fatigue, if one only takes care to lodge in a city rich in such records, or to have a library in one's neighborhood. You may then investigate any question while reclining on your couch, and compare the mistakes of former historians without any fatigue to yourself. But personal investigation demands great exertion and expense; though it is exceedingly advantageous, and in fact is the very cornerstone of history. (Polybius 2012, 12.27)

Much of interest emerges here. Perhaps the nodal formulation occurs when Polybius proposes to think the subjectivity, the human sensorium of the historian, by contrasting the eye and the ear as he does fully committed to a certain "visualism." As he makes clear, the purpose of this hierarchy is to motivate a distinction between a certain ethnographic model of history—that is, the idea not simply of witnessing events that such witnessing might then construe as historical, that is, as "really" having happened, but also of traveling *to* events (Polybius was caught up in the grind between Rome and Athens, notably the campaign against Carthage)—and an approach that relied on what is translated here as "hearsay." In other words, what Timaeus is faulted for is his willingness to rely on second-hand accounts of events, that is, for erroneously trusting the ear over the eye. Not far from this charge is another, namely, that of laziness or indolence. Thus, woven into the account of the subjectivity of the historian is also something we might call a work ethic, the contention that the truth of history is in some important sense tied to the exertion, the amount of labor expended in producing it. Although the point is not observed, the properly "theoretical" character of witnessing a debate or ritual (see the discussion of Ian Rutherford's work in "Theory in Limbo" above) is worth noting in this discussion of historiographic method.

At this juncture one might reasonably protest that what Polybius means by history is indistinguishable from what we would be inclined to call investigative reporting, or journalism. While this certainly invites us to hear something different in Foucault's self-characterization as a "historian of the present," it also obscures something of crucial importance, namely, the fact that *The Histories*—and nowhere more so than in the critique of Timaeus—is filled with textual citations, with readings. Indeed, Reynolds, among others, has argued that Polybius is one of the earliest writers to deploy the words of others not as examples (Socrates' quotations of Homer) but as evidence. Thus, while this attention to the written words of others would certainly follow from his preference for the eye, it also complicates what is meant by both eye-witnessing and traveling. Moreover, when one listens to Polybius fault Timaeus for not consulting others, for treating himself as the sole source of information about events, one not only realizes that Polybius includes talking to people, other sources, within what he understands by witnessing, but that in doing so he also appears willing to rescind his preference for the eye over the ear. Presumably he is not "signing" with his sources, he is speaking and therefore listening to them. Indeed, this would appear to be what is meant in the citation by "personal inquiries."

To stay focused, let me simply note that these complications—the erection of a hierarchy that is self-overturning—find expression in Polybius' characterization of the work of writing down what really happened in a particular debate, battle or, as we have seen, text. While it is certainly true that Polybius attaches what he means by history to events, he grasps that comprehending and thus learning about and from such events is crucial. To that end, he puts in play a distinction between grammar and rhetoric of the sort later to be heard echoing in Paul de Man, arguing that comprehension depends on a precise balance between factual description and what is translated as "eloquence." Even while one might argue that he does not do what he says, it is clear that his accent on the eye finds expression in his concern with how history will be rendered historigraphically for the reader. In other words, how is it to be *written* such that the object of visual attention is not language, but events? A fascinating section of Book 12 devotes its many lines to berating Timaeus for the use of "abusive language," a methodological error decried as much for its falsity as for its conspicuous lack of "eloquence." Indeed, if it makes sense to see Polybius as a decisive precursor to Bodin, it is because the former not only differentiates between events and writing but also derives the truthful character of events *from* a style of writing crafted so as to at once mobilize and contain the power of language.

In Julian Franklin's study of Bodin he places immediate emphasis on the fact that Bodin links the easy comprehension of history to the possibility of whether one can believe reports about the past, thereby establishing a distinction between reports and the past. His question has a dual provenance: pedagogy and jurisprudence. That is, in both fields the question of examples—whether in the form of instructive or juridical precedents—has become, in the course of the sixteenth century, decisive. Why? Because at issue is authority, and in particular, the authority of sources. In pedagogical terms this means that instruction might be compromised if examples deployed to carry it out are found to be based on or derived from nonauthoritative sources, thus ruining the pedagogical value of historical examples in one blow. Although Franklin makes little of it, one can see plainly that Bodin's approach to historiographic method is based on an interdisciplinary supplement: history must prop itself on the law-like principle of precedent, and vice versa. At issue is the crafting of reports that are not only believable, but believable *because* they secure and consolidate the authority of the sources upon which they are based and which they in turn qualify to become. Although this discloses, yet again (if anachronistically), the repressed interdisciplinarity of disciplines, I want to make a different point. Namely, that what Bodin repeats in Polybius—however differently—is the move to distinguish writing and events in order to produce a method for simultaneously policing this very distinction and producing the truth, or authority, of past events. By the time we get to Leopold von Ranke (Hegel's sparring partner), known for the historiographic formulation, "the way things properly (*Eigentlich*) happened," this policing of the distinction between writing and events has allied with the "science of policing" (*Polizeiwissenschaft*) that Foucault sees as having spawned "governmentality," a development that effects a mutation in the domain of biopolitics that prepares the inscription of the concept itself. In this sense, the trajectory of historiography transverses directly that of sociography.

To clarify, if only in provisional terms, how this discussion bears on my point of departure—the resonant substitution of "society" for "company" in Eliot's novella—I will observe that what the stress on policing invites is recognition that Bodin and Polybius are both illustrations of how a distinction like that between history and historiography involves a set of assumptions—notably assumptions about how a certain kind of writing must collaborate in its subordination to the precarious authority of events when laying the cornerstone of history—assumptions that might be brought to bear on a distinction of the sort I am attempting to draw between sociography and, to invoke an as yet untheorized term, the social. Earlier, I stressed the distinction apparent in Tönnies's work between sociography and statistics, and while this is necessary it steers one away from the capacious sort of problem that has been teased out of Polybius and Bodin.

To get at this I observe that in contrast to the almost obsessive attention paid to the critique of history in the last 70 years, comparatively little attention—at least in the theoretical literature—has been paid to the critique of sociology, and this despite the fact that it has been every bit as vigorous. Indeed, in Stanley Aronowitz's preface to Alain Touraine's *The Return of the Actor* he situates the novelty of this "return" in relation to a century-long unfolding of sociological theory, from the structuralist displacement of Durkheimian functionalism to an antitheoreticist backlash that sought to reduce the social totality to a configuration of social problems upon which legions of pragmatic sociologists might set their sights. Although he makes no mention of "sociography" per se, Aronowitz shows clearly that C. Wright Mills in *The Sociological Imagination* is expressly concerned with the cozy, and therefore politically reactionary, relation between the *writing* of pragmatic sociology and the *discourse* of social policy and planning in the United States. Suggestively, Aronowitz presents the freshness of Touraine's project in terms of its commitment to "historicity," that is, the belief that, in what Marx called the "socialization of society," the sequence of actions undertaken by social actors, indeed the effect of an action upon a later one (the logic of consecution), is of decisive import to the sociological description of society.

Such an observation invites consideration of whether the theoretical questions raised earlier about history belong in some as yet unspecified way to the sociological problematic that Aronowitz has traced. Is the geographic emphasis on spatiality, on contiguity rather than continuity, relevant both to the distinction between sociography and society, and to the labor of sociological contextualization? Posed in this way the question may be too narrow, but its virtue is that it prompts one to think in a more sustained way about formulations of "the social" that may enable one to engage and elaborate such a question.

Consider, in this spirit, two texts: Jacques Donzelot's "An Antisociology" from 1972 and Gilles Deleuze's "The Rise of the Social" from 1977. Donzelot's text is a review of the first volume of *Capitalism and Schizophrenia, Anti-Oedipus* and Deleuze's text is (in the French edition) the postface, the afterward, of Donzelot's *The Policing of Families*, and while one might recognize here what Eleanor Kaufman has called "the logic of praise," stopping there would do an injustice to both texts, for in the chiasmus that delinks them there arise some provocative formulations about what Deleuze and Guattari call "the socius."

At the heart of Donzelot's exposition stands a contrast between Jean Baudrillard's *For a Critique of the Political Economy of the Sign and Anti-Oedipus*. At issue is the question of how to theorize beyond the Freudo-Marxist impasse, or put in the form of a question, how might a critical theory of society avoid trying to use the social institution of the family to mediate between desire and labor, consciousness and life? For Donzelot, Baudrillard resolves this first by destroying the central distinction in Marx between use and exchange, then by discovering the logic of exchange in a distinctly Lacanian account of desire. In other words, Baudrillard avoids the Freudo-Marxist impasse by setting it on its side and having Freud cannibalize Marx. Society here begins to look the way it looked to Barthes in his early critique of Lévi-Strauss, "Sociology and Socio-Logic," like a twisted topography of logics. Although impressive, Baudrillard's project does not yet embody Donzelot's titular standard of "an antisociology."

What then constitutes the properly "antisociological" character of *Anti-Oedipus*, and Donzelot was one of the first to recognize it, is the fact that it allows the Freudo-Marxist synthesis to cannibalize itself. Yes, Deleuze and

Guattari to some extent reverse Baudrillard's procedure, but they do so in the spirit of kicking out, setting aside, the supports upon which the synthesis rested. Specifically, they undermine the sociologically charged distinction between functionalism and structuralism, the Marxian distinction between the infrastructure and the superstructure and the tendency, again important within sociology, to downplay the state as the decisive social actor. In doing so they anticipate an important tenet of Bruno Latour's "actor network theory," where nonagents, and not merely institutional structures, can act. It is this impulse that Donzelot celebrates as antisociological, without however entertaining Tiqqun's conclusion that there is no society. Instead, what he emphasizes is that *Anti-Oedipus*, through the concepts of the molecular and the molar, earth and territoriality, and its machinic account of the State, produces a *writing* of the social, of "the socius," that grasps the social as an effect of a becoming, of a spatiotemporal unfolding, that exceeds it. As if predicting my interest in his text, Donzelot puts special emphasis on the concept of territoriality writing:

> This [Deleuze and Guattari's account of coding, earth and territory] is more than mere literature, for this entire description is supported by a critique of representation which comes to serve as the basis for their analysis of territoriality. Delimiting a territory, marking out its limits, taking account of its resources, attributing a Center to it, amounts to representing it, leaving the surface of the earth in order to enter into the sphere of representation. Maps and charts constitute territory. (Donzelot 1977, 41)

The closing reformulation of Korzybski's distinction between map and territory is meant to show that the constitution of territory is caught up in the dynamics of representation. For that reason, and to prevent social theory from becoming "mere literature," it is crucial that beneath or before the map and its territory one posits the earth, that is, the condition of possibility for the charting, the representing, of territory. Significantly, furled within this critique of representation are charts and maps, that is, the figures of a certain spatial, if not specifically geographic, rhetoric. Elaborated prior to Jameson's foray into "mapping," Donzelot's reading of *Anti-Oedipus* (read by Jameson as an aesthetic) reminds us, among other things, that the challenge mapping places before representation is not entirely clear. Is a map a representation of a cognition, or is it the *medium* of cognition (of subjective experience) in its understanding of a given totality?

The theoretical implications of such geographic figures are spelled out in Deleuze's postface to *The Policing of Families*. Early in the piece Deleuze describes Donzelot's achievement thus: "At first glance, it [Donzelot's analysis of the juvenile court] might be taken for nothing more than a miniaturized jurisdiction; but, as sometimes happens when one studies an engraving (*une gravure*) through a magnifying glass, Donzelot discovers a different organization of space, other ends, other personages" (Donzelot 1979, ix). Having preceded this figure of the engraving with the claim that, in the juvenile court, Donzelot has found an instance that "exemplifies *the* social *par excellence*" (ibid., ix) it seems hard to overlook the fact that spatiality and the social are here conjoined deliberately. In fact, on the following page Deleuze spells out the methodological significance of the engraving writing: "In sum Donzelot's method is genealogical, functional and strategic, which bespeaks his considerable debt to Michel Foucault and also to Robert Castel. But the way Donzelot establishes his lines, the way he sets them working in a scene or a portrait, drafting an entire strategical map of the social, give his book a profound originality" (ibid. xi). Deleuze then sets out in the remainder of the postface to trace the "*pure little lines of mutation*" (ibid., x) that bespeak the originality of Donzelot's approach to the social. All of these lines—beginning with the family's detachment from domesticity and culminating in its productive relation to the "flotation device" of psychoanalysis—operate to erase the sociological position of the family as the institution that decisively mediates the encounter between consciousness and life.

It seems clear here that Donzelot and Deleuze (with or without Guattari) place a very high premium indeed on the problematization of the family and its disciplinary role in sustaining sociology. Clearly resonant with unacknowledged strains in materialist feminism (Christine Delphy comes to mind), it seems especially pertinent to note that the social, or in *Anti-Oedipus* "the *socius*," emerges as a different way to think the object of sociology once that object has fallen into the void created by the implosion of the family as a structure of mediation. Significantly, this other object is figured insistently as a spatial practice, indeed in his closing paragraph Deleuze picks up his earlier definition of the social—it is "located at the intersection of all these little lines"—and states, "Donzelot has made a map of the social, its emergence and its expansion," suggesting that geography (or is it, as it will be three years hence, geology?) is again playing a decisive role in squaring off against sociology. The fact that engraving, tracing of lines, mapping are so insistently part of this challenge would strongly suggest that Deleuze has envisioned something like what I have called "sociography," that is, a concept through which to think the interval between society and its writing, its inscription on a recording surface that it both is and is not.[2] What kind of a context is this interval? Is it a "social" context? If it isn't how might it engage the work of cultural studies, including as part of that work, the offering of Theory?

This provocative if inadequate distillation of sociology's Western emergence (does Ibn Khaldun's *Muqaddimah* fit?), I would argue, places before us an important word: *socius*. This is a term that floats across the pages of both volumes of the coauthored *Capitalism and Schizophrenia* without in any direct way encountering the problematic of sociology as a discipline or, in *A Thousand Plateaus*, a "war machine."

Why place the accent of my reading on this term? Aside from the way it seems to designate for Deleuze precisely a way of thinking the social as inscribed in writing—what he calls "engraving" (both as print and as technique)—there is also the fact that when translated from the Latin, *socius* means "companion," that is, someone or something who keeps one company. Thus, when Adolphe Quetlet coined the term "*sociologie*," he was, in effect, producing a *logos*, a body of words, about the companion, or companionship. Perhaps then Eliot's usage has its warrant in a disciplinary mutation that was gradually coming to be felt in the course of the nineteenth century in Western Europe. Be that as it may, what interests me here is the way the figure of the companion, which has no necessary relation to either family or nation, might be used to displace the enduring figures of reflection, or correspondence, or homology that have emerged along the frontier between sociology and literary study to describe the relation between, in this case, writing and social events. In other words, what happens if we characterize this relation by saying that literature "accompanies" events whether social or historical, and that the fitting term or concept for designating this type of companionship, this relation is sociography? Although this has the tone of a rhetorical question I want to propose that it is not *merely*, or simply that. To clarify, consider the following passage from Maurice Blanchot's *The One Who Was Standing Apart from Me*, or in French, *Celui qui ne m'accompagnait pas*, more literally rendered as, "this one who had not accompanied me."

> "I mean: aren't you expecting company until then?" Yes, it was astonishing, and this time I could not overcome my astonishment, except to repeat: "Company? People?" –which led him to repeat, also: "People, people!" in a way that dismissed the conversation, that obliged me to consider that it would not resume except from a completely different source that I would now have to look at. [...] The fact that he had led me to break with everything, as though with the promise that now the field would be open to us, certainly represented the type of illusion for which I could not hold him responsible, but only myself. It is true that when I associated with company, he seemed to keep himself at a distance because of the company, and the need to put an end to an unfortunate duality, to avail myself of a single loyalty, a single truth, had little by

little pushed me gently, ineluctably—where I was. As a result, company was lacking but the distance remained, even though thee was noting left to make us feel it, and, what was more, it didn't even remain, for it was the only one of the forms of this open field which I alone was to roam. (Blanchot 1993, 10–11)

In Tom Pepper's remarkable reading of Blanchot's "account" (following here Derrida's proposed rendering of the French *récit*) beyond commenting upon the perplexities of "accompanying," he teases out a detail that helps one engage the opacity of passages such as the one cited. Specifically, in "Because the nights," from *Singularities* Pepper picks up on Blanchot's excursus on third-person pronouns (pages 24–25) and thus urges us to "hear" in every "he" ("he seemed to keep himself at a distance because of the company") what Benveniste insisted was the impersonal personal pronoun of the third person (see here as well my discussion of this in *Sounds*, "Tercer sonido"). This helps take up what I have called the text's opacity in two ways. First, because Blanchot's account was drafted in the context of the 1950s it invites a reading that stresses the phenomenological, even existential, theme of mortality. In other words, the "I" of the narration emerges in such a reading as a "being toward death," where what accompanies the narrator by standing apart, by keeping its distance, is death. From this angle, Blanchot is tracing the algorithm that structures the "hypogram" of Bergman's *The Seventh Seal* (death as tenacious adversary). Against this, attention to the impersonal pronouns sounds the more distinctly structuralist theme of language. What accompanies the narration by standing apart from it is, to again invoke Benveniste, the discourse, that is, the inhuman system through which, and by which, the human sounds its name. It is not for nothing that Blanchot's narrator comes upon or lapses into "silence" (another of Bergman's great themes). Again, this is not the voice of the god Nietzsche insisted we had murdered, or, if it is, then it calls for a more rigorous onto-theological reflection than there is space for here. Instead, the "silence" of *The One Who Was Standing Apart from Me*, feels like, works like, the event of narration coming upon the apparatus of enunciation that both enables and evades communication. It accompanies narration without entering its company.

Second, a reading of Blanchot's account that attends to the choreography of its pronouns and ties this choreography to narration and the death drive, the being unto death, is a reading that, in opening a certain psychoanalytical line of reflection, urges one to recognize the Lacanian unconscious, the one *structured* like a language, in the narrator's encounter with the one (*celui*) who stands apart. While it is true that Lacan was always more taken with Jakobson than Benveniste, his early interest in the "subject of enunciation" was in deep dialogue with one of his most provocative metapsychological formulae, namely, the proposition that the unconscious is outside. From this angle, Blanchot's narration is about itself, the act of narration, but from an outside that is not in any simple way authorial. Indeed, the death in question here can be usefully reworded as the "death of the author," or, and this may be attributing more guile to Foucault than his abiding curiosity about Blanchot warrants, the "author function," where function floats between occupation, element or variable. Regardless, this reading precisely in feeling the untimely presence of "others" in the impersonal, yet definite (the or this one) "one," urges that we consider the extent to which Blanchot is already here thinking a modality of community in miniature, as if to propose that insofar as human subjects, beings in common, can belong to any context whatever, it is because they are always already woven into a company that keeps its distance.

If one reads in this enunciation of apartness, not just the clichés of being alone together, but of propositions about what being in someone or something's company might involve in general, then perhaps we have the grounds upon which to begin rethinking the distinction and encounter between events and writing, grounds that are more generatively rendered by a sociography of companionship, then a sociology of reflection with its dubious appeal to cognition as a surface on or in which an "outside" or "before" leaves its mark.

Readers inclined to accept the proposition that company, companion and "the *socius*" speak to each other may still wonder whether Blanchot cares at all about the sociopolitical questions I feel woven into his margins. Fair enough. I, however, will be far from the first to have drawn attention to Blanchot's sustained interest in communism in postwar France. His probing engagements with Bataille and Dionys Mascolo (see Blanchot's review of *Le Communisme, revolution et communication ou la dialectique des valeurs et des besoins*, published in the wake of his expulsion from the French communist party) makes this hard to ignore, even if, as Jeffrey Mehlman has argued, Blanchot's "politics" had also embraced a certain right-wing anti-Semitism. That said, the challenge of getting Blanchot's attention to language and to politics interwoven is a difficult one, although his fascination with Mascolo's articulation of communism and communication suggests that the difficulty is surmountable. Consider, in this spirit, Blanchot's fragment (itself an important generic gesture), "Marx's Three Voices" ("Les Trois paroles de Marx," so "sayings" might also be invited) one of the nearly 30 pieces gathered in his homage to his impossible friend Georges Bataille, *Friendship*.

A scant half a dozen paragraphs, three of them numbered, and situated in the wake of 1968, the piece offers a reading of Marx and thus a theory of Marxism woven into the events of May. In the opening paragraph Blanchot enumerates the voices, but just as importantly situates his own work, indeed the work of "everyone who speaks or writes" (Blanchot 1997, 98), after them and specifically after their "juxtaposition" in Marx. Two of the voices are characterized as "direct." The first, a lengthy voice, is the voice of thought. A voice that leads readers to read Marx as a humanist, a historicist, an atheist, an antihumanist even a nihilist, all readings of this voice that are troubled by its lack of a guiding question. Blanchot does not say as much but one might risk the designation "speculation" as a name for this genre of speaking.

The second voice Blanchot immediately calls, "political" (ibid., 99). It is similarly direct, but brief. In fact, it is a voice so brief that it short-circuits "every voice" (ibid.) and does so by manifesting as a call, an abrupt decision to say nothing. In associating this voice with the events of May, Blanchot is keen to situate the political between a platform on which gather particular demands, and the event of the demand, a word in French that also invokes the questioning Heidegger links to piousness in his well-combed essay on technology. Not, I would suggest, to be confused with the voice of a manifesto, this exorbitant call might also be heard as the corrosive gnawing of the "small fry" active in Kafka's *Bau* (burrow, but also "base") that Marx reads into the historical logic of a capitalism implacably digging its own grave.

The third voice is the only one to be designated as "indirect" and Blanchot designates it as the voice of science. As if laying an invisible hand on Jameson in his response to Nancy Fraser, Blanchot justifies the attribution of "indirection" to the voice of science, by treating the third voice as, in effect, a third person, that is, the impersonal person who speaks without rest or intermission. Interminably. But, as if also repudiating Althusser's reading of Marx directly (and the science/ideology distinction comes into play in the final paragraph), Blanchot nuances this evocation of science by sensing in the "thirdness" of its voice, "a mode of theoretical thinking that overturns the very idea of science" (ibid., 99). That this vocal quality invokes the mode of narration called "indirect" seems deliberate in that it links the overturning of science to its manifestation as narrative. Because *Capital* indulges, cultivates, this voice it deserves to be called subversive, and although Blanchot lets the matter rest, one might well want to ponder how the impersonal and the indirect speak to one another in the space of politics.

Blanchot draws the following conclusion from his characterizations of the three voices: "the communist voice is always at once tacit and violent, political and scholarly, direct, indirect, total and fragmentary, lengthy and almost instantaneous," adding, and the wording here is important, "Marx does not live comfortably with this plurality of languages, which always collide and disarticulate themselves in him" (ibid., 100). Put differently, he is held apart from what, in a reflexive construction, disarticulates him. In this, Blanchot is clearly pressing beyond the oft-repeated proposition that Marxism arose at the confluence of three discourses—bourgeois economic theory, Hegelian philosophy and the workers' movement—to situate Marxism in a "juxtaposition" of voices that he could not live comfortably with (Marx ne vit pas commodément avec …). In his review of Mascolo he reads him as advocating that "communism is the process of the materialist search for communication" (op. cit., 93) and here situates this search squarely in Marx's relation-of-separation to and with his own voices (*paroles*). For that very reason readers of Blanchot are compelled to appreciate how deeply active the politics of communism is in the staging of the "*socius*" that unfolds across the pages of *The One Who*. The "account" does not reflect these politics. By the same token, the account does not ask that we confuse it with industrial action. Instead, as offered to my reading, the account calls out to and for Theory. Specifically, Theory that struggles to formulate the terms of the site of inscription where cognitions and maps interweave, where bases and superstructures communicate, where homologies operate, where culture and its study encounter each other. In short, the site of a sociography that does not exist, but could.

Notes

1   An instructive airing of this controversy occurs in Neil Lazarus's "Representations of the Intellectual in *Representations of the Intellectual*" from 2005. The piece begins by noting that there has been an "academic and intellectual struggle over the meaning of Said" (Lazarus 2005, 112) and goes on to showcase this struggle in an effort to split heirs with Tim Brennan about whether there is any truth to the broadly held consensus both here and abroad that Said's work was foundational for postcolonial studies. Much hangs on how one defines postcolonial studies, and while Brennan and Lazarus disagree over the status of Foucault in Said's work, they agree in casting postcolonial studies as an anti-Marxist development in contemporary critical theory, one that "breathe[d] the air" of then emergent Western globalization, in Lazarus's perplexing colloquialism. This respiratory reformulation of contextualization brushes the entire critique back against its own grain. Needless to say, these have not been the last words on this matter, especially since Said's death, but they are important ones just the same.
2   It is useful to recall that two years before writing the postface, and five years before writing *A Thousand Plateaus*, Deleuze and Guattari write their study of Kafka. Although this text has been much discussed (and criticized) for the concept of "minority" that it produces, insufficient thought has been given to the "literary sociological" implications of the study as a whole. Given what I am arguing here it cannot be insignificant that they follow up *Anti-Oedipus* with a reading of literature that seeks explicitly to re: work what I am here calling the work of contextualization.

Chapter 8

CONCLUSION: THEORY IS OUT THERE

Interviewed on the pages of the *Los Angeles Review of Books*, Gayatri Spivak—certainly regarded as one of the preeminent theorists of her generation (Benedict Anderson might place her on the A team of postcolonial studies)—had the following to say about Theory and its instruction:

> But I don't apply theory when I'm actually teaching in these schools [her summer literacy programs for girls in India] of teaching at Columbia. It's like I have been thrown into water and I am learning to swim. Every time I am still terrified before I go to class. But the thing is that afterward, when I think of the experience, I can see how theory is nuanced by what I have learned from the teaching and what part of the theory survives because theorizing is also a practice. This is something that we have not been able to teach our students at the top. So even if one doesn't know that one is theorizing, one is doing so. If you generalize and speak to groups, you are theorizing. In fact, it is impossible to think without theorizing in one way or the other. (Spivak 2016, n.p.)

I conclude with a reading of this response. It contains pretty much everything and exemplifies the point about the odd "when" of Theory. What matters is not really her (although Spivak is remarkable in her dogged attention to teaching), but these sentences. The "where" they take us to.

The terror Spivak admits to will remind readers of *Death of a Discipline* and its urging that we allow "literature to teach us that there are no certainties, that the process [of teaching literature] is open, and that it may be altogether salutary that it is so" (Spivak 2003, 26), followed later with, "the most important thing, as far as I can tell, is knowing how to let go" (ibid., 34). As forms of what Benjamin might wish to call "counsel" (*Rat*), such formulations are designed to remind those who teach, especially those who teach reading, that the practice is only effective when the uncertain prevails. Crucial to this effect is the displacement of instructive agency: the teacher does not teach, the literary text does. Although easy to skip, post baccalaureate education does include instruction in how to teach, instruction that escapes mentoring and thus marking it with inadequacy, because it is never offered by the teacher. Given the many years that Spivak has taught (no "ageism" intended), the notion that she approaches each class "terrified" seems arch, even melodramatic until one attends to the figure she invokes: being thrown into water in order to learn how to swim. Sink or swim. The urgency this gives to instruction has much to do with the consequences of failing to learn. And teaching? Simply learning by doing? One has to listen structurally, as Adorno might say, to realize that if *Death* and the *LARB* interview are indeed "communicating vessels," then teaching surfaces in this figure through a formulation that has been echoing since page xii of the "acknowledgments" of *Death*: "I hope this book will be read as the last gasp of a dying discipline" (op. cit., xii). In other words, as with drowning, the failure to teach, as it were, in the open, in the *epistēmē* without guarantees, without letting go, spells the death of a discipline, in this case, the discipline of comparative literature. Although it appears random, or conversely dictated by cliché, the figure of swimming without previously knowing how fits. It is perfectly ordinary, if, properly, urgent.

As a diligent, although unforgiving, reader of Freud, Spivak will also know what he has to say about dreams involving swimming in *The Interpretation of Dreams*, namely, that they put in play the wish, even the pathological compulsion to repeat what Freud's colleague Otto Rank called "the trauma of birth." If, and this is merely a sketch, if submersion evokes intrauterine, that is, emphatically pre-Oedipal existence, then "learning to swim" involves escaping submersion and embracing, however ambivalently (and terror is an acute form of ambivalence), separation. Frankly, such speculations are less interesting than is a consideration of how the issues they raise might facilitate our understanding of how swimming and teaching might bear on the question of Theory. After all, Spivak's response is directly pitched at a query, not entirely friendly, about the role of Theory in her summer teaching. Several details bear emphasis as all of them are "generalizable."

But first, a final speculative turn. In fact, a hinge. If, as was argued in "Theory in Limbo," Barthes's formulation about the "birth of the reader" is a proposition about Theory, then might not Spivak's figure of swimming, of knowing how "to let go" (from the side, the hand of one's teacher), be read as a birthing of the reader, and specifically about the chiasmus Theory/reading— reading/Theory? Feasible, but what *urges* one to think such follows from what she has to say about the when and where of Theory, the first proposition of which arises when insisting that she does not apply Theory when teaching literacy. More than a passing auto-ethnographic declaration, this formulation repeats the oft-heard but seldom listened to claim that Theory is not the application of what Said would call a "system" to some object of attention. Indeed, if Theory is read, if it arises in reading, this is because its substance is identical to that which it is imagined to be applied to. Theory is "out there" with everything else. It is not a foreign body, bounded by unequivocal signs of its distinctive "systematicity." It is not something in the possession of its devotees, that is, a cult of those uniquely qualified to apply it to others. Thus, Spivak does not apply Theory when offering literacy to a subaltern who cannot read (much less speak) because it is too challenging. She does not apply it period. This is the point of immediately connecting this teaching to her "teaching at Columbia." To rephrase the matter in the terms I have been repeating, the when of Theory is not before the site of application, just as its where is not at an elite Northern university, or as she later puts it, "at the top."

In fact, Spivak is quite specific, saying, "But the thing is that afterward, when I think of the experience [presumably of teaching], I can see how theory is nuanced by what I have learned from the teaching and what part of the theory survives, because theorizing is also a practice" (Spivak 2016, n.p.). That this culminates in what many readers will consider an article of Marxist faith, namely, that all things valued by humans, including Theory, derive their value from the practice that produces them, should not be overemphasized and this despite the fact that she herself repeats it. What "we have not been able to teach our students at the top" is the "afterwardsness" of Theory. Here, I am urging that we not simply read "afterward" as the narrateme denoting a subsequent moment of reflection in the plot. Instead, recalling that Jean Laplanche (another analyst with whom Spivak is conversant), dissatisfied with the translation of Freud's *Nachträglichkeit* as "delayed effect," or, in Lacanian French *après-coup*, proposed "afterwardsness" as the English expression by which to grasp the perplexing temporality of metalepsis, might we not sense this resonance in the avoidance of "later" in Spivak's formulation? My point in so darkly underscoring "afterward" is that it is this, namely, the fact that Theory assumes what shape it has, after it is no longer what it was that matters, and not simply in the sense of a dialectic of Theory and practice. But, to be clear, the when of Theory is not either before or after teaching. It is the reading that takes place *as* this teaching and is thus spread over a joint that is out of time. And where is this joint? The "classrooms" strewn between India and the United States? The site of the interview and its teleopoetic conditions of possibility? Wherever it is that it is read? This page?

The answer to such rhetorical questions is: all of the above, but if we need a different concept of "context" to respond to such a joint—I have proposed the sociographic—then we will also want to respond to the challenge laid down when Spivak adds: "So even if one doesn't know that one is theorizing, one is doing so. If you generalize and speak to groups, you are theorizing. In fact, it is impossible to think without theorizing one way or the other" (Spivak 2016, n.p.). Here, a different intertext looms. Specifically, the proposition that one theorizes without knowing it evokes directly Marx's citation of Jesus when the former proposes that although humans do not know they are commodity fetishists, they do what fetishists do, a formulation that allowed Althusser to hear Pascal's "embodiment" of belief (kneel and ye shall believe) in Marx's theory of alienation. Also resonant with Gramsci's proposition that all people are intellectuals (invoked explicitly in the interview), Spivak's formulation invites the public "generalization," that Theory takes place where one least expects it, or at least where one is unaware that one is doing it. And where is that?

Two options present themselves. On the one hand, doing something without knowing it invites association with what Benjamin attempts to capture in his essay on Leskov ("The Storyteller: Observations on the Work of Nikolai Leskov") when he presents artisanal practice as a locus for the distracted formation of new habits. A similar point is made in "The Work of Art in the Age of its Technological Reproducibility," but in both cases what emerges around doing-without-knowing is the generativity of contingency, the notion that out of the essential ephemerality of an activity arises an unintended and certainly unforeseen effect or consequence. This is Theory?

On the other hand, inquiry into the where of a doing-without-knowing leads quickly past "doing something unconsciously," to being "done by the Unconscious," where the context of Theory fans out to include features that arise on "the other scene," that cryptic fold where unknown knowns fester seeking opportunity. From this angle, Theory is structured like an Unconscious, it happens as part of what stages any act engaged in by any teacher whatsoever. Which part? The thinking part. That is thinking insofar as it engages Theory one way or "the other." At one level, plainly enough, Spivak is here complicating the lives of those—like Knapp and Benn Michaels—who want to insist that lacking any consequences for thought Theory is an option scholars in the Humanities ought to avoid. Although nuanced, this is a version of the proposition that ignorance of Theory *is* a good excuse, and Spivak, never especially impressed by the against Theory chorus, is here insisting that if the members of the chorus are thinking at all, they are committed to Theory, one way or another. Actually not, "another," but *the* other. What of *this* other that Theory can be?

Something very quiet, almost still, happens here. The formulation "one way or another" operates a bit like "half a dozen of one, six of another," where its antemetabolic effect is to fold "half a dozen" and "six" on top of each other cancelling their difference. To invoke Spivak's teacher, de Man, the entire expression might be rephrased as "what's the difference?" By contrast, "*the* other," through the device of the definite article, keeps "way" from saturating its context. This suggests that there is at least one sense in which thinking is not a *way* of theorizing. Let's call it "the other" of ways of thinking, the thinking that is not a way of theorizing, where the accent falls on the importance of not confusing Theory with method, as in "way," or what lies after the path (*meta hodos*). In effect, the precision of this formulation operates as a restatement of the critique of application that in its own way invokes the figure of a recipe, that is, ingredients, measurements and preparations or procedures. While this is doubtless important, the author of *In Other Worlds* or *Other Asias* is likely frying other fish than merely that of method.

Other theorizing that thinking cannot escape except by becoming one way among others invites two types of elaboration: one that stresses Theory's commitment to the demands of the other and another that emphasizes Theory's constitutive relation to the other. In the first of these, Spivak, precisely in her restless relation to Eurocentrism, has insistently expressed the need—at once political and theoretical—to take responsibility for unthinking the other. Against nativists who act as though they can simply think otherwise, she has patiently sought to remind them that "thinking" is so freighted with the vestiges of Eurocentricity, it can hardly be trusted to deliver on its promise to engage the other on "its own" terms. By the same token, against Western and Northern cosmopolitans, she has illustrated time and again that humanist or even antihumanist goodwill can never get out in front of its sameness, a sameness in which the other survives only as diversity, not difference. Even if one remains unconvinced by the role she assigned to "deconstruction" in her engagement with the subaltern historians, what is hard to ignore is her nagging sense of the crushing gravity of the problem posed for thought by the other. If one theorizes, one way or the other by thinking, then Theory here designates a practice that is fully entangled in this problem. Not the other "as a problem," but thought as problematized by the demands of the other. How does reading persist under such circumstances? The "hermeneutic circle" formulated by Schleiermacher and radicalized by Heidegger is not so easily outmaneuvered. And then what?

The matter at hand is not simply prepositional. The difference between "for" (the other as a problem *for* thought) and "in" (the other as a problem *in* thought), while gesturing, perhaps even pointing, in productive directions leaves too much unstated. Especially as regards Theory. If one thinks in this context of recent work by Nahum Chandler (*X-The Problem of the Negro as a Problem for Thought*), Achille Mbembe (*Critique of Black Reason*) and the line of flight sketched by Lewis Gordon (in "Theory in Black: Teleological Suspensions in the Philosophy of Culture"), the scale of what calls for saying forces itself upon us. Since the precise status of Theory remains underdeveloped in these meditations—Chandler, for example, will rediscover the all too familiar theory/practice dyad in the wake of his spadework—lingering more patiently over Spivak's remark feels appropriate. If one is theorizing, even unconsciously (i.e., under its orders), while thinking one way *or* the other, then perhaps Theory itself is what operates as the other in a thinking whose guiding assumptions, even upon rational reconstruction, cannot be grasped as method. Gordon, in drawing attention to what is Black in Theory, is making a related insight. Stated in general terms, Spivak's "or the other," posits, even if unconsciously, the insight that if one is theorizing whenever one is thinking, then Theory marks an alterity *in* thinking that, as any astute deconstructionist would know, leaves its mark within Theory in turn. In her remarks, Spivak invites us to identify this mark with the when and where of teaching, referencing less the claims of practice than the distinctive effect of reading while generalizing in public. Earlier, indeed throughout this text, I have been condensing the challenge of this re-marking into the chiasmus of reading and Theory, and, if instead of saying "teaching" I have been saying "offering," it has been with an eye toward the value of sacrifice in comprehending how reading brings the reader into being as one who is ensnarled in and with "the" other. The offing of the author as a gambit to open oneself to the sociographic dispersion of the text is precisely what the offering of Theory needs to concern itself with. In this one sacrifices Theory properly.

Some (gross) generalizations in the guise of a conclusion.

Theory is not a canon. Even if proper names congregate in its presence these are not what matter except, perhaps, for the purposes of professional advancement, and the profession of professing (literature or anything else within the humanities and critical social sciences) is nearing its end. Put differently, a theorist is not an author. But nor is the theorist an adjective (Foucauldian, Fanonian, etc.). If Theory manifests when a text is offered to a reading, then a theorist may not even be a reader.

Theory is not (a) method. If by method one refers to a way of conducting oneself, a way of proceeding that formally vanishes into the clarity of results, in effect, a pure means to an end, then Theory is not a way. It is the other of way. As Derrida argued in his reading of Spinoza there may well be no offering without method, without steps (still or otherwise), but these do not arrive at Theory. Theory is already taking place.

Theory is neither not practice, nor a practice. It cannot evade the political, but nor need it conform to the forms within which the political is practiced in any empirically given time or place. Theory is the other of the way of thinking, but this other is non-denominational. It must be declared for. Reading weaves contexts and the "bias," the "slant" that arises is there to be owned. Theory may be (in) Black, but Black is not immediately "the Black

Radical Tradition" (chez Fred Moten). It leans left when read as leaning left. Put differently, Theory is not a compensation for politics. It is not Western in *that* sense (chez Merleau-Ponty and Perry Anderson).

Theory is not an application. It does not present itself as doctrine that can be used to guide research whether in the form of textual commentary, cultural analysis or the testing of hypotheses. The reading that Theory is arises from within that which it attends to, including reading itself. It is already out there with "things," not brought to them from some before.

Theory is not—Amanda Anderson's brilliant work notwithstanding—an argument. It cannot be extracted from things as a list of propositions, a list that a lame, thus Oedipal reading, seeks specifically to parse (from "part of an oration"). If much that passes for Theory is deemed by the impatient or uncharitable as "illogical" or "irrational," this may have to do with the fact that Theory is *not* an argument. This is not when Theory is happening. A reading may, to invoke a term put to work by de Certeau, effect "moves" (*coups*, blows). These are legible. But they cannot be represented in the grammatical algebra of Ss and Ps.

Theory is not a movement or tendency, in short, an "ism." Feminism is not Theory. Marxism is not Theory. Movements are abstractions, and not even concrete ones at that. To be sure, and the clarification matters, Feminism (French, Western, Post-) is *not* atheoretical. It is a profound and troubling form of reading, of thinking. It thus exhibits a rapport with Theory, one way or the other. But, it cannot be offered as Theory without putting to work concepts like canon, authors, arguments and so on, all features of what partisans and non-partisans alike would call *a* theory.

Theory is not from some places rather than others. Theory is out there. The offering that triggers it happens out there among the objects read. But Theory is, like the fugitive "truth" chased seasonally by Scully and Mulder, also *out* there. Alien to an enduring set of scholarly and academic (not the same) protocols but also "mad" or, at a minimum, deeply if not totally different. When I say my cat is "out there," he is with Theory. But, it turns out, so are most things, whether object, entities or subjects. When, in *Other Asias* Spivak writes of bringing Theory "to the Plains," she is, like Heidegger according to Derrida, falling behind the rigor of her own thought. Theory manifests when and wherever problems are stumbled upon, encountered and reading ensues. Ignorance of the other problems is no excuse.

Theory may also not be diplomacy. In "The Work of Theory: Thinking across Traditions," Banerjee, Nigam and Pandey sensibly propose that because Theory matters to so many diverse fields—and they discovered this in a properly pedagogical setting—it is in a position to isolate and negotiate contradictions and impasses. In doing so Theory grows in both insight and impact. While I embrace the notion that this enables Theory to form in "strange places and times" (Bannerjee, Nigam and Pandey 2016, 50), there is a remedial almost ambassadorial flavor to this offering that disappoints. Besides, the matter of when and where the relevant strangeness arises is left underdeveloped.

Above all Theory is not a list of generalizations gross or otherwise. It is metalepsis without the error, that is, it is not an effect "taken or mistaken for" a cause. It is the cause effect. When Althusser writes in part one of *Reading Capital*: "This then is the guilt (*coupable*, an evocation of Bataille and thus sacrifice) of our philosophical reading of *Capital*: it [our reading] reads Marx according to the rules of a reading in which he gave us a brilliant lesson in his own reading of classical political economy" (Althusser 1979, 30), he tenaciously traces through the when and where of "reading" the cause effect of Theory. Theory derives from the reading caused by learning the lesson in reading offered by what is read. Presciently, Althusser takes responsibility for his "guilt" over what is sacrificed (*la faute*, the transgression, offence) in or through his reading. He and Spivak are thus following, playing out, the same lesson.

But so what? Ultimately, if estranging "our" sense of what Theory is, has value it is because, as I have insisted throughout, it bears on the work of professing, work many readers will know has entered, through the portal of austerity, the wasteland of precarity. It grows, more aggressively for some, but it grows. In general. If we want to know how to handle Theory under such circumstances—should diminishing resources be committed to its offering; when and where should it be offered; by whom and for whom should it be offered?—then certainly we want to have a guess at what it is, what we are trying to get a handle on. If Spivak is correct that whenever we generalize in public we are "doing" Theory, then is the matter effectively moot, or is the point that some effort needs to be made to legitimize an offering of Theory that orders itself in the name of its ubiquity, its ambient insistence? As the term "ambient" might suggest, a defining aspect of its legitimation as an offering appeals to what we have long called, the humanities. Offering Theory is part of producing the humanities in their critical (urgent and posthumanist) iteration, and Theory is best handled here in fostering through collective exercise the work of reading. In effect, we humanists (anywhere on the planet) need to retrace our steps. If at some point we stopped "doing literature" (or, "whatever") to "do Theory," we need now to stop doing Theory, at least the Theory thought *not* be one's "primary" object of attention, and cultivate literacy (as before, whether "critical" or "transnational"). Offering Theory is developing the passion for sacrificing texts to reading, and this is the answer to the burning administrative query: why? As a 25-year-old Benjamin gnomically asserted: perception itself is impossible without reading (Benjamin 1996, 93). Skip the market. Who will animate it in the absence of perception?

Of the three Rs, only one actually starts with the letter. Reading. It is the only offering. It is Theory.

REFERENCES

Adorno, Theodor. 1973. *The Jargon of Authenticity*. Trans. Kurt Tarnowski and Frederic Will. Evanston, IL: Northwestern University Press.
———. 1981. *Prisms*. Trans. Samuel and Shierry Weber. Cambridge, MA: Cambridge University Press.
———. 1994. *Quasi una Fantasia: Essays on Modern Music*. Trans. Rodney Livingston. London: Verso.
Agamben, Giorgio. 1998. *Homo Sacer: Sovereign Power and Bare Life*. Trans. Daniel Heller-Roazen. Stanford, CA: Stanford University Press.
Ahmed, Sarah. 2000. *Strange Encounters: Embodied Others in Post-Coloniality*. London: Routledge.
Althusser, Louis. 1970. *For Marx*. Trans. Ben Brewster. New York: Vintage.
———. 1971. *Lenin and Philosophy and Other Essays*. Trans. Ben Brewster. New York: Monthly Review Press.
———. 1997. "The Only Materialist Tradition, Part 1: Spinoza," in *The New Spinoza*, ed. Warren Montag and Ted Stolze. Minneapolis: University of Minnesota Press.
———. 2006. *Philosophy of the Encounter: Later Writings 1978–87*. Trans. François Matheron et al. London: Verso.
Althusser, Louis, and Etienne Balibar. 1979. *Reading Capital*. Trans. Ben Brewster. London: Verso.
Anderson, Amanda. 2006. *The Way We Argue Now: A Study in the Cultures of Theory*. Princeton, NJ: Princeton University Press.
Anderson, Benedict. 1991. *Imagined Communities*. London: Verso.
Armstrong, Timothy. (ed.). 1992. *Michel Foucault Philosopher*. New York: Routledge.
Aronowitz, Stanley. 1981. *The Crisis in Historical Materialism: Class, Politics and Culture in Marxist Theory*. New York: Praeger.
———. 1988. "Forward." *The Return of the Actor: Social Theory in Postindustrial Society* by Alain Touraine. Minneapolis: University of Minnesota Press.
Austin, J. L. 1975. *How to Do Things with Words*. Ed. J. O. Urmson and Marina Sbisà. Cambridge, MA: Harvard University Press.
Badiou, Alain. 2010. *Cinema*. Ed. Antoine de Baecque and trans. Susan Spitzer. Cambridge, MA: Polity Press.
———. 2014. "People Cling to Identities … It Is a World Opposed to the Encounter," an interview with Clément Petitjean. Trans. David Broder. Verso Blog, April 14, 2014. www.versobooks.com. Accessed summer 2016.
Bannerjee, Prathama, Aditya Nigam and Rakesh Pandey. 2016. "The Work of Theory: Thinking Across Traditions." *Economic and Political Weekly* 51:37: 42–50.
Barthes, Roland. 1975. *The Pleasure of the Text*. Trans. Richard Howard. New York: Hill and Wang.

———. 1985. *The Responsibility of Forms: Critical Essays on Music, Art and Representation*. Trans. Richard Howard. New York: Hill and Wang.
———. 1986. *The Rustle of Language*. Trans. Richard Howard. New York: Hill and Wang.
———. 2015. *"A Very Fine Gift" and Other Writings on Theory*. Ed. and trans. Chris Turner. London: Seagull.
Beckett, Samuel. 1958. *Three Novels*. Trans. Samuel Beckett and Patrick Bowles. New York: Grove Press.
———. 1967. *Stories and Texts for Nothing*. Trans. Samuel Beckett and Richard Seaver. New York: Grove Press.
Benjamin, Walter. 1996. *Walter Benjamin Selected Writings Volume One 1913–1926*. Ed. Marcus Bullock and Michael Jennings. Cambridge, MA: Harvard University Press.
Bhabha, Homi (ed.) 1990. *Nation and Narration*. London: Routledge.
Blanchot, Maurice. 1993. *The One Who Was Standing Apart from Me*. Trans. Lydia Davis. New York: Station Hill Press.
———. 1997. *Friendship*. Trans. Elizabeth Rottenberg. Stanford, CA: Stanford University Press.
Bloch, Marc. 1961. *Feudal Society*. Trans. L. A. Manyon. Chicago, IL: University of Chicago Press.
Brennan, Timothy. 2000. "The Illusion of a Future: *Orientalism* as Traveling Theory." *Critical Inquiry* 26:3 (Spring): 558–83.
Brett, George, Gary Thomas and Elizabeth Wood. 1994. *Queering the Pitch: The New Gay and Lesbian Musicology*. London: Routledge.
Buchanan, James M. 1970. *Academia in Anarchy: An Economic Diagnosis*. New York: Basic.
Burchell, Graham et al. (eds.). 1991. *The Foucault Effect: Essays in Governmentality*. Chicago: University of Chicago Press.
Casarino, Cesare and Antonio Negri. 2008. *In Praise of the Common: A Conversation on Philosophy and Politics*. Ed. and trans. Cesare Casarino. Minneapolis: University of Minnesota Press.
Chandler, Nahum. 2014. *X The Problem of the Negro as a Problem for Thought*. New York: Fordham University Press.
De Certeau, Michel. 1984. *The Practice of Everyday Life*. Trans. Steven Rendall. Berkeley: University of California Press.
Cole, Andrew. 2014. *The Birth of Theory*. Chicago, IL: University of Chicago Press.
De Man, Paul. 1986. *The Resistance to Theory*. Minneapolis: University of Minnesota Press.
Deleuze, Gilles. 1979. "The Rise of the Social," in *The Policing of Families*. Trans. Robert Hurley. New York: Pantheon.
———. 1992. *Expressionism in Philosophy: Spinoza*. Trans. Martin Joughin. New York: Zone Books.
———. 1995. *Negotiations 1972–1990*. Trans. Martin Joughin. New York: Columbia University Press.
———. 2005. *Pure Immanence: Essays on a Life*. Trans. Ann Boyman. New York: Zone Books.
Derrida, Jacques. 1972. *Speech and Phenomena: And Other Essays on Husserl's Theory of Signs*. Trans. David Allison. Evanston: Northwestern University Press.
———. 1976. *Of Grammatology*. Trans. Gayatri Spivak. Baltimore, MD: Johns Hopkins University Press.
———. 1981–82. "Language and the Discourse on Method," University of California-Irvine, Special Collections, MS-C001 Folder 16: 13–14.

———. 1982. "Signature, Event, Context," in *Margins of Philosophy*. Trans. Alan Bass. Chicago, IL: University of Chicago Press.
———. 1991. *Cinders*. Trans. Ned Lukacher. Lincoln: Nebraska University Press.
———. 1994. *Specters of Marx: The Work of Mourning and the New International*. Trans. Peggy Kamuf. New York: Routledge.
———. 2001. "The Future of the Profession or the University without Conditions (Thanks to the 'Humanities,' What *Could Take Place* Tomorrow)," in *Jacques Derrida and the Humanities: A Critical Reader*. Ed. Tom Cohen. Cambridge: Cambridge University Press, pp. 24–57.
———. 2001. *The Work of Mourning*. Trans. Pascale-Anne Brault and Michael Naas. Chicago, IL: University of Chicago Press.
De Villiers, Nicholas. 2012. *Opacity and the Closet: Queer Tactics in Foucault, Barthes and Warhol*. Minneapolis: University of Minnesota Press.
Donzelot, Jacques. 1977. "An Antisociology." *Semiotext(e)* 2:3: 27–44.
Donzelot, Jacques. 1979. *The Policing of Families*. Trans. Robert Hurley. New York: Pantheon Books.
Du Bois, W. E. B. 1996. *The Philadelphia Negro: A Social Study*. Philadelphia: University of Pennsylvania Press.
Eagleton, Terry. 2003. *After Theory*. New York: Basic Books.
———. 2018. *Radical Sacrifice*. New Haven, CT: Yale University Press.
Eagleton, Terry et al. 1990. *Nationalism, Colonialism and Literature*. Minneapolis: University of Minnesota Press.
Eliot, George. 1999. *The Lifted Veil and Brother Jacob*. Ed. Helen Small. Oxford: Oxford University Press.
Fanon, Frantz. 1967. *Black Skin, White Masks*. Trans. Charles Lam Markmann. New York: Grove Press.
Felski, Rita (ed.). 2010. "New Sociologies of Literature," a special issue of *New Literary History* 41:2.
Fitch, Brian. 1988. *Beckett and Babel: An Investigation into the Status of the Bilingual Work*. Toronto: University of Toronto Press.
Foucault, Michel. 1969. "Untitled." *Revue de métaphysique et de morale* 74:2: 131–6.
———.1980. *Power/Knowledge: Selected Interviews and Other Writings 1972–1977*. Ed. Colin Gordon. New York: Pantheon Books.
———. 1981. "The Order of Discourse," in *Untying the Text: A Post-Structuralist Reader*. Ed. Robert Young. London: Routledge, Kegan, Paul.
———. 1984. *The Foucault Reader*. Ed. Paul Rabinow. New York: Pantheon Books.
———. 1998. *Michel Foucault: Aesthetics, Method, and Epistemology*. Ed. James Faubion. Trans. Robert Hurley et al. New York: New Press.
———. 2015. *Language, Madness, Desire: On Literature*. Ed. Philippe Artières et al. Trans. Robert Bonono. Minneapolis: University of Minnesota Press.
———. 2016. *Speech Begins after Death: A Conversation with Claude Bonnefoy*. Ed. Philippe Artières. Trans. Robert Bonono. Minneapolis: University of Minnesota Press.
Franklin, Julian. 1963. *Jean Bodin and the Sixteenth Century Revolution in the Methodology of Law and History*. New York: Columbia University Press.
Fraser, Nancy. 1990. "Rethinking the Public Sphere: A Contribution to the Critique of Actually Existing Democracy." *Social Text* 25/26: 56–80.
Freud, Sigmund. 1977. *The Origins of Psychoanalysis*. Ed. Marie Bonaparte et al. Trans. Eric Mosbacher and James Strachey. New York: Basic Books.

———. 2001. *Standard Edition of the Complete Psychoanalytical Works*, vols. 3, 6, 14, and 20–22. Ed. and trans. James Strachey. London: Vintage.
Gordon, Lewis. 2010. "Theory in Black: Theological Suspensions in the Philosophy of Culture." *Qui Parle* 18:2: 193–214.
Grossberg, Lawrence and Cary Nelson (eds.). 1988. *Marxism and the Interpretation of Culture*. Urbana Champagne: University of Illinois Press
Habermas, Jürgen. 1971. *Knowledge and Human Interests*. Trans. Jeremy Shapiro. Boston, MA: Beacon.
———. 1989. *The Structural Transformation of the Public Sphere: An Inquiry into a Category of Bourgeois Society*. Trans. Thomas Burger. Cambridge, MA: MIT Press.
Hoggart, Richard. 1970. "Schools of English and Contemporary Society," in *Speaking to Others*. New York: Oxford University Press, pp. 246–59.
Huffer, Lynne. 2010. *Mad for Foucault: Rethinking the Foundations of Queer Theory*. New York: Columbia University Press.
Hulme, T. E. 1924. "Cinders," in *Speculations: Essays on Humanism and the Philosophy of Art*. Ed. Herbert Read. New York: Harcourt Brace.
Iser, Wolfgang. 2006. *How to do Theory*. Oxford: Blackwell.
Jameson, Fredric. 1991. *Postmodernism or, the Cultural Logic of Late Capitalism*. London: Verso.
———. 1995. *The Geopolitical Aesthetic: Cinema and Space in the World System*. Bloomington: Indiana University Press.
———. 2016. *Raymond Chandler: The Detections of Totality*. London: Verso.
Kermode, Frank. 1979. "The Institutional Control of Interpretation." *Salmagundi* 43: 72–86.
Kim Cohen, Seth. 2016. *Against Ambience: and Other Essays*. London: Bloomsbury.
Kramer, Lawrence. 2019. *The Hum of the World: A Philosophy of Listening*. Berkeley: University of California Press.
Kristeva, Julia. 1986. *The Kristeva Reader*. Ed. Toril Moi. New York: Columbia University Press.
———. 1991. *Strangers to Ourselves*. Trans. Leon Roudiez. New York: Columbia University Press.
———. 1993. *Nations without Nationalism*. Trans. Leon Roudiez. New York: Columbia University Press.
———. 1995. "*Bulgarie, ma souffrance*." *L'Infini* (Fall): 42–52.
———. 1996a. *Julia Kristeva: Interviews*. Ed. Ross Mitchell Guberman. New York: Columbia University Press.
———. 1996b. "*Julia Kristeva: L'Urgence de la révolte*." *Magazine littéraire* 344 (June): 104–10.
Lacan, Jacques. 1988. *The Ego in Freud's Theory and in the Technique of Psychoanalysis*. Trans. Sylvana Tomaselli. New York: Norton.
Lacouture, Jean. 1970. "Le cours inaugural de M. Michel Foucault: Eloge du discours interdit." *Le Monde* (4 decembre): 8.
Lazarsfeld, Paul, and Marie Jahoda. 1972. *Marienthal: The Sociography of an Impoverished Community*. London: Tavistock.
Lazarus, Neil. 2005. "Representations of the Intellectual in *Representations of the Intellectual*." *Research in African Literatures* 36:3 (Autumn): 112–23.
Leader, Darian. 2018. *Hands*. London: Penguin.
Leroi-Gourhan, André. 1993. *Gesture and Speech*. Trans. Anna Bostock Berger. Cambridge, MA: MIT Press.
Lévi-Strauss, Claude, and Didier Eribon. 1991. *Conversations with Claude Lévi-Strauss*. Trans. Paula Wissing. Chicago, IL: University of Chicago Press.

Lewis, George E. 2004. "Improvised Music after 1950: Afrological and Eurological Perspectives," in *Audio Culture: Readings in Modern Music*. Ed. Christoph Cox and Daniel Warner. New York: Continuum.
Macherey, Pierre. 2011. *Hegel or Spinoza*. Trans. Susan Ruddick. Minneapolis: University of Minnesota Press.
Marley, Bob and the Wailers. "Jamming," Track 6 on *Exodus*, Island Records, 1977, LP record.
Mbembe, Achille. 2017. *The Critique of Black Reason*. Trans. Laurent Dubois. Durham, NC: Duke University Press.
McGinn, Colin. 2015. *Prehension: The Hand and the Emergence of Humanity*. Cambridge, MA: MIT Press.
Mehlman, Jeffrey. 1983. *Legacies: Of Anti-Semitism in France*. Minneapolis: University of Minnesota Press.
Melas, Natalie. 2007. *All the Difference in the World: Postcoloniality and the Ends of Comparison*. Stanford, CA: Stanford University Press.
Memmi, Albert. 1971. *New York Times Book Review* (March 14): 5 and 20.
Moten, Fred. 2003. *In the Break: The Aesthetics of the Black Radical Tradition*. Minneapolis: University of Minnesota Press.
Mowitt, John. 1989. "The Essay as Instance of the Social Character of Private Experience." *Prose Studies* 12:3: 274–84.
———. 1992. *Text: The Genealogy of an Antidisciplinary Object*. Durham, NC: Duke University Press.
———. 2013. *Radio: Essays in Bad Reception*. Berkeley: University of California Press.
Nancy, Jean-Luc. 1991. "The Unsacrificeable." Trans. Richard Livingston. *Yale French Studies* 79: 20–38.
———. 2007. *Listening*. Trans. Charlotte Mandell. New York: Fordham University Press.
Nationalism, Colonialism and Literature. 1990. Ed. Seamus Deane. Minneapolis: University of Minnesota Press.
Negri, Antonio. 1991. *The Savage Anomaly: The Power of Spinoza's Metaphysics and Politics*. Trans. Michael Hardt. Minneapolis: University of Minnesota Press.
Nietzsche, Friedrich. 2014. *Beyond Good and Evil: Prelude to a Philosophy of the Future*. Trans. Adrian Del Caro. Stanford, CA: Stanford University Press.
———. 2010. *Human All Too Human (I)*. Trans. Gary Handwerk. Stanford, CA: Stanford UP.
Peirce, Charles Sanders. 1894. "Spinoza's *Ethic*." *The Nation* 59: 1532, 344–45.
———. 1982. *The Writings of Charles Sanders Peirce: A Chronological Edition*, vol. 6. Ed. Max Frisch and Edward Moore. Bloomington: University of Indiana Press.
Pepper, Thomas. 1997. *Singularities: Extremes of Theory in the Twentieth Century*. Cambridge: Cambridge University Press.
Polybius. 2012. *The Histories* [Book XII]. Ed. and trans. S. Douglas Olson. Cambridge, MA: Harvard University Press.
Reynolds, Beatrice. 1945. "Introduction," in *Method for the Easy Comprehension of History* by Jean Bodin. New York: Columbia University Press.
Roudinesco, Elisabeth. 1990. *Jacques Lacan & Co: A History of Psychoanalysis in France 1925–85*. Trans. Jeffrey Mehlman. Chicago, IL: University of Chicago Press.
Rouvroy, Antoinette, and Bernard Stiegler. 2016. "The Digital Regime of Truth: From Algorithmic Governmentality to the New Rule of Law." Trans. Anaïs Nony and Benoît Dillet. *La Deleuziana* 3: 1–27.
Rutherford, Ian. 2013. *State Pilgrims and Sacred Observers in Ancient Greece: A Study of Theōriā and Theōroi*. Cambridge: Cambridge University Press.

Said, Edward. 1991. *The World, the Text and the Critic*. London: Vintage.
———. 1994. *Culture and Imperialism*. New York: Vintage.
———. 2000. *Reflections on Exile: and Other Essays*. Cambridge, MA: Harvard University Press.
Scott, David. 2017. *Stuart Hall's Voice: Intimations of an Ethics of Receptive Generosity*. Durham, NC: Duke University Press.
Spinoza, Baruch. 1951. *The Chief Works of Benedict de Spinoza*. Trans. R. H. M. Elwes. New York: Dover.
———. 1963. *Earlier Philosophical Writings*. Trans. Frank Hayes. New York: Bobbs-Merrill.
Spivak, Gayatri C. 1999. *The Critique of Postcolonial Reason: A History of the Vanishing Present*. Cambridge, MA: Cambridge University Press.
———. 2003. *The Death of a Discipline*. New York: Columbia University Press.
———. 2008. *Other Asias*. Malden, MA: Blackwell.
———. (with Steve Paulson). 2016. "Critical Itinerary: An Interview with Gayatri Spivak," in *Los Angeles Review of Books* (July 29, 2016).
Tiqqun. 2010. *An Introduction to Civil War*. Trans. Alexander Galloway and Jason Smith. Cambridge, MA: MIT Press.
Tönnies, Ferdinand. 1929. "Statistik und Soziographie," *Allgemeines Statistisches Archiv 18*. Ed. Friedrich Zahn. Jena: Gustav Fischer, pp. 546–58.
Williams, Raymond. 1989. *The Politics of Modernism*. Ed. Tony Pinkney. London: Verso Books.
———. 2001. *The Raymond Williams Reader*. Ed. John Higgins. London: Blackwell.

INDEX

Academia in Anarchy (Buchanan) 4
"actor network theory" (Latour) 155
Adorno, Theodor: and authenticity 17;
  on "exaggerations" 45; and Frankfurt
  School 72; on language and music
  59–60; on logic of devotion 1; on
  Nietzsche 1; and play(ing) 86; on politics
  of engagement 123; on "structural
  listening" 103, 164; and Theory 1, 122
aesthetic(s): and analytic technique 74;
  and contextualization 146; and cultural
  studies 144; and ideology 145; and
  music 123; and reason 74; Said's reading
  of 146–47; and the West 65
affect 15, 45, 77, 121
After Theory (Eagleton) 3, 5, 7–8,
  13–14
Agamben, Giorgio 1, 6–8, 13, 116
Ahmed, Sara 74, 84n3
Ahmed, Siraj 139
Alienation and Freedom (Fanon) 102n3
allegory (de Man) 39, 133; *see also* symbol
Allison, David 134
A Lover's Discourse (Barthes) 20
Althusser, Hélène 93
Althusser, Louis: on the encounter 13n2,
  55, 93, 96; on ideology 118, 144–45;
  reading(s) of Marx/Lenin 112, 160, 166;
  on (aleatory) materialism, 93–94, 96,
  117n5; concept of overdetermination
  40, 55–57; and philosophy as practice
  111; psychotic episode 93; reading of
  Spinoza 117n5; on science 144; and
  Theory 170; see also *clinamen* (Lucretius);
  determination; improvisation; Marxism;
  psychoanalysis; sacrifice
ambience 94–96; *see also* humanities, the
Anderson, Amanda 169

Anderson, Benedict 61, 133, 163
Anderson, Perry 169
"An Open Letter to Harlem Désir"
  (Kristeva) 68, 75
anthropology 21, 148
Anti-Oedipus: Capitalism and Schizophrenia
  (Deleuze and Guattari) 154–56, 161
anti-Semitism 41, 55, 159
antisociology (Donzelot) 154–56, 159
anxiety: about borders 61; in Foucault's
  inaugural Collège de France lecture
  21; Freud's experiences of 41, 43,
  53; anxiety of influence (Bloom) in
  Said's work 121–23, 125; *see also* affect;
  nation(alism); psychoanalysis
apparatus 18, 31, 52, 118n7, 158; see also
  dispositif (Foucault)
Archaeology of Babel, The (Ahmed) 139
Arendt, Hannah 5
Aronowitz, Stanley 23, 153–54
Artaud, Antonin 18
art 86, 94–95, 144
Art Ensemble of Chicago, The 98
arts, the 88, 96–99, 101; *see also* humanities,
  the; science(s)
Asclepius 23
*A Thousand Plateaus: Capitalism and
  Schizophrenia* (Deleuze and Guattari)
  157, 161n2
Austin, J.-L. 97
authenticity: Adorno's reading of 17; and
  Foucault's inaugural Collège de France
  lecture 27, 30–32; and immigration 67;
  and inauthenticity 18–19
author(s): "author function" (Foucault) 22,
  26–27; "death of the author" (Barthes)
  9, 31, 159; in Deleuze's letter to Cressole
  32–33; and Foucault's inaugural Collège

de France lecture 22, 26–27; and sexuality 19; and Theory 168; work-author distinction 97–98; *see also* autobiography; body/bodies; offering; queer theory
autobiography 57, 63, 83n1, 122

"Bach Defended Against his Devotees" (Adorno) 1
Badiou, Alain 13, 18, 85, 101
Bailey, Derek 88
Bakhtin, Mikhail 125, 127
Banerjee, Prathama 169
Barthes, Roland: concept of "cruising" in 19; concept of "death of the author" 9; and improvisation 86; reading of Kristeva 63; critique of Lévi-Strauss 154; and listening 81; and "overdetermination" 12; and reading 9–12, 83, 138; and sexuality 19–20; and Theory 9–12, 83, 164; work-author distinction 97; *see also* author(s); body/bodies; determination; humanities, the; psychoanalysis; queer theory; society; virtuality
Basque independence struggle 61
Bataille, Georges 10, 13, 18, 132, 159, 170
Baudouin, Francis 150
Baudrillard, Jean 154–55
Beckett and Babel (Fitch) 34
Beckett, Samuel: role in Foucault's inaugural Collège de France lecture 19, 21–22, 25–28, 31; *see also* literature; modernism
Benjamin, Walter: "brushing against the grain" formulation in 78; on "counsel" 163; essay on Leskov 166; on radio 84; on reading as perception 171; and Theory 171
Benn Michaels, Walter 166
Bennett, Jonathan 117n3
Bennington, Geoffrey 104
Benveniste, Émile 89, 158
Bergson, Henri 33
Beyond Good and Evil (Nietzsche) 13
Bhabha, Homi K. 69, 124
Black Skin, White Masks (Fanon) 89

Blanchot, Maurice 105–6, 111, 157–61
Bloch, Marc 34n4
Bloom, Harold 121
body/bodies: and concept of "cruising" (Barthes) 19; facticity of 14n4; and *logos* 157; maternal/feminine body 66, 83n1, 84n4; mind/body problem (Freud) 42; and resistance (Foucault) 28; scriptor's body 19; and Theory 14n4, 15, 165; *see also* LGBTQ; power; queer theory; sexuality
Bolton, Brydon (musician) 87
Le Bon, Gustav 69
Bonnefoy, Claude 34n2
Borges, Jorges Luis 99
Bouteldja, Houria 79
Brecht, Bertolt 84n5, 102n2
Brennan, Tim 128, 161
Brett, Philip 16
Brexit (UK referendum vote) ix, 63
Bryer, J. J. 35n5
Buchanan, James 4
"*Bulgarie, ma souffrance*" (Kristeva) 83n1, 84n4
Bullitt, William C. 75
Burchell, Graham 26
Butler, Judith 11, 17, 31, 96, 112

Cage, John 60, 70, 82, 98
Canguilhem, Georges 23, 29
Capital I (Marx) 142
capital(ism): Althusser's reading of 9, 12, 145, 170; and commodities 13n2, 143; and *conatus* 142; gothic register of 7–8; historical logic of 160; and ideology 145; and multinational(ism) 79; and reading 12; and sovereignty 60–61; and Theory 4; transnational flows of 61–62; and world system 61; *see also* class(es); communism; globalization; logic; Marxism; materialism
Caputo, John 116n1
Casarino, Cesare 114–15, 117n7
Castel, Robert 156
Catterall, Bob 139n1
Caute, David 73
Cavell, Stanley 59–60, 86

INDEX

Centre for Contemporary Cultural Studies (CCCS, Birmingham, UK) 37, 142–43
Centre for Humanities Research (Cape Town) 87, 102
De Certeau, Michel 43, 52, 56, 169
Cervantes, Miguel de 99
Césaire, Aimé 61, 147
Chakrabarty, Dipesh 139
Chandler, Nahum 167
Chandler, Raymond 145
Chatterjee, Partha 139
Chomsky, Noam 122
cinema 41, 78, 85, 104, 117n6
Civilization and its Discontents (Freud) 51, 66
Cixous, Hélène 104
Clark, Suzanne 83
class(es): 54, 58, 73, 149; *see also* capital(ism); cultural studies
clinamen (Lucretius) 93
Cocteau Twins (music group) 60
"Cogito and History" (Derrida) 106, 127
Cole, Andrew 2, 5
Coleman, Ornette 87
colonialism 61, 73
Coltrane, John 98
Commonwealth (Hardt and Negri) 113
communication 59, 90–91, 158, 161
communism: 68, 112–13, 159, 161
Communists Like Us (Guattari and Negri) 113
Community and Society (Tönnies) 148
Condition of the Working Classes in England, The (Engels) 149
Conrad, Joseph 92
context(ualization): concept of xii, 119, 141; and cultural studies 141–42; history-as-context 119; and labor xii; "problem" of 37, 80, 142, 144; signature/event/context gesture (Derrida) 108; and sociology 141–42, 145–46, 154; and Theory xi–xiii, 5, 15, 119, 141, 145, 147; and thinking 1, 15; *see also* antisociology; geography; globalization; history; logic; map(s)/mapping; philosophy; re: working; society; sociography; textuality; "the socius"
contingency 38, 45–46, 166
"Contradiction and Overdetermination" (Althusser) 55–56

Country and the City, The (dir. Dibbs) 119–20
Covering Islam (Said) 6
Cox, Christophe 94
creolization 61, 99
Cressole, Michel 33
"Criticism Between System and Culture" (Said) 124, 126
Critique of Black Reason (Mbembe) 167
Crowd, The (Le Bon) 69
"cruising" (Barthes) 19–20; *see also* body/bodies; homosexuality; LGBTQ; queer theory
"Cultural Strangeness and the Subject in Crisis" (Kristeva interview) 83n1
cultural studies: founding of Centre for Contemporary Cultural Studies (CCCS) 142–43; and class(es) 56; and contextualization 141; and everyday life 37, 40; Hoggart's inaugural Birmingham University lecture in 144; object of 50, 54; and psychoanalysis 40–41, 56–57; and Theory 37–39, 54, 156; *see also* discipline(s); Marxism; nation(alism); postcolonialism; post-Marxism
Culture and Imperialism (Said) 121, 126, 129–30, 140, 146

Darwin, Charles 82
Dasein (Heidegger) 93
Dea, Stephanie 117n6
Death of a Discipline (Spivak) 163–64
Decolonizing the Mind (Ngugi) 147
deconstruction 106, 139, 167–68
Defert, Daniel 27
Deleuze, Gilles: role in 1960s Nietzsche revival 18; writings on cinema 117n6; letter to Cressole 33–34; commentary on Donzelot 154–56; "Intellectuals and Power" (with Foucault) 114; and sociology 157; and Spinoza 104, 109, 117n4; and Theory xiii; on "the socius" 154–57; and concept of "war machine" (with Guattari) 157; *see also* immanence; philosophy; queer theory; sociography
Delphy, Christine 156
De Man, Paul: on allegory 39, 133; and resistance to theory 13, 38, 121; on

Rousseau 134; concept of symbol 39, 133; and Theory 38–39, 56, 121; *see also* reading; rhetoric; time/temporality

Derrida, Jacques: on animal-human relation(s) 92–93; death of 3; on grammatology 80; on the hand 92–93; on the "new humanities" 95, 97; and psychoanalysis 50; Said's reading of 124, 126–30, 133–40; seminar on Spinoza 103–16, 117n2, 118n8; and Theory xiii, 5, 10, 168–69; La Villette collaboration with Coleman 87; and writing 80, 149; *see also* author(s); cultural studies; deconstruction; humanities, the; improvisation; listening; offering; philosophy; reading; sociography

Descartes, René: concept of *cogito* 92; Derrida's seminar on 103–10, 112, 115; Descartes-Mersenne correspondence 105; on language 117n3

Désir, Harlem 62, 68, 75

desire: and the family 154; in Foucault's inaugural Collège de France lecture 20–21, 25, 28–29, 31–32; and psychoanalysis 72–73, 77; in Spinoza's work 113; subject of (Butler) 112; *see also* hermeneutics; queer theory; sexuality; Theory

determination: concept of 38; and critique 56; in cultural studies 40; economic determination 37; historical determination 127; overdetermination 11–12, 40, 45–46, 54–56; problem of 39; and psychoanalysis 50, 56, 93; and reading 11; "vulgar" determination 128; Williams on 125; *see also* everyday life; psychoanalysis; society; Theory

Devereux, George 73

Dibbs, Mike 119–20

Dickens, Charles 137

Diderot, Denis 33

"Différance" (Derrida) 135

Diken, Bülent 84n3

discipline(s): and cultural studies 37; death of 163–64; disciplinary object 37, 41, 57; in work of Foucault 16, 18; and interdisciplinarity 153; in work of Said 120, 124, 130–31, 133, 148; of sociology 157; and Theory 9

Discipline and Punish (Foucault) 18, 131

discourse(s): Derrida's reading of Descartes 104–7, 110–11, 115–16; discursivity 40, 46, 51, 82, 119, 124; and Foucault's inaugural Collège de France lecture 16–23, 25, 27, 29, 31; and jurisprudence 127; and mapping 147; and Marxism 160–1; and medicine 127; and national(ism) 70, 75; and Orientalism 120; of psychoanalysis 47, 64–65, 75, 82; of social policy 154; and Theory xiii, 2; and world system 145; *see also* language; literature; modernism; religion

Domenach, Jean 26–27, 29

Don Quixote (Cervantes) 99

Donzelot, Jacques 154–56

DuBois, W. E. B. 149

Dumézil, Georges 22, 29

Dumont, Louis 83n2

Dunlap, Geoff 119

Durkheim, Émile 149, 153

Eagleton, Terry: on death 13–14n4; and Marxism 39; on nation(alism) 145–47; and Theory 1, 3–5, 7–8; *see also* literature; map(s)/mapping; modernism; offering; sacrifice

Echographies of Television (Derrida and Stiegler) 80

Ego in Freud's Theory and in the Technique of Psychoanalysis, The (Lacan) 88

Einstein, Albert 75, 82

Elden, Stuart 34n1

Elementary Structures of Kinship, The (Lévi-Strauss) 89

Eliot, George 141, 153, 157

empire 129, 136, 139, 142

Empire (Hardt and Negri) 113

Engels, Friedrich 92, 142, 149

Enlightenment, the 66

Eno, Brian 94

Eribon, Didier 21, 27

Ethics, The (Spinoza) 104, 107–11, 116

Euclid 109, 117n6

Eurocentrism 18, 89, 133, 136, 147, 167; *see also* West, the
everyday life: and improvising 112; in life and work of Freud 40–41, 44–46, 50, 52, 54, 57, 79; and Theory 37–46, 79; *see also* cultural studies; determination; discipline(s); psychoanalysis; reading; speech/speaking
Everything You Always Wanted to Know About Sex (dir. Allen) 85
Exodus (Marley) 88
Expressionism in Philosophy: Spinoza (Deleuze) 109

Fabian, Johannes 133
Fanon, Frantz: review of Geismar and Caute's books on 73; reading of Lacan 89, 91, 102; link with Lukács 123; Said's reading of 123, 140n2; and Theory 122; *see also* colonialism; nation(alism); psychoanalysis
Faust II (Goethe) 46
Felski, Rita 142
feminism 17, 101, 156, 169; *see also* post-feminism
Fennesz, Christian 86, 96
feudalism 24, 34, 53
Feuerbach, Ludwig 118
fiction: in Derrida's Spinoza seminar 107–12; in work of Foucault 18; in Kristeva's writings 77; Theory vs 78, 125; *see also* literature; rhetoric
Fitch, Brian 34n5
Fliess, Wilhelm: Freud's break with 49; correspondence with Freud 41–42, 45, 47, 50–52, 82
Fluss, Diana 52
For a Critique of the Political Economy of the Sign (Baudrillard) 154
Forget English! (Mufti) 139
Forster, E. M. 146
Foucault, Michel: role in 1960s Nietzsche revival 18–19, 41; concept of "apparatus" (*dispositif*) 20; concept of "author function" 159; concept of "break" (episteme) 13, 19; collaboration with Deleuze 114; on discourse/discursivity 18, 21–23, 25, 27, 29, 31, 40; Donzelot's debt to 156; exchange with Derrida 105–6, 115; and homage(s) 22–27, 29–34; inaugural lecture at Collège de France 19–35; and knowledge 18, 20, 33–34; and power 19, 24, 28–34, 71; and psychoanalysis 40–41, 47; and resistance 18–19, 28–34; Said's reading of 124–34, 137–38, 161n1; and Theory xiii, 20, 22, 29; *see also* author(s); governmentality; history; literature; madness; philosophy; queer theory; sexuality; speech/speaking
Franklin, Julian 152
Fraser, Elizabeth (Cocteau Twins) 60
Fraser, Nancy 73, 144, 146, 160
Friendship (Blanchot) 159
"Freud and the Scene of Writing" (Derrida) 135
Freud, Sigmund: and anti-Semitism 55; concept of "delayed effect" (*Nachträglichkeit*) 165; Dora case 47; correspondence with Einstein 75; relationship with Fliess 41–42, 45, 47, 49–52, 82; influence on Habermas 72; role of work in Kristeva 62–67, 69–70; and Marxism 154; and nation(alism) 77; concept of Oedipus complex 57; concept of overdetermination 11, 40, 55–56; theory of parapraxis (*Fehlleistung*) 37–38, 41, 44–49; personal and professional life 38, 41–54; Spivak's reading of 164; concept of splitting (*Spaltung*) 10–11; and Theory 2, 11, 56, 79, 82–83; relationship to Vienna 41, 44, 46, 50–54; Wolf Man case 74; *see also* cultural studies; determination; everyday life; feminism; psychoanalysis; queer theory; science(s); sexuality; uncanny, the
Frost, David 68
Fukuyama, Francis 59
"Function and Field of Speech and Language in Psychoanalysis" (Lacan) 45

Gangle, Rocco 117n6
Gastarbeiten 73
Geismar, Peter 73

gender 24, 106
Genealogy of Psychoanalysis, The (Henry) 40
geography: and geology 156; and history 121, 130–32, 135, 141; psycho-geography 145; and Theory 11; *see also* cultural studies; discipline(s); Eurocentrism; sociography; space(s)/spatiality; "the socius"; West, the
Geopolitical Aesthetic, The (Jameson) 145
gesture(s): enunciative gesture(s) 61, 79; and everyday life 37; in Foucault's inaugural Collège de France lecture 22, 24–25, 27, 30, 33; in "Jamming" (Marley) 101; pedagogical gesture 75; of reading 11; rhetorical gesture(s) 138, 150, and sacrifice 7–8; sonic gestures 87; and Spinoza 107–9, 117n4; and Theory 10, 22; *see also* context(ualizaton); feudalism; religion; space(s)/spatiality
Gesture and Speech (Leroi-Gourhan) 92
Ginzberg, Carlo 115
globalization 62, 161
Godzich, Wlad 83
Goethe, Johann Wolfgang von 48, 139
Goldmann, Lucien 121, 129, 142
Gordon, Colin 34n3
Gordon, Lewis 167–68
governmentality 89, 149, 153
Graff, Gerald 4
Grafton, Tony 150
Gramsci, Antonio 128–30, 132, 135, 166
Great Expectations (Dickens) 137
Grégoire, Ménie 78, 84n
Grey, Daniel (musician) 87
Grossberg, Lawrence 144
"Group Psychology and the Analysis of the Ego" (Freud) 69
Guattari, Félix 113, 154–56, 161

Habermas, Jürgen: and education 76; influence of 19; on nation(alism) 74; on public sphere 43, 53, 72–73, 78, 79; and Theory 79; *see also* pedagogy; psychoanalysis; uncanny, the
Haizmann, Johann Christoph 82
Hall, Stuart 15, 21, 40, 82, 118n7, 142
Hamacher, Werner 139
Hamlet (Shakespeare) 82, 137
Hammett, Dashiell 146
Hands (Leader) 92
Hani, Chris 137
Havas, Roland 81
Hegel, Georg Wilhelm Friedrich: influence on French thought 23–24, 29, 55; logic(s) of the "concept"/recognition in 24, 74; and Marxism 85, 93, 115–16; and Spinoza 108–9, 112; *see also* determination; history; idealism; ideology; phenomenology; philosophy
Hegel or Spinoza? (Macherey) 108
Heidegger, Martin: concept of *Dasein* 92–93; Derrida's critique of 92–93; and dwelling 77; on the hand 92–93; concept of "hearkening" 81; motif of "the open" 118n7; rectoral address 105; on sacrifice 13n3; on technology 160; and Theory 169; *see also* cultural studies; hermeneutics; humanities, the; music; phenomenology; philosophy
Henry, Michel 40
hermeneutics 41, 56, 69, 81
Hertz, Robert 93
Hesiod 29
higher education 3, 81, 96; *see also* university, the
Histories, The (Polybius) 150–3
history: "bad history" (Hoggart) 144; concept of 84n3, 124, 129; and contextualization 119; "end of history" (Fukuyama) 137; in work of Foucault 13, 18, 23, 26–29, 33n1, 132, 137; and geography 130–31, 141; historicism 2, 38, 127; historicity 13, 63, 106, 137, 154; historiography 38, 146, 150–51, 153; intellectual history 41; personal history 63, 66; of philosophy 32; and psychoanalysis 38, 64, 71, 84n3; and representation 119, 125–27, 130, 135–36; in work of Said 120–1, 123–33, 136–39, 146; and Theory xi, 120–21, 128, 138, 141, 154; urban history 54; *see also* class(es); determination; disciplines(s); discourse(s); idealism; madness; Marxism; materialism; nation(alism); West, the

History and Class Consciousness (Lukács) 121, 123, 129
"History, Literature and Geography" (Said) 129–30, 133, 135
History of Madness, The (Foucault) 23, 33n1, 106
History of Sexuality, The (Foucault) 18, 28–29
Hitchcock, Alfred 78, 85, 103
HIV/AIDS 33
Hjelmslev, Louis 60
Hocquenghem, Guy 31
Hoggart, Richard 143–44
Hölderlin, Friedrich 18
holocaust 5, 7
homage(s): and Blanchot's friendship with Bataille 159; in Foucault's work 22–34, 131; and ritual (Bloch) 34nn3–4
"Homeostasis and Insistence" (Lacan) 91
Homo Sacer (Agamben) 6–8
How To Do Theory (Iser) 2
How to do Things with Words (Austin) 97
Huffer, Lynne 27, 33–34n1
Hulley, Kathleen 83n1
Hulme, T. E. 5
Hum (Kramer) 95
human(s): and animal(s) 89–92, 94; and cybernetics 89; and humanism 1, 89, 93, 95; and machine(s) 89–92, 94; *see also* humanities, the
Human, All Too Human (Nietzsche) 1
humanities, the: in academia 86–87, 97–98, 166, 168; "ambient humanities" 81, 86, 94–95; critical humanities xiii, 4, 86, 101, 136; and the hand 92–93; and the human 95; and human science(s) 88–89; and jamming 94, 99; and improvisation 88, 96; and "Left-leaning" 3, 86, 93–94, 99; "new humanities" (Derrida) 95, 97; "sinister humanities" 92–94; and subjectivity 85; and Theory xiii, 4, 166, 168, 170; *see also* ambience; arts, the; cultural studies; globalization; science(s)
Hume, David 33
Husserl, Edmund 81, 113, 126, 134–35
Hyppolite, Jean 23–25, 29, 131

idealism 46, 93, 112; *see also* materialism
identity: and criticism 135–6; and cultural studies 15; familial origins of 66; identity politics 67, 135; and intersectionality 16; LGBTQ 16; and nation(alism) 66–67; personal and professional identity 26, 83n1, 120; and sexuality 31; and Theory 2, 4–6, 13n1, 15, 82, 136; *see also* discourse(s); feminism; gender; psychoanalysis; queer theory; sexuality
ideology: and apparatuses (Althusser) 118n7; and globalization 62; and psychoanalysis 63, 68; and science 144–45, 160; and Theory 12; *see also* aesthetics; history; Marxism; nation(alism)
"Ideology and Ideological State Apparatuses" (Althusser) 118n7
Imagined Communities (Anderson) 61
immanence 7, 101, 136
imperialism 147; *see also* colonialism; empire; nation(alism); postcolonialism
improvisation: between the arts and social sciences 88; as concept and practice 87–88; and fiction 111; and the humanities 94, 96, 98; and jamming 85–86, 92, 101; and pedagogy 12; and Theory 101; *see also* materialism; human(s); machine(s); music; re: working; teaching; time/temporality
"Improvised Music after 1950: Afrological and Eurological Perspectives" (Lewis) 98
"*indigène*" (Bouteldja) 78
In Other Worlds (Spivak) 167
In Praise of the Commons (Cesarino and Negri) 114
"Intellectuals and Power" (Deleuze and Foucault) 114
intentionality 59; *see also* phenomenology
Interpretation of Dreams, The (Freud) 41–42, 91, 164
Introduction to Civil War (Tiqqun) 142
Iser, Wolfgang 2–4
Italian War and the Task of Prussia, The (Lassale) 50

Jakobson, Roland 158
Jameson, Fredric: on cognitive mapping 144–46, 155; on nation(alism) 133; Q&A with Fraser 144; *see also* capital(ism);

imperialism; logic; postmodernism; sociography
jamming: and cybernetics 89–91; and human-animal relation 92–93; and the humanities 94–95; and improvisation 88; and lyrics to Marley's song 99–101; and Theory 85; *see also* human(s); machine(s); materialism; music
"Jamming" (Marley) 86, 88, 99–101
Jesus 104, 116n1, 166
Johnson, Boris 6
Jones, Ernest 42, 44
Joyce, James 148
Julia Kristeva: Interviews (Kristeva) 83n1

Kafka, Franz 160, 161n2
Kalifa, Jean 102n3
Kamuf, Peggy 104
Kant, Immanuel 13n3, 33, 93, 95
Kassovitz, Matthieu 70
Kaufman, Eleanor 154
Kerouac, Jack 87
Khaldun, Ibn 157
Khashoggi, Jamal 13n4
Khota, Reza (musician) 87, 96, 102
Kim-Cohen, Seth 94
Klossowski, Pierre 18
Knapp, Steven 166
Knowledge and Human Interests (Habermas) 72
Kojève, Alexandre 23, 112, 116
Korzybsky, Alfred 146
Kramer, Lawrence 95
Kristeva, Julia: and foreigner(s) 61–62, 64–67, 71, 73–75, 76, 79, 83n1; and language 60; and maternal memory 83n1, 84n3 n. 3–5, and music 59–60, 64–65, 68, 71, 74, 76–79, 83n1; and nation(alism) 59, 61–62, 66–71, 73–79, 84n4; and stranger(s) 59–63, 65, 67–71, 73, 75–79, 84n3, and technique 62–65, 70–71, 73–78; and Theory xiii; *see also* geography; history; identity; literature; postcolonialism; psychoanalysis; subject(s)/subjectivity; touch(ing); uncanny, the

labor: academic labor 17, 97; and collaboration 19; and cognition 93; and contextualization xii; and cultural studies 38; and Foucault's inaugural Collège de France lecture 31; free flow of 61; and human-animal relation 92; intellectual labor 95, 143; and philosophy 115; and truth of history 151; *see also* capital(ism); history; human(s); Marxism; pedagogy; sociology; teaching
Lacan, Jacques: role in 1960s Nietzsche revival 18; on "afterwardness" (*après coup*) 165; and cybernetics 89; concept of ego 66; exchange with Derrida 133; Fanon's commentary on 102n3; and film 78; and jamming 90–92; concept of *jouissance* 78; and Lacanianism 34n3, 75, 154; 91–93; concept of the Other 87; radio broadcast by 84n5; concept of the Real 95; and the speaking subject 145; teaching of 88; and Theory xiii; concept of the Unconscious 90, 158; *see also* human(s); improvisation; machine(s); nation(alism); psychoanalysis; re: working, uncanny, the
Lacouture, Jean 21, 29
language: and being 17–18; and cybernetics 89; in Derrida's seminar on Spinoza 104–11, 115–16; in Descartes's letter to Mersenne 117n3; and Foucault's inaugural Collège de France lecture 24, 27; and the humanities 97; and human linguistic communication 59; and the human sciences 92; and literature 125, 142, 144; and music 59–60; and politics 159; power of 152; psychoanalysis 45–46, 74, 89–91; social forces in 125; and speech 34n2; and structuralism 158; and Theory 12, 15, 142; and the unconscious 158; *see also* communication; discourse(s); logic; Marxism; psychoanalysis; rhetoric
"Language (*langue*) and the Discourse on Method" (Derrida): and nation(alism) 104–5; and philosophy 104–5; reading of Spinoza in 105–6, 110–11, 115–16
Language, Madness and Desire: On Literature (Foucault) 34n2
Laplanche, Jean 165
Lasalle, Ferdinand 50

Latour, Bruno 155
La Villette (Paris venue) 87
Laws (Plato) 13n1
Lazarsfeld, Paul 149
Lazarus, Neil 161n1
Leader, Darien 92
"Left Leaning: Towards a Sinister Humanities" (Mowitt) 102n4
Lenin, Vladimir Ilyich 68, 71, 94, 112; *see also* Marxist-Leninism
Leroi-Gourhan, André 92
Levinas, Emmanuel 116–18
Lévi-Strauss, Claude 21, 89, 90, 154
Lewis, Charles 111
Lewis, George E. 98
LGBTQ 16
libidinal economy 27
Lifted Veil, The (Eliot) 141
Lillevan (video artist) 87
listening: and "Jamming" (Marley) 100; and reading 45, 80–81, 86; and speaking 19, 45, 152; "structural listening" (Adorno) 103; and Theory 83; "transferential" listening 82; *see also* body/bodies; contingency; communication; improvisation; music; psychoanalysis; reading; speech/speaking
"Listening" (Barthes and Havas) 81
Literary Theory: An Introduction (Eagleton) 3
literature: and being 18; and contextualization 161n2; and fiction 115; in work of Foucault 19, 34n2; and language 18; and literary theory 17; and music 78; and philosophy 106; and postcolonialism 61; and psychoanalysis 43; sociology of 141, 143–45, 157; and teaching 163; and Theory 168, 170; travel literature 64; Western literature 136; world literature 62, 139, 148; *see also* colonialism; cultural studies; discipline(s); modernism; psychoanalysis; re: working
"Living On: Borderlines" (Derrida) 106
logic: of belatedness (Freud) 55; of capitalism 160; of the concept (Hegel) 24, 74; of devotion xii, 1; of dreams 43; of everyday life 38, 50, 53; of identification 44; logical positivism 59, 97; "logic of praise" (Kaufman) 154; of narrativity 134; of nation(alism) 70; and philosophy 13n2, 113–14; of reconciliation (Said) 123; of the supplement (Derrida) 110; of tonality 65, 68; of the uncanny 75; *see also* capital(ism); cultural studies; deconstruction; language; music; psychoanalysis
Lowy, Emmanuel 51
Lukács, György: influence on Habermas 72; postepical novel by 66; in Said's work 121–25, 129, 130, 135; and sociology of literature 145; *see also* literature; Marxism; reflection theory; sociology
Lucretius, Titus Carus 93
Lyotard, Jean-François 40

Macherey, Pierre 108–9, 112–13, 117n5
machine(s): and cybernetics 89; and human-machine relation(s) 92–93, 96; and jamming 90–94; and reading 81; and the supplement (Derrida) 80; and Theory 81, 101; "war machine" (Deleuze/Guattari) 81; and writing 83; *see also* human(s); sociology; technology
madness 15, 19, 116, 127; *see also* reason
Madness of the Day (Blanchot) 105, 111
magic 49
Mahler, Gustav 86
map(s)/mapping: and cognitive mapping (Jameson) 144–47; map-territory distinction (Korzybsky) 146, 155; and the social (Donzelot) 155–56; theorist's map 127; *see also* antisociology; sociography; sociology; space(s)/spatiality; "the socius"
Marchais, Georges 114
Marcus, Steven 49
Marienthal: a Sociography of an Unemployed Community (Lazarsfeld) 149
Marley, Bob: and god ("jah") 99–101; and improvisation 101; and jamming 90, 92, 99; recording of "Jamming" 85, 88–89; *see also* Wailers
Marx, Karl: on alienation 143, 166; on commodities 143; and cultural

expression 142; on "externalization" 85;
  relation to Freud 63; "ghosts" of 137;
  legacy of 115; on life and consciousness
  141; relation to Spinoza 93–94, 112;
  and Theory 170
Marxism: and cultural studies 39–40,
  117n7; and everyday life 56; Hegelian
  tradition of 112, 116, 129; and
  modernism 68; and concept of "open
  Marxism" (Derrida) 115, 117n7;
  and May '68 159; "socialization of
  society" 154; and Spinoza 104, 112;
  "spirit of Marxism" (Derrida) 137;
  and Theory 12, 169; vulgar Marxism
  125; *see also* determination; discourse(s);
  idealism; ideology; Marxist-Leninism;
  materialism; post-Marxism
Marxism and the Interpretation of Culture
  (Grossberg and Nelson) 144
Marxist-Leninism 146
Mascolo, Dionys 159, 161
masculinity 24–25, 34
materialism: aleatory materialism 94,
  98; and communication 161; and
  communism 112; cultural materialism
  40; dialectical materialism 55, 63; and
  feminism 156; historical materialism
  137; machinic materialism 89; new
  materialism(s) 38; and ontology 118;
  and Spinoza 177n5; and Theory 38;
  and the university 93; *see also clinamen*
  (Lucretius); history; humanities, the;
  idealism; improvisation; Marxism
May '68 uprisings 21, 114
McGinn, Colin 92
McLuhan, Marshall 103
Mayr, Georg von 148
Mbembe, Achille 1, 167
Meaning of Sarkozy, The (Badiou) 13n2
media: mass media 71, 75, 78; in work of
  McLuhan 103; and nation(ality) 67, 75;
  and philosophy 111; and sociography
  19; and the supplement (Derrida) 80;
  and telephonic communication 87;
  see also communication
"Media, Margins and Modernity" (Said
  and Williams) 120, 125, 139
Mehlman, Jeffrey 159

Melas, Natalie 148
Memmi, Albert 73, 148
Meno (Plato) 108
Merleau-Ponty, Maurice 89, 135
Mes Pensées (Montesquieu) 76
metaphysics 16, 94, 116
Method for the Easy Comprehension of History
  (Bodin) 150, 152
Middle East 136
Miller, Jacques-Alain 40, 78
modernism: and literature 19, 30–31,
  34–35n5, 146; and Marxism 68;
  practices of 82; and reading/writing
  138; *see also* arts, the; discourse(s);
  empire; imperialism; postmodernism;
  time/temporality
"Modernism and Imperialism"
  (Jameson) 146
Montesquieu, Baron 62, 66, 76–77
Morton, Timothy 94
Moses and Monotheism (Freud) 64
Moten, Fred 88
Mthiyane, Thomas (artist) 87
Mufti, Aamir 139
Mulligan, Gerry 87
Multitude (Hardt and Negri) 113
Muselman, the 6, 8
music: analysis of "Jamming" (Marley)
  99–101; and composition 123;
  counterpoint in 68, 132–33; fugue in
  64–65, 71, 74–77; and improvisation
  88, 98; and indeterminacy 98; in
  Kristeva's writing 64–65, 68, 71,
  74, 76–79, 83n1; and musicology
  16, 132; and nation(alism) 71, 74,
  77; performance of 85–87, 98; and
  psychoanalysis 77–78; "queering the
  pitch" 16; and sound 60; and Theory
  xiii, 79, 85; *see also* art; discipline(s);
  Eurocentrism; jamming; logic;
  psychoanalysis; queer theory
"Music and Language" (Adorno) 59
Must We Mean What We Say? (Cavell) 59
Mzayiya, Dathini (artist) 87

Nancy, Jean-Luc 13n3, 81, 115
Napolin, Julie Beth 92
narrativity 134, 137

nation(alism): and determination 39–40, 55; and *l'ésprit général* 75–9; and the human 66; and internationalism 61–62, 69–70, 79; Kristeva's writing on 59, 61–62, 66, 69–71, 74–75, 77–78; nation-state 61; and philosophy 105, 117; and Theory 79; *see also* allegory; empire; imperialism; literature; psychoanalysis; postcolonialism; reading; symbol

Nationalism, Colonialism and Literature (Eagleton et al.) 61, 147

"Nationalism: Irony and Commitment" (Eagleton) 146

Nations Without Nationalism (Kristeva) 62, 68

Negotiations (Deleuze) 33

Negri, Antonio 112–17

Nelson, Cary 144

neoliberalism 97

Neruda, Pablo 147

"New Humanities" (Derrida) 95

New Left Church (Eagleton) 7

Ngugi, wa Thiong'o 147

Nietzsche, Friedrich: 1960s revival of 18; aphorism 55 (*Beyond Good and Evil*) 13n3; declaration of death of god 158; in Deleuze's philosophy 33, 104; Foucault's reading of 23, 41, 131–32; and Theory 1

"Nietzsche, Genealogy, History" (Foucault) 23, 132

Nigam, Aditya 169–70

offering: and holocaust 5, 7; and *homo sacer* (Agamben) 6–8; practice of 2; and sacrifice 1–2, 5–11, 132, 168–70; and Spinoza 116; and Theory xiii, 1–7, 10–11, 13n1, 85, 107, 148, 156, 168–71; *see also* author(s); humanities, the; pedagogy; reading; teaching

Of Grammatology (Derrida) 9, 105, 110, 117n2

One Who Was Standing Apart from Me, The (Blanchot) 157–58

"On Narcissism" (Freud) 69

"On the Improvement of the Understanding" (Spinoza) 104, 108–10

"On the One Hand, and the Other" (Mowitt) 102n4

"open Marxism" (Derrida) 115, 117–18

Order of Things, The (Foucault) 18

Orientalism (Said) 61, 124

Other Asias (Spivak) 167, 169

otherness 65, 74, 87, 89, 167–68

Palestinian independence struggle 61, 140n2

Pandey, Rakesh 169–70

Pascal, Blaise 84, 166

Patrizzi, Francesco 150

pedagogy 4, 6–8, 11, 15

Peeters, Benoît 105

Peirce, Charles Sanders xii, 112, 117

Pepper, Thomas 158

performativity 117, 97–98

Petitjean, Clément 13n2

phenomenology 40, 89, 116, 135

Phenomenology of Mind (Hegel) 24

Philadelphia Negro: A Sociological Study, The (DuBois) 149

philosophy: and deconstruction 103; and Deleuze's letter to Cressole 32–33; and Derrida's critique of Heidegger 92–93; and disagreement between Derrida and Foucault 127; and discourse(s) 127; and education 103; of the encounter (Althusser) 93; Foucault's relationship to 18, 23–24, 27; and listening 81; and literature 106, 144; and nation(alism) 105; of praxis 17; and reason 113–15, 127; and sociology 144; and Spinoza 106, 108–12, 117n4; and Theory xii, 4, 9, 13n1, 101, 167; *see also* discipline(s); discourse(s); history; improvisation; materialism; metaphysics; performativity

Plato 13n1, 108

Pleasure of the Text, The (Barthes) 10, 19

Poe, Edgar Allan 133

Policing of Families, The (Donzelot) 154–55

politics: and anthropocentrism 114; biopolitics 153; and communities 16; of engagement 123; geopolitics 66, 68, 115, 124; and homosexuality 28; identity politics 67, 135; of independence 147; of killing 13n4; of the Left 62, 149; and nation(alism) 68, 70; and psychoanalysis 68; and queer theory 17, 32; of representation 17; and sacrifice 14n4; and sociology 76, 145, 148, 154, 159; and space

53, 55, 139, 160; and Spinoza 112; and Theory 6, 14n4, 169; *see also* anti-Semitism; class(es); capital(ism); communism; context(ualization); cultural studies; discourse(s); globalization; ideology; Marxism; reflection theory; sexuality
Politics of Modernism, The (Williams) 119
Polybius 150–53
Post-Card, The (Derrida) 50
postcolonialism: and class(es) 73; and cultural studies 61; and decolonization 1, 146–48; and history 121, 123; and literature 147–48; and nation(alism) 74, 79; postcoloniality 139, 148; postcolonial studies 62, 119, 124, 161n1; and queer theory 17; and Theory 2, 5, 139; *see also* colonialism; empire; imperialism
post-feminism 5; *see also* feminism
post-Marxism 5, 40; *see also* Marxism
postmodernism 5, 17, 145–46; *see also* modernism
Postmodernism, or the Cultural Logic of Late Capitalism (Jameson) 145
poststructuralism xii, 17; *see also* structuralism
power: and culture 124; and embodiment 93; in work of Foucault 16, 18–19, 28–34, 71; of language 152; and psychoanalysis 44; and queer resistance 29–32; and sovereignty 13–14n4; and Spinoza 111–14; and Theory xi; *see also* ; discipline(s); discourse(s); hermeneutics; music
Preface to Film (Williams) 40
Prehension (McGinn) 92
"Presentation on Psychical Causality" (Lacan) 102n3
Principles of Philosophy (Descartes) 106
"Project for a Scientific Psychology" (Freud) 41, 91
Proust, Marcel 83n1
psychoanalysis: and cultural studies 56; and cybernetics 89; and dreams 42; and everyday life 37–38, 40–41, 43–44, 52, 79; and the family 156; concept of *jouissance* in 69, 78; as mind-reading (Fliess) 50; and nation(alism) 62, 66, 69–71, 77; and/as parapraxis (*Fehlleistung*) 37–38, 41, 44–49; and politics 68; and the public sphere 72, 74, 76, 79; and superstition 46–48, 53; and Theory 79; and urban space 51, 79; *see also* queer theory; religion; sexuality; sociography; space(s)/spatiality; technique
"Psychoanalysis and Cybernetics, or, On the Nature of Language" (Lacan) 89
"Psychoanalysis and the Polis" (Kristeva) 77, 82
Psychoanalytic Politics (Turkle) 84n3
Psychopathology of Everyday Life, The (Freud) 38, 40–41, 44–46, 52
public sphere: and nation(alism) 67; and psychoanalysis 43, 72–74, 76, 78; and urban space 53; and Theory 79

queer theory: and "cruising" 19–20; and Foucault's inaugural Collège de France lecture 20, 30, 32, 33–34n1; and resistance 16–19; and homosexuality 30–32; and Theory 20; *see also* LGBTQ; sexuality
Quetelet, Adolphe 157

Rabelais, François 65
Radical Sacrifice (Eagleton) 7–8
radio 78, 84n1n5
Radio: Essays in Bad Reception (Mowitt) 84n5, 102n2, 143
"*Radiophonie*" (Lacan) 84n5
"Rameau's Nephew" (Diderot) 33n1
Rank, Otto 164
Ranke, Leopold von 153
reading: and work of Blanchot 158–61; chiasmus with Theory 11–12, 80, 103; contrapuntal reading (Said) 132–33; and Derrida's Spinoza seminar 106–9, 111–15; and Foucault's inaugural Collège de France lecture 16, 19, 20–25, 33, 34n1; of improvisation 101; and mapping 155; and musical performance 85; and psychoanalysis 45–46, 48–50, 52, 54, 66, 69; and queer resistance 16, 19–20;

Said's reading of Derrida and Foucault
126, 129, 138–39; and sociography
19, 28; and Theory xii–xiii, 1, 7–12,
13n2, 15, 22, 37–40, 54, 56, 60, 80,
103, 119, 121, 148, 161–62, 164–65,
167–71; *see also* allegory; determination;
hermeneutics; listening; music; symbol
Reading Capital (Althusser) 9, 12, 170
Readings, Bill 101
Reaganism 128
reason: dialectical reason(ing) 94, 112–13,
115, 143; disciplinary reason 133; and
imagination 114; "instrumental reason"
89; and madness 127; and saying/playing
74; *see also* history; philosophy
reception theory 2
reflection theory 142–43
religion 13n2, 23–24, 47, 51, 113; *see also* superstition
Renan, Ernest 69–70
representation: and geography 130,
135; and history 118–20, 125–26,
130, 135–36; and philosophy 108,
127–28, 131, 135–37, 155; politics
of 17; and reading 39; and reflection
142; and space/time 131, 135–36; and
Theory 136; *see also* map(s)/mapping; modernism
"Representations of the Intellectual
in *Representations of the Intellectual*"
(Lazarus) 161n1
"Resurrection Symphony" (Mahler) 86
Return of the Actor, The (Touraine) 153
re: working 88, 93
Reynolds, Beatrice 150–1
rhetoric: of debt 24; in Derrida's Spinoza
seminar 108–9; of dying (Eagleton) 7,
13–14n4; of geography 130–31; and
grammar 152; and psychoanalysis 50;
of sanguinity 8, 13–14n4; and space/
spatiality 133–35, 155; of statecraft 6;
and Theory 129; *see also* discourse(s); language
Rilke, Rainer Maria 118n7
Robbe-Grillet, Alain 9
Rolland, Romain 51
Roudiez, Leon 68
Roudinesco, Elizabeth 71

Rousseau, Jean-Jacques 94, 134
Roussel, Raymond 18, 34n2
Rouvroy, Antoinette 89
Rutherford, Ian 12–13n1, 151

sacrifice: of the author 9; and holocaust
5, 7; and *homo sacer* (Agamben) 6–8; and
instruction 104; lyric in "Jamming"
(Marley) 99; and reading 80, 83, 170; and
scapegoat 6, 8; and Theory 1–2, 5–8,
10–11, 12n1, 13n1, 80, 168, 170; *see also*
anti-Semitism; offering; politics; rhetoric
Sade, Marquis de 18
Said, Edward: on "critical consciousness"
122–24, 131, 134–36; on (the) critic(ism)
123–24, 126–31, 133, 135–36, 138–39,
139n1; debate with Williams 119–26,
128–30, 135–36; and geography 121,
130–35, 141; and history 119–33,
136–42; and nation(alism) 123, 133,
135, 139, 140n1 n. 1–2; and Palestinian
cause 140n2; and postcolonialism 2,
61, 119, 121, 123–24, 139, 161n1;
reading of Derrida/Foucault 124–38;
and Theory xiii, 2, 119–25, 129, 138;
see also colonialism; cultural studies;
determination; empire; imperialism;
literature; space(s)/spatiality;
subject(s)/subjectivity
Samourai, The (Kristeva) 140n3
Sartre, Jean-Paul 108, 115–16, 123,
127, 144
De Saussure, Ferdinand 60, 110, 117n6
Savage Anomaly, The (Negri) 112, 114, 116
Schaeffer, Pierre 81
Schiller, Friedrich 144
Schleiermacher, Friedrich 167
Schmitt, Carl 6
Schönberg, Arnold 123
Schorske, Carl 50
science(s): applied sciences 97; human
science(s) 92; and ideology 144–45;
linguistic science 110; natural
science 95; political science 148; and
psychoanalysis 37, 42–44, 46–48, 50,
52; "science of policing" 153; and the
social sciences 4, 86, 88, 144–45, 149,
168; and Theory xiii, 4, 168; *see also* arts,

the; governmentality; humanities, the; map(s)/mapping
Scott, David 82, 142
Searle, John 97
Semeiotiké (Kristeva) 63
Seminar II (Lacan) 88, 92
Sense et non-sense de la revolté (Kristeva) 83n1
Seventh Seal, The (dir. Bergman) 158
sexuality: and apparatus 18; and "cruising" (Barthes) 19–20; heterosexuality 27; homosexuality 30–2; Foucault's reading of 16, 19–20, 25, 27–32; *see also* body/bodies; gender; LGBTQ; power; queer theory; speech/speaking
Shadow of the West, The (dir. Dunlap) 119
Shelley, Percy Byshe 106
Shore, Daniel 104, 116n1
Short Treatise on God, Man and His Well Being (Spinoza) 117n1
Simmel, Georg 79
Singularities (Pepper) 158
socialism 12, 61
society: and cultural studies 56; and culture 148; and discourse(s) 146–47; in work of Donzelot on 154–6; in Eliot's novella 153; feudal society 34n4; and postcoloniality 148; and sacrifice 6; and science 91–92; social character of 141; and Theory xi, 3, 38, 148; *see also* antisociology; map(s)/mapping; sociography; sociology; "the socius"
sociography: and companionship 159; and contextualization 145, 154, 165; and cultural studies 37; and historiography 153; history of 148–49; and knowledge 149; and literature 157; and psychoanalysis 37–38, 52; society-sociology distinction 154; "sociographic" echo chamber 19, 28, 31; and sociology 146, 148; and Theory xiii, 38, 119, 141, 156, 161, 168; *see also* map(s)/mapping; nation(alism); postcolonialism; representation; "the socius"
Sociological Imagination, The (Wright Mills) 153
sociology: critique of 153–59; of culture 146; of literature 141, 143–45; and society-culture relation 148; *see also* antisociology; cultural studies; discipline(s); politics; reflection theory; science(s); society; sociography; "the socius"
"Sociology and Socio-Logic" (Barthes) 154
Socrates 23, 150–51
S.O.S. Racisme 83n1
Sounds: the Ambient Humanities (Mowitt) 81
sound studies 81, 94
sovereignty 6, 60–61, 150
Soziographie (Steinmetz) 148
space(s)/spatiality: of ambience 96; and architecture 19; and class(es) 56; in Derrida's reading of Spinoza 108–9 and everyday life 38, 57; of Foucault's inaugural Collège de France lecture 22; Freud's office space 52–53; and improvisation 88; and map(s)/mapping 146, 156; and nation(alism) 78; and politics 53, 160; and representation 120; in work of Said 120–4, 126, 128–36; and sociography 154, 156; spatial orientation of the human (Kant) 93; and Theory 121–23, 129, 138, 156; of the university 93; urban space 51–55, 79; *see also* anti-Semitism; "the socius"; time/temporality
speech/speaking: of the analysand 82; everyday acts of 45; and Foucault's reading of Beckett 22, 27; "ideal speech situation" 74; and listening 152; and sexuality 31–32; speaking beings 66; and the subject 63, 65, 89, 145; and thinking 92; and writing 110; *see also* language; masculinity; psychoanalysis; subject(s)/subjectivity; voice(s); writing
Speech Begins After Death (Foucault and Bonnefoy) 34n2
Spinoza, Baruch: Deleuze's reading of 109, 117n4; Derrida's seminar on 103–16, 117n2, 168; and immanence 101; "intellectual love of god" 100; and Marx(ism) 94, 118n7; Negri's reading of 112–17; (non-)method of *more geometrico* 107, 109, 116, 117n2; revival of 93
Spivak, Gayatri: and national(ism) 62, 83, 139; and postcolonial studies 62, 124,

INDEX

163; and teaching 164–68; and Theory xii, 83, 163–70
"Statistics and Sociography" (Tönnies) 148
Steinmetz, Rudolf 148
Stiegler, Bernard 80, 111
Strachey, James 41, 57n1
Strangers to Ourselves (Kristeva) 59, 62
Stuart Hall's Voice (Scott) 82, 142
subject(s)/subjectivity: Althusser's writing on 145; "becoming-subject" 7; consumer-subject 13n2; of cultural studies 40; and death 97; of desire 112; entry into language of 24; enunciative subject 158; and foreigner(s) 65, 71; 83n1; fugal subject(s) (Kristeva) 71; and the human 91, 151, 159; and *jouissance* 69; and listening 81; and nation(alism) 70–71; and neurosis 43; and object(s) 21, 85, 93, 123; post-Cartesian subject 106; and psychoanalysis 63, 70–71, 75; and queer resistance 16–17; speaking subject 63, 89; in Spinoza's work 113; splitting (*Spaltung*) of 10; Subject and Answer (Kristeva) 65, 68; and time 134; and Theory 138, 169; Western "super-subject" (Said) 132
Subterraneans, The (Kerouac) 87
superstition: and psychoanalysis 46–50, 53; in Spinoza's work 114; *see also* religion
symbol (de Man) 34n4, 39, 81, 95, 133; *see also* allegory
S/Z (Barthes) 10–11

teaching: and Derrida's Spinoza seminar 103, 105, 107, 111–12, 116, 117n4; in Lacan's Seminar II 88; as performative 98; of Spivak 163–65, 168; and Theory 163–65, 168; in work of Williams 120; *see also* cultural studies; higher education; improvisation; pedagogy; psychoanalysis; university, the
technique: in work of Kristeva 62–5, 68, 70–1, 73–8; queering as 15; and reading 138
technology 15, 84n5; *see also* machine(s)
Texts for Nothing (Beckett) 22

textuality 38, 115, 126, 138, 150; *see also* context(ualization)
"The Antithetical Sense of Primal Words" (Freud) 88
"The Cogito and the History of Madness" (Foucault) 106, 127
"The Ethics for the Nation" (White) 117n6
"The Future of Cultural Studies" (Williams) 40
"The Only Materialist Tradition, Part 1: Spinoza" (Althusser) 117n5
"The Order of Discourse" (Foucault) 16
Theory: "afterwardness of" 165; chiasmus with reading 11–12, 80, 103; and critical consciousness 122–24, 134, 136; and cultural critique 56; death of 3–4; and decolonization 148; and fiction 77–78; in Foucault's inaugural Collège de France lecture 29–30; and geography 133; and history 133; and improvisation 101; and map(s)/mapping 161; and musical performance 85, 88; and nation(alism) 69–70; and offering xiii, 1–7, 10–11, 13n2, 107, 148, 155, 169; and (the) other(ness) 167–68; and psychoanalysis 52, 54, 57n1, 69–70, 79, 82–3; and queer theory 15–18, 20, 30, 32; and reading xiii, 1, 7, 11–12, 9–13, 15, 22, 60, 80–83, 103, 169–70; and sacrifice 1–2, 5–14, 80, 141; and thinking 166; and traveling theory (Said) 123, 125; when/where of xi–xiii, 1–2, 11–12, 20, 33n1, 37, 79, 83, 85, 88, 119, 141, 147, 164; *see also* reception theory; reflection theory
"Theory in Black: Teleological Suspensions in the Philosophy of Culture" (Gordon) 167
"The Part Played by Labor in the Becoming Human of the Ape" (Engels) 92
"The Purloined Letter" (Poe) 133
"The Rise of the Social" (Deleuze) 154
"the socius" (Deleuze/Guattari) 154–59, 161

Theological-Political Treatise, The (Spinoza) 104, 107, 113
"The Storyteller: Observations on the Work of Nikolai Leskov" (Benjamin) 166
"Thoughts for the Times on War and Death" (Freud) 69
"The Unsacrificeable" (Nancy) 13n3
"The Work of Art in the Age of its Technological Reproducibility" (Benjamin) 166
"The Work of Theory: Thinking Across Traditions" (Banerjee et al.) 169
time/temporality: and allegory-symbol relation (de Man) 39, 133; Derrida's problematization of 137; general temporality 121; and history 51, 135; and improvisation 98; lived time 100; and metalepsis 165 and modernism 21; "real time" 87; suspension of 140n2; and Theory 129; *see also* space(s)/spatiality
Tiqqun (French collective) 142–43, 155
Tomaselli, Sylvana 89–90
Tönnies, Ferdinand 148–49, 153
Toop, David 88, 92
touch(ing): between arts and humanities 99, 101; and "brushing" (Benjamin) xiii, 67, 74; and improvisation 98; and myth of origins 77; and public discourse 78; and technique in Kristeva 64, 71, 74, 76
Touraine, Alain 153–54
transcendence 70, 79
"Traveling Theory" (Said): and contextualization 139; and critical consciousness 122; and (the) critic(ism) 124; "reculmination" of 121; and Theory 4, 148; and exchange with Williams 119; *see also* colonialism; geography; imperialism; postcolonialism; space(s)/spatiality
"Traveling Theory Reconsidered" (Said) 122–23, 148
Trilling, Lionel 140n1
truth: and Derrida's Spinoza seminar 108, 111; in the work of Foucault 18; of history 151; of (the) past (events) 150, 153; and psychoanalysis 44; and Theory 169

Turkle, Sherry 84n5
Turner, Ted 68, 71

uncanny, the: and Freud 66–67; in work of Kristeva 66–8, 70, 84n4; logic of 75; and Theory 7, 15; *see also* psychoanalysis
Understanding Media: The Extensions of Man (McLuhan) 103
university, the: and Heidegger's rectoral address 105; and neoliberalism 97; and Theory xiii, 4, 6–7, 9; *see also* Centre for Contemporary Cultural Studies (CCCS); higher education; humanities, the; labor; pedagogy; teaching
Unnamable, The (Beckett) 15, 21, 25, 27

De Villiers, Nicholas 17
virtuality 10, 72–3
voice(s): and work of Blanchot 158–61; and Foucault's inaugural Collège de France lecture 20–31; in work of Kristeva 63, 67–68; of the other 81; voice of Stuart Hall 82, 142; Western European voices 115; *see also* phenomenology; West, the
Voice and Phenomenon (Derrida) 113, 134

Wailers (group) 88, 99–101
Weltliteratur (Goethe) 139
West, the: history of 64; and music 65, 74; and non-Western national projects 61; Northern, Western canon of "great ideas" 5; and otherness 66, 133; and philosophy 115; Said's writing on 121–23, 129–36; and Theory xiii–xiv, 1, 129; Western "super subject" (Said) 132; *see also* colonialism; discourse(s); geography; globalization; imperialism; literature; postcolonialism; subject(s)/subjectivity; voice(s)
Westphal, Bertrand 130
"What is an Author?" (Foucault) 22, 27
"What of Tomorrow's Nation?" (Kristeva) 68
"What Would Jesus Deconstruct?" (Caputo) 116n1
White, Hale 117n6
"Why War?" (Freud) 70, 75

Williams, Raymond: and anxiety of influence (Bloom) 121; concept of culture of 37; on determination 125; exchange with Said 119–26, 128–30, 135–36, 144; and Marxism 56; and reading 39–40; and Theory xiii; *see also* cultural studies; everyday life; literature; reflection theory; sociology

Wolfson, Harry Austryn 104

Wolfson, Louis 74, 117

World, the Text, and the Critic, The (Said) 119

Wright Mills, C. 153

writing: Derrida's concept of 34n2, 80–81; and engraving 156–57; and events 152, 154, 159; and everyday life 38, 54; and Foucault's inaugural Collège de France lecture 22–23, 30, 34n2; Heidegger's approach to 93; and Kristeva's work 65–66, 76, 83n1; and modernism 22 and nation(alism) 62, 64–65, 76; as practice 30; and reading xii, 52, 138; "scene of writing" (Freud) 53; and sociography 149; and Theory xii, 8, 156; and "the socius" 155–57; and truth 150; *see also* discourse(s); politics; psychoanalysis; speech/speaking; virtuality

"WWJD: Genealogy of a Syntactic Form" (Shore) 116n1

X – The Problem of the Negro as a Problem for Thought (Chandler) 167

Yeats, W. B. 146–48

"Yeats and Decolonization" (Said) 147–48

Young, Robert 23, 102n3

Žižek, Slavoj 62, 72, 78, 86

www.ingramcontent.com/pod-product-compliance
Lightning Source LLC
Chambersburg PA
CBHW021828300426
44114CB00009BA/369